Contract Law

FOR

DUMMIES®

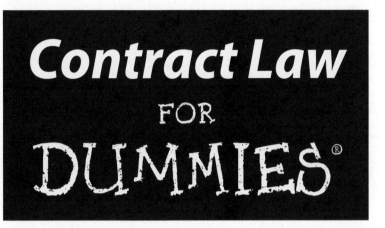

Contract Law
FOR
DUMMIES®

by Scott J. Burnham
with Joe Kraynak

WILEY

John Wiley & Sons, Inc.

Contract Law For Dummies®

Published by
John Wiley & Sons, Inc.
111 River St.
Hoboken, NJ 07030-5774
www.wiley.com

Copyright © 2012 by John Wiley & Sons, Inc., Hoboken, New Jersey
Published simultaneously in Canada

Library of Congress Control Number:

ISBN 978-1-118-09273-6 (pbk); ISBN 978-1-118-19555-0 (ebk); ISBN 978-1-118-19544-4 (ebk); ISBN 978-1-118-19547-5 (ebk)

Manufactured in the United States of America

10 9 8 7 6 5 4 3

WILEY

About the Author

Scott J. Burnham, a graduate of New York University School of Law, is the Curley Professor of Commercial Law at Gonzaga University School of Law in Spokane, Washington. For 30 years, he has taught Contracts at law schools throughout the U.S. and internationally. As a practicing lawyer and consultant on contract matters, he has a good sense of the practical application of contracts principles, and as a prolific writer on legal topics, he has the ability to convey those principles with clarity.

Dedication

To everyone who studies contract law — may you grow to love her as much as I do!

Author's Acknowledgments

Thanks to acquisitions editors Michael Lewis and David Lutton, who chose me to author this book and ironed out all the preliminary details to make it possible, and to Larry Garvin, who recommended me for the gig.

Elizabeth Rea, my project editor, deserves a loud cheer for serving as a gifted and patient collaborator and editor — shuffling chapters back and forth, shepherding the text and graphics through production, making sure any technical issues were properly resolved, and serving as the unofficial quality control manager. Copy editor Danielle Voirol earns the editor of the year award for ferreting out my typos, misspellings, grammatical errors, and other language foe paws (or is it faux pas?), in addition to assisting Elizabeth as reader advocate. I also tip my hat to the Composition crew for doing such an outstanding job of transforming my text and graphics into such an attractive book. My deepest thanks go to wordsmith Joe Kraynak, who was able to successfully blend my knowledge of Contracts with his knowledge of writing.

Publisher's Acknowledgments

We're proud of this book; please send us your comments at http://dummies.custhelp.com. For other comments, please contact our Customer Care Department within the U.S. at 877-762-2974, outside the U.S. at 317-572-3993, or fax 317-572-4002.

Some of the people who helped bring this book to market include the following:

Acquisitions, Editorial, and Vertical Websites

Project Editor: Elizabeth Rea

Acquisitions Editor: Michael Lewis

Senior Copy Editor: Danielle Voirol

Development Editor: Joe Kraynak

Assistant Editor: David Lutton

Editorial Program Coordinator: Joe Niesen

Technical Editors: James P. Nehf, Jeremy Telman

Editorial Manager: Michelle Hacker

Editorial Assistant: Alexa Koschier

Cover Photo: © iStockphoto.com/Pali Rao

Cartoons: Rich Tennant (www.the5thwave.com)

Composition Services

Project Coordinator: Nikki Gee

Layout and Graphics: Joyce Haughey, Christin Swinford, Laura Westhuis

Proofreaders: Melissa Cossell, Bonnie Mikkelson

Indexer: Valerie Haynes Perry

Publishing and Editorial for Consumer Dummies

    Kathleen Nebenhaus, Vice President and Executive Publisher

    Kristin Ferguson-Wagstaffe, Product Development Director

    Ensley Eikenburg, Associate Publisher, Travel

    Kelly Regan, Editorial Director, Travel

Publishing for Technology Dummies

    Andy Cummings, Vice President and Publisher

Composition Services

    Debbie Stailey, Director of Composition Services

Contents at a Glance

Table of Contents

Introduction

● ●

*I*n *The Paper Chase,* a TV series based on a 1973 movie about the adventures of first-year law students at Harvard, Professor Kingsfield, the Contracts professor, tells his students the following:

> The study of law is something new and unfamiliar to most of you, unlike any other schooling you have ever known before. You teach yourselves the law, but I train your minds. You come in here with a skull full of mush, and, if you survive, you leave thinking like a lawyer.

Getting you to think like a lawyer is the goal of law school, but reaching that goal can seem more arduous than it has to be. When you take the course called Contracts, for example, you'll probably find that you're mostly reading cases, and you never see a contract.

One reason for this disconnect is that the course in Contracts is traditionally designed to teach you "legal method" — skills such as reading cases, analysis, and synthesis — and not the substance of contract law, which is often sort of incidental. The only problem is that you have to know the rules and principles of contract law in order to have some grist for the analytical mill.

Because your casebook may not present the material in an easily accessible and understandable format, *Contract Law For Dummies* is designed to plug that gap. It can help you wrap your brain around the most fundamental concepts and help you see the forest, not just the trees. Consider this book your step-stool up to the higher-complexity coverage you'll encounter in your classes.

About This Book

Contract law isn't exactly a science or an art; it's a little of each. As a science, contract law is governed by certain principles and rules. As an art, contract law often requires creativity as courts apply the rules and interpret the language of contracts. Because of this, *Contract Law For Dummies* contains a little of both. It presents the rules that govern contracts and provides numerous examples to help you apply those rules to different fact situations. This presentation enables you, as a budding contract lawyer, to do the following:

> ✔ More accurately predict a court's ruling on any given contract dispute.
>
> ✔ Know when you have to follow a rule and when you can change it.
>
> ✔ Draft contracts that more effectively protect your clients' interests.
>
> ✔ Pass your law school and bar exams.

This book is organized so you can read it from cover to cover or skip around to only those parts, chapters, or sections that capture your current fancy or serve your present needs. I've been teaching contract law for 30 years and practiced it for 7 years before that, and I've developed a unique approach that has been very successful for my students. This book follows that approach, presenting what you need to know in the order that tends to be most effective.

As you'll soon discover, however, developing the skills required for understanding and practicing contract law — and doing it well — isn't always a linear path. While discovering new concepts and ways to interpret the language of contracts, you often must skip back to review what you thought you already knew and understood. This book is optimized for skipping around to find exactly what you need whenever you happen to need it.

Conventions Used in This Book

I use several conventions in this book to call your attention to certain items. For example:

- ✔ *Italic* highlights new, somewhat technical terms (such as *objective manifestation* and *parol evidence*), which I follow up with straightforward, easy-to-understand definitions.
- ✔ **Boldface** text indicates keywords and phrases in bulleted and numbered lists.
- ✔ Monofont highlights web addresses.
- ✔ A *widget* is a hypothetical good bought and sold in Contracts classes.
- ✔ *Contracts* with a capital *C* refers to the study of the subject, and *contracts* with a small *c* refers to agreements.
- ✔ I generally cite the North Carolina version of the Uniform Commercial Code (UCC), because the Uniform version is under copyright, whereas an enacted statute is in the public domain.
- ✔ When I refer to "the Code," I mean the UCC. And when you see "the Restatement," I'm referring to the Second Restatement of Contracts.

What You're Not to Read

You can safely skip anything you see in a gray shaded box. We stuck this material in a box (called a *sidebar*) for the same reason that most people stick stuff in boxes: to get it out of the way so you don't trip over it. However, you may find the brief asides in the sidebars engaging, entertaining, and perhaps even mildly informative.

Foolish Assumptions

In writing this book, I made a few foolish assumptions, mostly about your motivation and how you're going to use this book:

- ✔ You're planning to master U.S. contract law. This book mentions English law, international law, and the contract law of other countries only in passing.

- ✔ You're eager to tackle contract law.

- ✔ You're probably going to supplement this text with more formal study, including coursework, additional reading, assignments, and briefing the cases.

- ✔ You understand that my approach to teaching contract law is only one of many effective ways.

- ✔ In class, you won't say, "But Burnham says. . . ."

I make no assumptions concerning how much you already know about contract law — you needn't know anything to get started.

How This Book Is Organized

To assist you in navigating this book's contents, I divvied up the chapters that comprise this book into seven distinct parts. This section provides a quick overview of what I cover in each part.

Part I: Introducing Contract Law and Contract Formation

In a contract law case, one of the first things the court has to determine is whether the parties even have a contract. The chapters in this part introduce and explain the essential elements of contract formation (offer, acceptance, and consideration) along with notable exceptions — promises that are enforceable without a contract.

As a bonus, Chapter 1 provides an overview of contract law and introduces you to the two sources of governing rules: the Restatement of Contracts and the Uniform Commercial Code (UCC).

Part II: Determining Whether a Contract Is Void, Voidable, or Unenforceable

To challenge the formation of a contract in the court of law, a party may present a *contract defense* — proof claiming that certain additional facts undermine the contract's formation and destroy its enforceability. This part explains different contract defenses, including whether a party did anything illegal or unfair and whether the parties had the ability to make a contract, as well as the factors that determine whether an oral agreement is enforceable.

Part III: Analyzing Contract Terms and Their Meaning

Contract disputes arise when the parties don't concur on which terms they agreed to or what the terms mean. One party may claim that the parties agreed to a term that doesn't appear in the written contract. A contract may have gaps that fail to address unforeseen circumstances. Or the language in a contract may be ambiguous. The chapters in this part discuss several strategies that the courts use to plug the gaps in a contract and interpret what the language really means . . . or at least what it would mean to reasonable people standing in the parties' shoes.

Part IV: Performing the Contract or Breaching It

Whether the parties formed a contract is only half the story. The other half deals with the performance of that contract. The chapters in this part tackle nonperformance issues. Here you find out whether changes made to a contract after formation are enforceable, whether the occurrence of unforeseen events or the nonoccurrence of certain conditions excuses performance, and how one party may breach a contract even before performance is due.

Part V: Exploring Remedies for Breach of Contract

If a party breaches the contract, the courts must decide how to remedy the breach in a way that's fair for both parties. This isn't tort law, where the courts try to punish the wrongdoer. In contract law, the goal is to give the non-breaching party what she expected from the performance of the contract but no more than that. The non-breaching party shouldn't get a windfall at the expense of the breaching party.

The chapters in this part introduce and explain the various methods available to the courts to remedy a breach.

Part VI: Bringing Third Parties into the Picture

A contract often affects more than the parties who made it. A contract is like a piece of property that can be carved up and bought and sold. When parts are transferred, third parties can get involved in performance and enforcement of the contract. The chapters in this part help you recognize the rights and duties of those third parties and decide under which circumstances third parties are allowed to enforce contracts and may have duties to perform under a contract.

Part VII: The Part of Tens

Every *For Dummies* book includes a Part of Tens — chapters containing ten bite-sized, easily digestible tips, tricks, or insights. Here I offer ten key questions to ask when analyzing a contract problem and ten famous people and philosophies in contract law.

Icons Used in This Book

Throughout this book, icons appear in the margins to call your attention to different types of information. Here are the icons and a brief description of each.

Everything in this book is important (except for the stuff in the shaded boxes), but some information is even *more* important. When you see this icon, read the text next to it not once but two or three times to tattoo it on your gray matter.

Tips provide insider insight from behind the scenes. When you're looking for a better, faster way to do something, check out these tips.

This icon appears when you need to be extra vigilant or seek additional guidance before moving forward. Don't skip this important information — I'm warning you!

Certain cases have strongly influenced contract law and how the courts interpret the law and language of contracts. To spot these key cases, look for the Key Case icon.

Contract law makes a lot more sense when you see how it applies to fact situations, so I use hypothetical situations liberally throughout the book to illustrate and simplify the explanation of certain concepts. The Example icon flags these hypotheticals so you can easily spot them.

Where to Go From Here

Contract Law For Dummies is designed to take you from ground zero to a fundamental understanding of contract law. If you're interested in the big-picture view of contract law in theory and practice, check out Chapter 1. Otherwise, read the book from cover to cover, skip around by using the table of contents as your guide, or head to the index if you need guidance on a more specific topic.

Part I

Introducing Contract Law and Contract Formation

"Here at Don's, we seal a deal with a straight look, a handshake and a reverse Step-Over Toe-Hold."

In this part . . .

Chapter 1 begins by exploring the fundamentals of contract law — what it is, how it came into being, and which sources provide the rules and principles that govern contracts. Here, you discover the basics of contract formation, contract defenses, and contract interpretation, and you find out what generally happens when parties don't fulfill their contractual obligations.

The remaining chapters in this part focus on contract formation. You encounter the three essential elements of contract formation — offer, acceptance, and consideration — and find out when promises are enforceable even if parties haven't met the requirements to form a contract.

Chapter 1

Getting the Lowdown on Contract Law

In This Chapter

▶ Wrapping your brain around the concept of contract law

▶ Grasping the fundamental rules and principles that govern contracts

▶ Understanding contract formation, defenses, and interpretation

▶ Getting up to speed on performance, breach, and remedies

Contract law may feel overwhelming, especially when you're in a class that reads and analyzes case after case after case. Adding to that load are the many sources of contract law, including the common law, the Restatement of Contracts (Restatement), the Uniform Commercial Code (UCC), federal and state statutes, and rules that govern when parties are allowed or prohibited from coming up with their own contract terms.

Although all the details swirling around the topic of contract law are important, placing those details in context makes them more manageable and enables you to see the big picture. That's what this chapter is all about. Here, you get the eye-in-the-sky view of contract law and a framework on which to hang the rich tapestry of policies, principles, and rules collectively referred to as *contract law*.

Grasping the Concept of Contract Law

Contrary to popular belief, contract law isn't just a bunch of rules and regulations that govern agreements between people. It's not developed and imposed from above by some rule-making authority. It developed naturally over the course of thousands of years through the interactions and transactions between people like you and me — the parties who form contracts.

In this section, I explain what a contract is, present a few different perspectives on the principles that should drive the formation of contract rules, and briefly explore how contract law developed into what it is today.

From coconuts to contracts: Grasping the purpose of contracts

To begin to grasp what contract law is all about, imagine a group of people on a desert island trying to figure out ways to govern their relationships. They want to be a community, but they also want each person to have autonomy. Collectively, they decide that each person may own property and make agreements about what to do with that property. They discover that the free exchange of property increases the wealth and well-being of both parties; for example, if one person has a surplus of coconuts and a shortage of fish and another person has a surplus of fish but no coconuts, the two may exchange goods for their mutual benefit.

If the parties take the next step and decide that they can promise in advance to perform such exchanges, their agreement indicates the beginnings of contract law. As certain issues arise, the islanders form rules that address those issues, such as how quickly the parties must perform, the acceptable quality of the coconuts and fish, and the consequences for nonperformance. Their system of contract law grows organically from the ground up, not from the top down.

Defining contract

A *contract* is simply a promise or set of promises enforceable by law. Which agreements are enforceable by law varies from culture to culture — what's acceptable in one culture may not be acceptable in another. If I agree to sell you my house, for example, the house-selling culture says that I can't make any untruthful statements about the house. But if I agree to play a hand in the World Series of Poker, then the poker culture says that I can't make any *truthful* statements about my hand.

The United States doesn't have a monolithic contract law with uniform rules. Contract law is nuanced and fact intensive. A "rule" may differ, for example, depending on whether the parties are two giant corporations having their lawyers negotiate an agreement or family members making an agreement over the dinner table.

Comparing different schools of thought on contract rules

The overriding principles that guide the formation of contract rules vary according to different schools of thought. Depending on your perspective, you may think that the rules should be based on what is

✔ **Customary and reasonable:** In most systems of contract law, the rule that develops is usually based on what's customary and reasonable. With nearly every issue that arises in contract law, just think about what's reasonable, and you'll usually discover the "rule."

✔ **Economically efficient:** My economist friends think that rules should be based on what's most economically efficient. According to the economists, people enter contracts for their mutual financial benefit; for example, you agree to sell and I agree to buy your car for $7,000, because right now, the $7,000 is worth more to you than the car, and the car is worth more to me than the $7,000 I have in my piggy bank. Throughout this book, I sometimes share the economist's perspective, but if you haven't studied Econ (or read *Economics For Dummies* [Wiley]), stick with asking what's reasonable and you'll come up with the rule most of the time.

✔ **Fair for the little guy:** According to my friends in the Critical Studies movement, the people in power, who happened to be rich white men, made the rules. The rich guys came up with rules that are favorable to them, so contract law needs to watch out for the little guy, who gets the worst of it in contracts.

Regardless of view, everyone would probably agree that one of the most difficult problems facing contract law today is the ease with which consumers can bind themselves to contracts by clicking I AGREE to the "terms and conditions" that nobody reads. This is quite different from the contract created by a carefully negotiated exchange of drafts. Or is it? Throughout your career in contract law, you'll struggle to determine whether the same rules apply to both situations.

Tracing contract law's roots

Most contract law in the United States comes from England, where it was largely based on the tradition commonly referred to as the *common law,* meaning the law made by judges. Many of the rules of commercial law that govern buying, selling, and financing come from medieval times. Anytime parties traded, they had to have an understanding of the deal they were making. They made their own rules, called the *law merchant,* to govern their situation.

As the law became more specialized, various areas of contract law were spun off and now stand on their own. Insurance law, banking law, and government procurement law are all areas of contract law that you don't study in a standard Contracts course. One authority has called contract law "the law of leftovers" — general principles that remain irrespective of the substance of the transaction.

Meeting the Key Players: Common Law, the Restatement, and the UCC

Although you'll find no definitive collection of the rules and regulations that govern contracts, you can find guidance from three primary resources: the common law, the Restatement of Contracts, and the Uniform Commercial Code (UCC, or the Code). I refer to these resources throughout the book, so you need to have a general understanding of how each resource contributes to contract law.

Exploring the common law: Tradition and precedent

In the Anglo-American (meaning English and American) tradition, contract law was *common law* — judges decided each dispute on the basis of tradition and recorded precedent. Imagine yourself the lord of the manor in Merrie Olde England, and the parties to a dispute look to you for wisdom. You'd likely ask, "What have we done in the past? Does it make sense today?" — the same questions today's judges ask!

In a common-law system, if you want to find out what the outcome is likely to be under a particular fact pattern, you have to read all the applicable cases (the reported court decisions) and synthesize them. That's what you do in your legal research and writing class and you sometimes do in your Contracts class when you have a string of cases to read. You don't read them in isolation; you try to see the connections and be prepared to say why one case came out one way and one came out another way.

Because of the common-law rule of *stare decisis* ("let the decision stand"), courts generally follow precedent. Therefore, you can fairly accurately predict what a court will do in the future based on what courts have done in the past. Because that predictive power is important to businesses entering transactions, contract law is slow to change.

Capturing general rules in the Restatement

Although the common-law approach is effective, sometimes you just want to know what the general rule is, devoid of any particular fact situation. Having to read all the cases on point to find a rule would be a pain. Fortunately, someone has always been willing to read all those cases and try to synthesize them into *black-letter rules* — attempts to capture the essence of each rule. In the 18th century, that someone was Sir William Blackstone, who wrote *Commentaries on the Laws of England* (1765–1769). In those days, lawyers, including many of our Founding Fathers, relied on Blackstone for this purpose. Now contract law has the Restatement.

The *Restatements of Law* are an effort by the American Law Institute (a group of law professors, lawyers, judges, and other interested parties) to reduce the law to workable sets of black-letter rules. The First Restatement of Contracts came out in 1932. The principal reporter was Samuel Williston, who wrote one of the great multivolume treatises on contract law. The rules in this Restatement are somewhat rigid and don't always reflect modern legal thinking, which often takes into consideration a number of mushy factors instead of drawing bright lines.

A Second Restatement of Contracts was promulgated in 1981, with Allan Farnsworth as reporter. When I refer to "the Restatement," I mean the Second Restatement.

Although the Restatement is a great resource, recognize its limitations:

- ✔ **It's not enacted law, so it has only persuasive authority.** If you're citing law to a judge, the judge wants to know what the higher courts in that jurisdiction have held, not what the Restatement says.

- ✔ **It represents a limited number of views.** People hold conflicting views of what should be the rule, with some jurisdictions following one line of reasoning and others following another. The Restatement generally chooses the majority view in this situation, so you may get the misimpression from its statement of a rule that the law is more settled than it is. And on a few occasions, the Restatement states the minority view because the drafters thought it represented the better view.

  Many publications of the Restatement for students contain only the rules. The complete edition includes commentaries and illustrations to help you more fully understand each rule.

Statutes: Supplanting common law with codes

Although contract law is traditionally common law, statutes enacted by legislatures are increasingly taking over the role of common law. The courts have to follow the laws enacted by the legislature, so if the law has a statute on point, that should be the starting point for a court.

As you're probably aware, many European countries have civil law systems based largely on systematic arrangements of statutes called *codes.* Such systems have an authoritative source to go to in order to find the governing contract law. Louisiana, because of its French origins, has a civil code of Contracts, and so do many other states.

In the mid-19th century, a "codification" movement in England and the U.S. sought to codify the law in order to make it more accessible, and the codifiers won out in a number of states, including California, which has codified the law of Contracts in its Civil Code. But these codes often just state common-law rules and principles, leaving the courts plenty of room to interpret the statute and apply it to a particular situation.

Contract law is mostly state law rather than federal law. Although no federal common law of contracts exists, a number of federal statutes govern contracts. Most of these are in the consumer and credit areas, so when you have a transaction in these areas, check for any relevant federal statutes.

Brushing up on the Uniform Commercial Code (UCC)

If each state had the same statutes governing contracts, then the law would be easier to find and more predictable, which is especially important in commercial law that applies to many interstate transactions. Congress could probably enact an American Commercial Code based on its authority to regulate interstate commerce, but Congress has left this project to the states. The states have turned to the assistance of the Uniform Law Commission (ULC) — a private group with representatives from every state that aspires to write model statutes that get the law right and that are enactable.

When the ULC agrees on a model statute, the process is only just beginning, because the model statute isn't yet law. State legislatures must enact the statutes for them to become law.

The ULC, with the assistance of the American Law Institute (the folks responsible for the Restatements) has had great success getting states to enact the Uniform Commercial Code (UCC), which contains a number of Articles addressing various aspects of commercial law. Karl Llewellyn first drafted this model statute in the 1940s, and states began to enact it in the 1960s. Article 2, which deals with the sale of goods, is the Article most relevant to contract law.

Varying the model statutes in state laws

The ULC is frequently unable to achieve its goal of uniformity, because states can and often do alter the Uniform version. So although every state has enacted the UCC (Louisiana has not enacted Article 2), they've all enacted slightly different versions. In this book, I generally cite the North Carolina version, not out of some love for the First-in-Flight state but because the Uniform version is under copyright, whereas an enacted statute is in the public domain.

In your law studies, you'll probably be working with the Restatement and the Uniform version of the UCC as promulgated by the ULC. But remember, when you have a research question in a certain jurisdiction, you need to look up the law in that state to make sure that it's the same.

Note: Attempts to revise UCC Article 2 have come to an end, but Article 1 underwent a revision process in 2001. Most states have enacted Revised Article 1, which is also used on the Multistate Bar Exam, so that's the version of Article 1 that I refer to. Again, when doing research in a jurisdiction, you must find out which is the applicable law in your jurisdiction.

Looking at some important UCC principles

Although UCC Article 2 gets the most press in this book, you also encounter references to UCC Article 1, which deals with basic principles and definitions that apply throughout the Code, including Article 2.

Some of the basic principles found in Article 1 are so important that I cite them repeatedly. I discuss two of the most significant provisions next.

Freedom of contract: Letting parties agree to a different rule

One important principle of UCC Article 1 is what I call the *freedom of contract provision.* Section 1-302(a), as enacted in North Carolina at 25-1-302(a), provides the following:

> § 25-1-302. Variation by agreement.
>
> (a) Except as otherwise provided in subsection (b) of this section or elsewhere in [the Uniform Commercial Code], the effect of provisions of [the Uniform Commercial Code] may be varied by agreement.

This important rule offers guidance on how to think of "the law." Contract law is not a bunch of regulations that parties to a contract must follow. Often, contract law facilitates a transaction by providing a rule that kicks in if the parties neglect to provide their own rule. These rules are often called *default rules* because, like the default settings on your computer, they apply unless you change them. But very often, as UCC § 1-302(a) states, contract law gives the parties the freedom of contract to come up with their own rule. Some of the rules are regulatory, and unfortunately the Code isn't always helpful in identifying whether a particular rule is regulatory (can't be changed) or facilitatory (can be changed by the parties' mutual agreement).

Note, for example, that § 1-302(b) states some obligations that the parties can't get out of by agreement. But that same provision goes on to say that you can "determine standards by which the performance of those obligations is to be measured." You can't, for example, agree not to be reasonable, but you can agree, "It is to be considered reasonable if we do A, B, and C." Figuring out the interplay between what is permissible in some circumstances and not permissible in others is one of the greatest challenges in studying contract law.

As you study Contracts, try to identify which are the regulatory rules that have to be followed and which are the facilitatory rules that the parties are free to change. Take a nuanced view. If the court doesn't let the parties change the rule, ask why — was it because the parties were in a particular state? Entered into a particular kind of transaction? Had an imbalance of power?

Supplementing the UCC with common law

Another important provision in Article 1 is § 1-103(b), which points out that the Code is not the exclusive law applicable to a transaction. As enacted in North Carolina at § 25-1-103(b), it provides the following:

> (b) Unless displaced by the particular provisions of this Chapter [the Uniform Commercial Code], the principles of law and equity [. . .] supplement its provisions.

This rule makes clear that the Code doesn't address every topic, and where it's incomplete, courts will fill in gaps in the Code with rules derived from the common law. For example, the Code says very little about the defenses to contract formation that I explain in Chapters 5 through 7 of this book. Section 1-103(b) says that in a case involving the sale of goods, those defenses apply, but you have to look to the common law to see what they are.

Applying state law in federal court

Many contracts cases are heard in federal court. Most of those cases got there on the jurisdictional basis of *diversity* — under federal law, parties who are citizens of different states are allowed to use the federal courts if the amount of money at issue is over a certain dollar amount set by Congress. In such cases, the federal court uses the principles of Choice of Law (as I explain in Chapter 18) to decide which state's law governs the transaction. The federal court is in effect sitting as the state's highest court and asking, "What would the judges on that court do in this situation?"

Whenever you see that a contracts case is in federal court, ask how that court got jurisdiction. If the answer is diversity, then identify the state whose law the court is applying. If the court got jurisdiction in some other way — for example, because it's a matter of *admiralty law* (law on the high seas) or because the United States is a party — then the court follows general principles of contract law rather than the law of any particular state.

Be careful when you research contract law questions, particularly online. Your search results for the decisions of a particular state often include federal court decisions from the circuit in which the state is located. But you have to read the federal court decision carefully to find out which state's law it's applying. If it's not applying the law of your state, the federal court isn't a very good authority. And even if the court applies your state's laws, remember that the federal court decision is only persuasive authority in your state.

Inferring a state rule that makes little sense

When federal courts take a contract case on the basis of diversity, the federal courts defer to state law, regardless of whether they agree with it. A good example of how this plays out in the real world is in the case of *Northrop Corp. v. Litronic Industries,* 29 F.3d 1173 (7th Cir. 1994).

In this case, Judge Richard Posner of the 7th circuit Federal Court of Appeals was given the task of ruling on a case where Illinois law applied. The rule in issue had three possible interpretations, but the Illinois courts had not yet expressed their opinion on the matter. Although Judge Posner preferred the view adopted only in California, his job was to try to figure out how the courts in Illinois would decide the case.

Judge Posner concluded that Illinois would probably not agree with his preferred view and said in effect, *We are hearing this case because of diversity, and Illinois law applies. Illinois would likely follow a rule that makes less sense, but I am going to have to hold my nose and go along with the state rule because that is what a federal judge has to do in a diversity case.*

You might think it would make more sense for the federal court judges to ask the state court judges what they would do, and many states have a procedure for doing that. Sometimes when the state has insufficient precedent, the state court takes a "certified question" from the federal court in order to assist the federal court in resolving a dispute.

Applying different sources of contract law

When you look at a contract case, you often need to consider several different sources of contract laws, including common law, the Restatement, the UCC, and federal and state statutes.

Suppose a client in Montana purchased a wheelchair for personal use and the seller refuses to fix it, even though it came with a warranty. Is she entitled to relief? At first glance, the case seems pretty simple, but it gets complicated in a hurry when you start to consider all sources of law that may come into play, which include the following:

- Federal consumer protection law, because the case involves a consumer
- The federal Magnuson-Moss Warranty Act, because it involves a warranty
- Montana UCC Article 2, because it involves the sale of goods
- The Montana Wheelchair Warranty Act, a statute that specifically addresses this transaction
- State consumer protection statutes and other relevant statutes
- General principles of contract law in Montana, found both in statutes and in cases

A word about international law and the CISG

Uniformity is helpful in governing both inter-state and international transactions. More than 70 countries, including the United States, have adopted the United Nations Convention on Contracts for the International Sale of Goods (CISG). By default, the CISG applies to transactions for the sale of goods between businesses located in countries that have adopted it. You can find the text of the CISG at www.uncitral.org/uncitral/en/uncitral_texts/sale_goods/1980CISG.html.

Many U.S. lawyers contract around application of the CISG by putting in their international con-tracts a choice of law provision (see Chapter 18) specifying that the UCC of a particular state gov-erns the agreement. Other lawyers, particularly in contracts that contain an arbitration clause (see Chapter 18), specify that the UNIDROIT Principles of International Commercial Contracts will apply. For the text of the UNIDROIT Principles, promul-gated by the International Chamber of Commerce, visit www.unidroit.org/english/principles/contracts/main.htm.

✔ The parties' contract, because it's part of their own private contract law (You'd have to examine the contract terms carefully; the parties' agree-ment to a term doesn't necessarily make it enforceable. To the extent the federal and state law is regulatory, the contract would have to follow that law, but to the extent it's facilitatory, the parties would be free to provide their own rules.)

If you like solving puzzles like this, welcome to the world of contracts!

Forming, Defending, and Interpreting Contracts: The Basics

Knowing the rules that govern contracts is only half the battle. You have to be able to apply those rules to different situations. Because contract law is so fact dependent, it's always coming up with exceptions to the rules to deal with par-ticular circumstances. No book covers all the possible variables and exceptions, but knowing the rules and the principles behind them gives you a firm founda-tion to build on. This section provides a framework for understanding Contracts.

Look at the big picture. Doing so may be difficult because no one agrees on a single best way to organize the study of Contracts. The topics are like a deck of cards that you can shuffle up and deal in various ways. Whether you start with remedies or with consideration, what's important is seeing how the pieces all fit together.

Understanding contract formation

Every contract starts at the point of formation. As I explain in Chapters 2 and 3, a *contract* is a bargained-for exchange that requires the following three ingredients:

- ✔ **Offer:** Party A's promise to Party B in exchange for something
- ✔ **Acceptance:** Party B's assent to Party A's offer
- ✔ **Consideration:** What each party offers in exchange for the other party's promise

If the parties didn't form a contract (because one of the essential ingredients was missing), that may not be the end of the story. Based on the theories of reliance and restitution (see Chapter 4), even in the absence of a contract, parties may be required by law to compensate another party because they made a promise or received a benefit:

- ✔ **Reliance:** If one person relies on another person's promise, the promise may be enforceable even in the absence of a bargain. For example, I promise to give you my car when you graduate, and you pass up another free-car offer as a result. I may be required to compensate you for your loss. Contract law uses reliance to restore the injured party to the position she was in before she relied on the promise.
- ✔ **Restitution:** If Party A confers a benefit on Party B without forcing it on her and without intending it as a gift, then even though Party B never offered consideration in exchange for that benefit, Party A may have a right to receive restitution. Contract law uses restitution to make the benefitted party give up the benefit, restoring her to the position she was in before the benefit was conferred.

Checking out attack and defense maneuvers

When a deal fulfills the requirements of offer, acceptance, and consideration, the agreement is presumptively an enforceable contract, but either party may challenge the contract via a *contract defense,* otherwise known as a *defense to formation.* A party may base its contract defense on different grounds, such as the characteristics of one of the parties (under the age of 18 or having impaired judgment), something one party did to the other (fraud, duress, or undue influence), or something wrong with the contract itself (mutual mistake, illegality, unconscionability, or an oral contract when the law requires the contract to be evidenced by a writing). Chapter 5 introduces contract defenses, and Chapters 6 through 8 discuss the specifics.

Finding the terms of the contract and building contract-interpretation skills

A contract rarely contains a comprehensive list of terms the parties agreed to, nor does it provide for everything that might happen in the future. If the contract is indefinite or incomplete, contract law provides ways to clarify the terms and fill the gaps. If the agreement is part written and part oral, contract law uses the parol evidence rule to determine which unwritten terms to include. Some terms not included in the contract may need to be added due to *course of performance* (a history of how the parties acted under the present agreement), *course of dealing* (how the parties performed under other, similar contracts), or *trade usage* (how other parties in the industry perform). Finally, even after finding all the terms, the parties may have a disagreement regarding interpretation of unclear language in the contract. Chapters 9 through 11 address these issues.

Examining Contract Performance, Breach, and Remedies

After parties form a contract, the parties must *perform* (do what they promised to do). If a party doesn't perform and she's in breach, then contract law must determine a just remedy for the breach — usually an amount of money sufficient to compensate the non-breaching party for what he lost as a result of the breach. This section explores breach, remedies for breach, and the role of third parties.

Recognizing breach of contract

Breach of contract is a deceptively easy concept to grasp — it means that the party didn't keep his promise. Sometimes, however, a party who didn't keep his promise may actually not be in breach, as in the following situations:

- ✓ **The parties didn't actually have a contract.** One of the best and most common responses to an allegation of breach of contract is to launch a contract defense to try to prove that contract formation never happened. A party accused of breach may say, "Ha-ha! I can't be in breach because we never had a contract!"

- ✓ **The parties modified the contract, omitting the promise.** See Chapter 12 for details on making changes to a contract.

✔ **Performance was excused.** Performance may be excused because of an unanticipated event that prevented it or because performance was conditional and the condition never occurred. The most common condition is the other party's performance: The claim is that if you didn't perform, then I don't have to perform. See Chapters 13 and 14 for details on circumstances that excuse performance.

✔ **The other party repudiated prior to the performance deadline.** One of the other parties may have made an *anticipatory repudiation* — telling the other party in advance of the time for performance that he doesn't plan to perform the contract and thus letting the non-repudiating party off the hook. Chapter 15 covers anticipatory repudiation.

Formulating remedies and establishing losses

If parties have a contract and one party breaches, then the injured, non-breaching party is entitled to a remedy. The goal here is to give the injured party the *expectancy* — the position the party would've been in had the contract been performed. In addition to the expectancy, reliance and restitution come back as two additional remedies for breach. Chapters 16 to 18 cover the various remedies in greater detail.

In contract law, the principal remedy, the expectancy, puts the non-breaching party where she would've been had the contract been performed, not back where she was before the contract was formed.

Exploring the role of third parties in contract law

Third parties are people who aren't parties to the contract but who are affected by it in some way. They may be *third-party beneficiaries* of the contract (they stand to receive something), or they may have rights assigned or duties delegated to them by parties to the contract. Contracts classes rarely cover the role of third parties in contract law, but this is an important topic in the real world. Chapters 19 and 20 explain what you need to know.

Practicing in the Real World of Contracts

Getting lost in the study of Contracts or any legal subject is easy. The rules keep piling up, you can't keep them all straight, and pretty soon you're drowning under them. Take a deep breath and try to see the big picture as I present it in this chapter.

Most contract issues are solved through negotiation, not litigation, so contract lawyers, especially the most skillful of them, rarely see the inside of a courtroom. As you're studying case after case — the way Contracts is typically taught — fight the urge to become overly litigation-oriented and bogged down in minutiae.

 Use your skills to see how you can use contract law in planning and drafting agreements. Contracts then becomes a matter of preventive law: Having read how people screwed up in past cases, you're going to get it right so you and your clients don't end up in court. When you think of Contracts as planning and drafting, you appreciate more the principle of freedom of contract. If you know the rules, then you're better able to draft around them.

Chapter 2

Let's Make a Deal: Offer and Acceptance

A contract is a promise or set of promises enforceable by law. The waters get a little murky, however, when you begin to explore how the law determines whether parties have formed a contract. Questions arise, such as *What constitutes an offer? Did the offeree signal acceptance? Was the offer still open when the acceptance occurred?*

Questions also arise regarding the manner and method of acceptance. Was the agreement formed by *promise* (a commitment to do something) or *performance* (actually doing something)? Does clicking the Agree button on a website or entering an electronic signature count as acceptance? What if the party on the receiving end of a form offer signals acceptance with a form of her own, complete with additional or different terms? This chapter answers these questions and more.

Contract Formation: Getting a Handle on the Essentials

In the Anglo-American legal system, a contract is binding if it fulfills the following three contract formation requirements:

✔ **Offer:** One party (the *offeror*) promises the other party (the *offeree*) something in return for something else. To legally qualify as an offer, it must specify what the offeror wants in return.

What's binding? It's a cultural thing

Each culture may draw the line between non-binding talk and binding commitments in a different place. In theory, a society could treat all promises as legally enforceable. Five-year-olds seem to live in such a culture — they scream, "But, Mommy, you *promised*," as though that alone were sufficient to require enforcement. Other societies may make entering into an enforceable agreement very difficult. A few hundred years ago, English society required that you put a seal on a document to make it binding.

Fortunately for the practice of international law, most societies accept written agreements signed by both parties as a sufficient indication of intent to make a binding commitment, but exceptions do exist. The counsel for a multinational company recently told me about a deal he made in which the other country's law required that both parties sign every page and have the signing witnessed by a team of notaries.

Currently in the U.S. and elsewhere, electronic contracting challenges the tradition of signing contracts by hand. Society must now determine how parties can form binding contracts in the culture of cyberspace.

Don't let the -or and -ee suffixes confuse you. Just remember that the -or is on the giving end, as in *promisor* (the party making the promise), and the -ee is on the receiving end, as in *promisee* (the party to whom the promise is made).

✔ **Acceptance:** The offeree gives the offeror whatever was requested in the offer.

✔ **Consideration:** The consideration is whatever each party brings to the table. For example, if I contract with you to be your attorney, you bring money, and I bring my services.

Mix all three ingredients, and you have a contract. The rest of this chapter explains how to determine whether the requirements of offer and acceptance have been satisfied. Chapter 3 tackles the third requirement: consideration.

A contract signals the end of "just talk" and the beginning of serious business. After a contract is made, if a dispute arises, one party can take the other to court to seek enforcement. Contract formation is all about distinguishing between "just talk" and the binding commitment that has legal ramifications.

Forming a Contract: Promises, Offers, and Mutual Assent

It takes two parties to make a contract. A *party* is a person or entity who agrees to be bound by the contract. (See how much fun contract law can be? One person is a party!) Part VI explains how a *third party,* one who's not bound by the contract, may become involved.

To make a contract, both parties must give their *mutual assent;* that is, they must willingly agree to the terms of the contract. To determine whether the parties have formed a contract, you must carefully examine the facts to find assent by both parties. This section describes how parties give their assent and reveals that not all promises are legally binding commitments.

Making a commitment by making a promise

A *promise* is a commitment to do or not to do something, regardless of whether the word *promise* is actually used. So to determine whether a party has made a promise, look for the commitment behind the words.

For example, if Joe says to Mary, "I promise to give you $200 tomorrow," that's a commitment; Joe has pledged to do something. If Mary says to Joe, "I'll give you my bicycle tomorrow," that's also a commitment, even though Mary didn't utter the word *promise.*

When one person promises something to another as in this example, it's a *gift promise.* It may be morally binding, but it's not legally binding. To become legally binding, the promise must be accompanied by a request for something in return, as I explain in the next section.

Turning a promise into an offer by asking for something in return

To turn a gift promise into an *offer,* add the condition that the offeree must do or give something in return. That *something* can be either a promise (a commitment to do something) or a performance (actually doing something).

When Joe says to Mary, "I promise to give you $200 tomorrow," that's just a gift promise. But if Joe says to Mary, "I promise to give you $200 tomorrow if you promise to give me your bicycle tomorrow," now he's made an offer. He's promised to do something but only if she promises to do something in return.

Note: To my economist friends, contracts are exchanges that *maximize utility* — the usefulness of whatever the parties agree to exchange. Joe makes his offer because Mary's bicycle is more useful for him than is his $200. If Mary can make better use of the $200 than she can her bicycle, she's likely to agree to the exchange. With both parties better off than they were, the exchange has increased the sum total of human happiness. It's a win-win situation. Way to go, Contracts!

Giving acceptance by giving or agreeing to give what was requested in return

Acceptance occurs when the offeree gives or agrees to give the offeror whatever he asked for in return for his promise (see the section "Acceptance must match the offer: The mirror-image rule," later in this chapter). As with the offer, the acceptance requires no formal language. If Joe offers to buy Mary's bicycle for $200 and she says, "It's a deal!" that's all it takes. At that very moment, Boom! — a contract falls from the sky.

Don't make the mistake of confusing contract formation with contract performance. As soon as Joe presents his offer and Mary accepts it, they've formed a contract. If Joe comes to get the bicycle the next day and Mary says, "Ha-ha! I changed my mind. I'm not selling you my bicycle," then she has breached the contract. See Part IV for info on breach of contract.

Assenting in action or thought: Objective manifestation versus subjective intent

One of the great debates in contract law revolves around whether assent is found in the parties' subjective intent to form a contract or in their objective manifestations:

- ✔ **Subjective intent:** What the parties were *thinking* when they formed the contract
- ✔ **Objective manifestation:** What the parties *did*, such as their words or their outward expressions

Meeting of the minds? Nonsense!

Courts sometimes speak of the need for a "meeting of the minds" in order to establish the intent to be legally bound. But courts don't really mean that. Because they don't know whether the minds actually met, judges look for words or conduct that a disinterested (impartial) observer would regard as indicating agreement to the contract. Such words or conduct constitute the "objective manifestation of assent" that can bind the parties.

Don't describe assent by using that offensive expression (which I refuse to repeat here, because I don't want to encourage you to say it). Instead, say that a contract requires an "objective manifestation of assent." This doesn't exactly roll off your tongue as easily as that other expression, but that's how you should say it and how judges should, too.

Verifying what's going on in someone's mind is impossible, so courts look for assent in the objective manifestations of the parties, not in their intent. This section explains how the objective theory of assent plays out in practice and highlights its importance.

Seeing objective manifestation in practice

The reason I use so many examples in explaining Contracts is that the rules mean something only in context, and seeing a rule applied in different contexts is how you come to understand the law in action. This section contains two examples of how objective manifestation of assent plays out in practice: In one example, someone claims the agreement was a joke, and in the other, someone makes an inadvertent arm movement at an auction.

Suppose that the day after Mary agreed to sell her bicycle to Joe, she has a change of heart and says, "I didn't really mean it when I said, 'It's a deal.' I was just joking." Mary is claiming that no contract was formed because in her mind, she didn't intend her words to be taken seriously.

Unfortunately for Mary, contract law isn't concerned with what was or wasn't in her head but with her objective manifestations. The question is not whether she thought she was serious — that would involve looking at subjective thoughts. The question is whether a reasonable person standing in Joe's shoes would've thought she was serious by looking at her objective manifestations — whether she appeared to be serious when she spoke the words. If the answer is yes, then based on the objective theory of assent, Mary is bound to the contract even if in her heart of hearts she was joking.

A TV commercial for a dandruff shampoo contained a wonderful example of the objective theory of assent. The setting is an auction, which is a great place to explore contract-formation essentials and the nuances of assent. The auctioneer opens the bidding by saying, "Who will give $2,000 for a date with supermodel Cindy?" A guy in the audience lifts his paddle with #18 on it in order to use it to scratch his head. The auctioneer immediately slams down his gavel and says, "Sold to number 18 for $2,000!"

As soon as the auctioneer opens the bidding, he's inviting bids or offers from the attendees. As soon as the guy in the audience lifts his paddle, which everyone knows is how you enter a bid, he has made his offer. When the auctioneer brings his hammer down and says, "Sold!" that's acceptance.

The commercial ends there, but imagine the winning bidder's response: "Hey, wait a minute. I didn't intend to make an offer — my intention was to scratch my head." But contract law would say, "Sorry. We don't care what your subjective intention was. You objectively manifested your assent when you raised the paddle. A reasonable person in the shoes of the auctioneer would think you had made an offer, and he accepted it, so a contract was formed!"

Leonard v. Pepsico: Collecting for a jet

In the case of *Leonard v. Pepsico,* Pepsi issued a catalog of items a person could buy with Pepsi Points. Consumers could buy Pepsi products to earn points, and although people had to submit a minimum of 15 Pepsi Points with their order, they could purchase additional points for 10 cents each. To advertise the promotion, Pepsi ran a commercial in which a teenager is buying all sorts of stuff with Pepsi points — a T-shirt for 75 points, a leather jacket for 1,450 points, sunglasses for 175 points — and finally he descends from the sky and lands in front of his school in his own Harrier Jump Jet (one of those jet planes that can descend straight down). As he lands, the commercial displays "HARRIER FIGHTER 7,000,000 PEPSI POINTS."

After watching the ad, Mr. Leonard sent in an order form with 15 Pepsi Points plus $700,000 and change (to cover postage and handling) and demanded the Harrier Jump Jet. Pepsi claimed no contract had been formed. One of Pepsi's defenses was that because the ad and the catalog didn't constitute an offer but were invitations to make an offer, they could decline to accept Leonard's offer. They also defended on the grounds that even if they had made an offer, it wasn't a serious offer. They argued that Leonard's thinking it was serious didn't matter.

The court decided in favor of Pepsico. It held that Pepsi's objective manifestations in the ad would lead a reasonable person to conclude that Pepsi was joking. Leonard was tossed out of court. To decide for yourself whether a reasonable person would think Pepsi was joking, watch the Pepsi Harrier Jet Commercial video on YouTube.

Appreciating the importance of objective manifestation of assent

The theory of objective manifestation of assent has significant consequences. Because a contract is formed objectively, whether a party reads or understands it is irrelevant. For example, if I sign a ten-page contract and then claim no contract was formed because I never read it or didn't understand it, I'd have no case. The court would look for objective manifestation of assent and find it in my signature.

Similarly, when I travel to Uruguay and rent a car, I have to sign a rental agreement that's written in Spanish. Claiming that no contract was formed, I might say, "No hablo español!" But contract law would point to my signature on the contract and respond, "¡Manifestación objetiva de consentimiento mutuo!" which translates to "Objective manifestation of assent!"

Objective manifestation of assent also comes into play with online contracts. The offeree usually has an opportunity to read the Terms and Conditions but skips that part and clicks the Agree button or its equivalent. That qualifies as an objective manifestation of assent.

Although objective manifestation seals the deal, it doesn't necessarily mean that the contract is enforceable. In some cases, the offeror, knowing that the offeree won't read or understand the contract, slips one-sided terms into it to take unfair advantage. Contract law has ways of dealing with this, as I explain in Chapter 6. However, although the courts may scrutinize such a contract more carefully and may not enforce all the terms, they usually conclude that a contract was formed.

Forming contracts without words: The implied-in-fact contract

As long as other objective manifestations are present, you don't even need words to form a contract. Parties may, through their actions, form an *implied-in-fact contract* — a real contract (that is, a bargained-for contract) found in the conduct of the parties rather than in their words. For example, suppose you go into your favorite fast-food restaurant and see that the manager is busy with customers. You grab a bottle of water out of the cooler, and, catching her eye, you point to the bottle and she nods. You then take a seat and start drinking the water. Even though the two of you have not exchanged words, little doubt exists that you entered into a contract to pay for that water. This is an implied-in-fact contract.

Determining Whether Language Constitutes an Offer

An offer requires a promise, and a promise requires a commitment, but sometimes what a person says doesn't rise to the level of commitment and is therefore not an offer. The test is whether the language is so complete that it requires nothing more than acceptance to form a contract. If the language requires something more than acceptance, then it's probably not an offer. Using this test typically disqualifies the following as offers:

- Preliminary inquiries
- Advertisements
- Circulars (offers that were sent to multiple persons) if the offerees know they were sent to multiple persons
- Catalogs

Of these four, preliminary inquiries and advertisements are the most common. The following sections explain how to distinguish inquiries and advertisements from genuine offers and how circulars and catalog listings fit in with advertisements.

Distinguishing a preliminary inquiry from an offer

A *preliminary inquiry* is like a fishing expedition: The parties merely discuss what they'd hypothetically be willing to offer or accept. To test whether a party has presented an offer, ask whether a reasonable person would think that no more than an acceptance is required to form a contract. Carefully scrutinize the language and the context.

Suppose Mary says to Tom, "How much would you sell your house for?" Tom responds, "I'd like to get $100,000 for it." Mary says, "I accept!" Have the two parties formed a contract? Mary clearly uttered a manifestation of acceptance, but does what Tom said constitute an offer? The test is whether a reasonable person observing this conversation would think that when Tom said, "I'd like to get $100,000 for it," he was committing to sell his house for $100,000. I think a reasonable person would conclude that this isn't the language of an offer. He was expecting Mary to make him an offer. It's not the same as saying something like, "Give me $100,000 for it, and it's yours." Tom's statement is more along the lines of a preliminary inquiry than an offer.

Similarly, if Tom puts a sign outside his house that says, "For Sale. $100,000," that's not an offer. Mary can't simply accept the offer by handing Tom a suitcase with $100,000 in it, because that's not the customary practice for this type of transaction. Customary practice is to put a for-sale sign outside a house to solicit offers to buy the house, not to get people to give an acceptance. Based on the language and the context, more than acceptance is required to form a contract.

Ads, catalogs, and circulars: Distinguishing advertisements from offers

An advertisement is generally not an offer. It's an invitation to make an offer. Assume a store advertised in the newspaper, "Golden 50" HDTVs $500." If this were an offer, the store would legally be obligated to sell a TV to everyone who accepted the offer, even if the store ran out of those TVs. If the store couldn't deliver on its commitment, it would be found in breach.

Contract law comes to the aid of the store by saying that the ad is merely an invitation to make an offer. Technically, when a customer goes to the store and says, "I'd like to buy one of those TVs you advertised," the customer is making an offer. The store can then either accept or reject it.

Similarly, a catalog is not an offer but an invitation to make an offer. For example, if I order something from a store catalog and they're unable to supply it, the store isn't in breach. I make my offer when I submit my order. If they can't fill my order, they decline my offer.

What's a widget?

In Contracts classes, professors are always coming up with hypotheticals that involve buying and selling widgets. This may lead you to wonder, What's a widget? The answer: A *widget* is a hypothetical good bought and sold in Contracts and Economics classes. Think of it as a gadget, a whatchamacallit, or a thingamajig.

Of course, stores could take advantage of this arrangement by employing the bait and switch — advertise an incredible deal (the bait) and then offer a deal that's not so great (the switch). Contract law has no solution for this problem, but most jurisdictions have enacted consumer protection laws that make the bait and switch a legal violation. This is why stores often add language to their advertisements, such as "while supplies last" or "quantities limited."

Another way to resolve the issue of multiple acceptances and limited supplies is to make an item available only to the first person who accepts. If I have six friends over to my house, for example, and say to them, "I'll sell this widget for $10," five of them may accept. I'd be in trouble if the remaining four filed a breach of contract claim against me. A reasonable person in this situation would probably say that because the six offerees knew I had only one widget for sale, a reasonable way to resolve which of them got it would be the first to accept.

An advertisement may be an offer if it's so clear and definite that only acceptance is required to form the contract. Circulars are especially vulnerable because each recipient might not reasonably know that others have received the same circular. If I send a letter to six friends offering to sell a widget for $10, this may constitute an offer. If each recipient didn't know I'd sent the offer to others, then I could be bound by multiple acceptances, because each offeree might reasonably think I had one widget and was offering it to him or her exclusively.

Deciding How Long an Offer Remains Open

An offer remains open for whatever time period is *reasonable*. What's reasonable varies according to facts and circumstances. If late in the day on Friday I offer to sell you 1,000 shares of Megalomart stock for $20 a share, you may reasonably expect the offer to remain open until the opening bell on Monday, because the share value won't change over the weekend. If we're standing on the floor of the New York Stock Exchange during the trading day, however, and I say the same thing to you, the offer may be open for only a few seconds, because values may be very volatile. (Some old cases state that an offer made during a face-to-face meeting lapses when that meeting ends.)

The offeror may override the "reasonable period" rule by setting a specific time period. On Friday, for example, I can say to you, "I'll sell you 1,000 shares of Megalomart stock for $20 a share, and this offer is open until Tuesday noon." Unless another offer-terminating rule applies, the offer remains open until that time. One of those rules is that the death of the offeror or offeree terminates the offer.

Determining Whether the Offeror Can Back Out: Revoking the Offer

Keeping an offer open indefinitely would result in keeping the offeror on the hook until the offeree got around to accepting it, which is obviously unfair to the offeror. Because of this, contract law allows the offeror to back out under certain conditions. The following sections explain how and under what circumstances an offeror is allowed to back out and how the offeror and offeree may use an option contract to keep the offer open for an extended period.

After making the offer, the offeror may *revoke* (take back) the offer any time before acceptance. For example, if I say, "I'll sell you 1,000 shares of Megalomart stock for $20 a share," and while you're thinking about it, I say, "I take it back!" then I've effectively revoked the offer and it's no longer available for you to accept.

Even if the offeror promises to keep the offer open for a specific time, she may revoke the offer before the time expires. For example, if on Friday, I say, "I'll sell you 1,000 shares of Megalomart stock for $20 a share, and this offer is open until Tuesday noon," and then I say, "I take it back," I've successfully revoked the offer, because I merely made you a *gift promise* to keep the offer open until Tuesday. In U.S. law, gift promises are not enforceable.

The rule that the offeror may revoke the offer any time before acceptance has several exceptions, including the following:

- ✔ Option contracts
- ✔ Statutes that create an option
- ✔ Reliance on the offer

The following sections discuss these exceptions in greater detail.

Making an option contract

For an offer to remain open, a party must make an enforceable promise — a promise given in exchange for something from the other party. One way to keep an offer open is through the use of an *option contract:* One party agrees to keep the option open in exchange for something, often money.

Assume that after I make the offer on Friday, you say, "I promise you a dollar to keep that offer open until Tuesday noon." You made an offer to give me a dollar for my agreeing to keep my offer open until Tuesday. If I accept, then we have an enforceable option contract.

Recognizing statutes that create an option

Through a statute, the legislature is free to change the common-law rule. The law may disallow an offeror from revoking an offer under certain conditions. In situations in which the specified conditions exist, parties make an option contract without meeting the common-law requirements. The legislature has done this in UCC § 2-205, which is called the *firm offer rule.*

As enacted in North Carolina, the statute provides the following:

> § 30-2-205. Firm offers.
>
> An offer by a merchant to buy or sell goods in a signed writing which by its terms gives assurance that it will be held open is not revocable, for lack of consideration, during the time stated or if no time is stated for a reasonable time, but in no event may such period of irrevocability exceed 3 months; but any such term of assurance on a form supplied by the offeree must be separately signed by the offeror.

This statue essentially creates an option contract without the offeree's having to pay for it. Note, however, the limited context for this rule. Because it's found in Article 2 of the UCC, it applies only to the sale of goods. And by its language, it applies only to merchants — parties experienced in business practices. And it applies only when the merchant makes the offer in writing. Finally, the offer must state that it will be held open. This rule reflects the standard business practice — merchants expect that if they make a written statement that an offer will be open, they've made a commitment.

This statute would not apply, however, if the merchant put an ad in the newspaper stating, "This price is good until Tuesday," because the ad is merely an invitation to make an offer. For more about ads, see the earlier section "Ads, catalogs, and circulars: Distinguishing advertisements from offers."

The legislature may enact a *statute* to change the *common law* — the rules that govern contracts as established by the body of cases judges have decided. The statutes you encounter most frequently in contract law are in the Uniform Commercial Code (UCC), particularly Article 2, which deals with the sale of goods. (*Tip:* When you see a statute number in the form 2-###, the *2* refers to Article 2.)

Relying on the offer

As a general rule, an offeree shouldn't rely on an offer. For example, assume I offered you 10,000 pens for $1 each. Offer in hand, you go out and rent space to open a pen store, buy pencils, and take out advertising. As you're headed back to me, I revoke the offer before you accept. I had no idea you were going to do all that. If you wanted to bind me, you could've negotiated for an option to keep the offer open. You didn't, so you're out of luck.

The exception arose in the case of *Drennan v. Star Paving.* Drennan was a contractor who bid to get a job building a school. In his bid, which is an offer, he used Star Paving's bid on the paving portion of the contract. After Drennan was awarded the job to build the school but before he could accept Star Paving's bid for the paving, Star Paving tried to revoke its offer. The court created an exception to the general rule that an offeror can revoke at any time before acceptance. In this case, Drennan couldn't accept Star Paving's bid until he knew (1) Star Paving had made the low bid for paving and (2) Drennan's bid on the school-building job was accepted. A reasonable person in Star Paving's shoes would've known that, so the court held that Star Paving's bid was open for a reasonable time until after Drennan found out whether he had won the contract.

Deciding Whether the Offer Has Been Accepted

Assuming that an offer has been made and not yet terminated, the offeree has the power to form a contract by accepting the offer. Not every action by the offeree constitutes an acceptance, however. This section explains the rules that govern acceptance.

Acceptance must match the offer: The mirror-image rule

The offeror is the master of the offer, so the offeree's acceptance must be the *mirror image* of the offer, matching it in every respect. If the offeror states that the offer's open until Tuesday and the offeree tries to accept it on Wednesday, that doesn't qualify as acceptance, because the offer lapsed on Tuesday. If the offer is to sell shares of stock for $20 and the offeree responds, "It's a deal for $19 a share," that's not acceptance, because it fails to match the offer's terms.

Any attempted acceptance that fails to adhere to the mirror-image rule is a rejection of the offer and is considered to be a counteroffer.

When the offeree in the preceding example tries to accept at $19 a share, she rejects the offer to sell at $20 a share, becomes the offeror, and presents a counteroffer to purchase shares at $19 each. If that counteroffer is rejected, the party making the counteroffer can't bind the offeror by saying, "Then I accept your offer of $20 a share," because that offer's no longer on the table. It terminated upon rejection.

To retain the power of acceptance, the offeree can make an inquiry. Instead of offering $19 per share, the offeree could say something like, "While keeping your offer of $20 open, may I inquire as to whether you would consider selling for $19 a share?" If the offeree does that, then the original offer probably remains open.

Acceptance is effective on dispatch: The mailbox rule

One of the more ancient rules of offer and acceptance is the *mailbox rule*. According to this rule, acceptance is effective on dispatch — that is, when it leaves the offeree's hands, not when the offeror receives it.

For example, suppose I present an offer to you by mail. You receive the offer on Wednesday, and on Thursday, when the offer is still open, you mail your acceptance. On Friday, you have second thoughts, and you send me a fax that says, "I reject your offer." On Saturday, I get your letter that says, "I accept your offer." Even though I received your rejection by fax first, your acceptance was effective when you put it in the mailbox, so at that moment we had a contract.

The mailbox rule is designed to prevent the offeree from gaining an unfair advantage by accepting and then having additional time to speculate on whether she has made a wise decision.

Looking at various forms of acceptance

As the master of the offer, the offeror determines the *medium* of acceptance, such as postal mail, e-mail, or fax, when presenting the offer. The offeree must communicate acceptance using a medium that's as good or better. So if the offeror presents the offer by postal mail, the offeree may accept via postal mail or a better method, such as fax or e-mail. The offeror may also determine the *manner* of acceptance:

✔ Promise

✔ Performance

✔ Promise or performance (letting the offeree choose)

Following the usual rule, the manner is whatever's reasonable in the circumstances unless the offeror specifies the manner. This section explains the three manners of acceptance in greater detail.

Accepting by promise: Bilateral contracts

Usually, the offeror wants a *promissory acceptance* — a return promise that seals the deal. A promissory acceptance gives the offeror the security of having a contractual commitment that the offeree will do something. When Joe says to Mary, "I'll buy your bicycle for $200," he reasonably expects her to respond by saying something like, "It's a deal." When she does, a contract is formed, in this case a *bilateral* (two-sided) *contract.* Each party has promised something to the other, and each is immediately bound when the contract is formed.

When both parties sign a contract, they form a bilateral contract. Technically, the first to sign is the offeror, saying in effect, "I promise to do all the things I'm obligated to do in this writing if you promise to do all the things you're obligated to do in this writing." When the second person signs, that's the acceptance, and they're now both obligated to perform.

Accepting by performance: Unilateral contracts

Sometimes the offeror wants *acceptance by performance,* meaning acceptance is conditional upon the offeree's taking some action that's specified in the offer. Acceptance by performance is described as a *unilateral* (one-sided) *contract,* which is somewhat of a misnomer, because it describes only the offer, which is always one-sided. *Unilateral contract* really means an offer to be accepted by performance.

Unilateral contracts are common in reward, prize, and game situations. If my dog goes missing, for example, I may put up posters that say, "Lost dog. Reward $100." I'm promising offerees $100 on condition that they accept by giving me the performance of finding my dog. Notice I don't have the security of knowing that any party has committed to finding my dog. I'm just hoping that the offer will induce performance. If I want the assurance of performance, I could make a bilateral contract by offering to pay someone $50 if he promises to look for my dog and having him agree to it.

The offeror's right to revoke the offer any time before acceptance can cause problems in a unilateral contract, because acceptance occurs only upon completion of performance. The offeror could revoke after the offeree has begun performance but not completed it, thus causing the offeree hardship. To help prevent situations like this, contract law has a rule: If the offeree begins performance and the offeror either knows this or reasonably wouldn't require notice, an option contract is created and the offeror can't revoke the offer during the reasonable time that the offeree would complete performance.

For example, suppose I offer $10,000 to the first person who runs from Boston to Los Angeles in 30 days or less. If you promise me you'll do it, I would reasonably say that your promise is irrelevant because this is a contract to be accepted by performance, not by promise. So you begin running. On the 30th day, you're totally exhausted, but you see a big sign ahead that says "Welcome to L.A." As you approach, I jump out from behind it and say, "Ha-ha! I revoke my offer." You then run past the sign.

According to the general rule, the offer terminated because I revoked it before acceptance by performance — before you reached L.A. With the exception, however, as soon as you start running, we have an option contract that binds me not to revoke, though it didn't bind you to complete performance. I can't revoke after you've begun performance, and assuming you complete the run, thus completing performance, I owe you $10,000.

Accepting by promise or performance: Offeree's choice

When an offer can be accepted by either *promise or performance,* then as soon as the offeree begins performance, both parties are bound as if they had made a bilateral contract.

For example, suppose I say to you, "I'm going on vacation for a month. It would be great if you could paint my garage while I'm gone for $2,000. You can either tell me you're going to do it or just do it." You could reasonably promise to do it, in which case a bilateral contract would be formed at that moment, or you could reasonably not say anything and just do it. Because this offer can be accepted by either promise or performance, at the moment you begin slapping paint on my garage, a contract is formed. If you then decide to stop, you're in breach.

If an offer can reasonably be accepted either by promise or performance, then the offeree's beginning of performance binds both parties just as if the offeree had promised to do it. Distinguish that situation from the offer that can be accepted *only* by performance. In that case, the offeree's beginning of performance prevents the offeror from revoking the offer but doesn't bind the offeree to complete.

Changing the rules by statute: UCC § 2-206

Just as the UCC changes the rule for option contracts in § 2-205 by creating an option contract without consideration (see the earlier section "Recognizing statutes that create an option"), UCC § 2-206(1)(b) creates a change of rules with respect to contracts to be accepted by performance. As enacted in North Carolina, it provides:

§ 25-2-206.

An order or other offer to buy goods for prompt or current shipment shall be construed as inviting acceptance either by a prompt promise to ship or by the prompt or current shipment of conforming or nonconforming goods, but such a shipment of nonconforming goods does not constitute an acceptance if the seller seasonably notifies the buyer that the shipment is offered only as an accommodation to the buyer.

This means that a merchant may accept by promise or performance, with performance being the shipping of what the purchaser ordered *or something different* ("nonconforming goods"). Note that this changes the common-law mirror-image rule — the rule that an acceptance that is different from the offer is not an acceptance (see the earlier section "Acceptance must match the offer: The mirror-image rule"). Here, it *is* an acceptance. However, if the seller ships a different product and says something like, "I know this isn't what you ordered, but that item was out of stock, so I'm shipping you a slightly higher quality replacement for your convenience," then the seller's performance doesn't qualify as acceptance. The seller has now made a counteroffer, which the buyer can accept or reject.

Suppose a customer (offeror) orders ten Type A widgets. According to the statute, the offeree may accept either by promising to ship the goods or by actually shipping the goods (performance). If the offeree promises to ship the goods, the parties have formed a contract for the sale of ten Type A widgets.

Alternatively, suppose the offeree ships Type B widgets rather than Type A widgets. In common law, this isn't acceptance, because the mirror-image rule says that acceptance must exactly match the offer. Technically, it's a counteroffer, which the buyer doesn't have to accept. But the drafters of the Code wanted to make life a little harder for the seller who ships the wrong goods, so instead of treating the shipment of wrong goods as a counteroffer, the Code says that the "shipment of conforming or *nonconforming* goods" qualifies as acceptance. As soon as the seller ships those Type B widgets, the contract is formed for Type A widgets, and the seller is in breach.

The Code cleverly provides a way out for the innocent seller. If the seller has no Type A widgets but thinks the buyer would rather have Type B widgets than no widgets at all, the seller may ship the nonconforming items as long as he notifies the buyer that they're being sent as an accommodation. If the seller does this, the shipment of nonconforming goods is not a breach but a counteroffer that the buyer may accept or refuse.

Making Sense of the "Battle of the Forms" and UCC § 2-207

Drafters of the UCC knew that parties often don't read their contracts. Even worse, when a business receives a form contract from another party, they may not read or sign it. Instead, they send their own form contract in response, which the other party doesn't read or sign. When a dispute breaks out, one party points to a term in its form as the governing term for the contract, and the other party makes the same claim. The Battle of the Forms is on!

Common law had a simple solution to this problem: the offeree's form rules. If the offeree's form differed in any way, according to the mirror-image rule, it didn't qualify as acceptance but as a counteroffer. If the parties then shipped goods and paid for them, it looked like they'd assented to the terms of that counteroffer. But the UCC's drafters didn't think it was fair that the offeree should always get its terms in a situation where no one bothered to read the forms, so the UCC set out to restore some balance.

The drafters of the UCC brought their tinkering with the common-law rules to new heights with § 2-207, making it undoubtedly the most difficult Contracts topic to wrap your brain around. This section provides the following, as enacted in North Carolina:

> § 25-2-207. Additional terms in acceptance of confirmation.
>
> (1) A definite and seasonable expression of acceptance or a written confirmation which is sent within a reasonable time operates as an acceptance even though it states terms additional to or different from those offered or agreed upon, unless acceptance is expressly made conditional on assent to the additional or different terms.
>
> (2) The additional terms are to be construed as proposals for addition to the contract. Between merchants such terms become part of the contract unless:
>
>> (a) the offer expressly limits acceptance to the terms of the offer;
>>
>> (b) they materially alter it; or
>>
>> (c) notification of objection to them has already been given or is given within a reasonable time after notice of them is received.
>
> (3) Conduct by both parties which recognizes the existence of a contract is sufficient to establish a contract for sale although the writings of the parties do not otherwise establish a contract. In such case the terms of the particular contract consist of those terms on which the writings of the parties agree, together with any supplementary terms incorporated under any other provisions of this code.

If you don't get it, don't feel inferior. UCC § 2-207 leaves even the most serious Contracts scholars puzzled. Part of the problem is that the section is very poorly drafted. When it addresses a fork in the road, it often explains what happens if you travel down one fork but not what happens if you go down the other.

In this section, I reveal the UCC's solution and explain some of the problems that occur when

    ✔ A party refuses to contract unless the other party agrees to its terms

    ✔ The offeree includes an additional term in its form

    ✔ The offeree includes a different term in its form

Deciding whether acceptance is conditional

Section 2-207(1) starts out by referring to "a definite and seasonable expression of acceptance," without explaining what that means. Most authorities think this means that for the exchanged forms to make a contract, the parties have to at least agree to the same essential terms, such as the quantity, description of the goods, and price. In fact, the parties usually read those terms and make sure that they agree with them. The terms they don't read are the "boilerplate" terms that follow. So when 2-207 refers to "additional or different terms," it probably means the boilerplate terms.

Subsection (1) of UCC § 2-207 essentially tosses out the mirror-image rule. So when a party's response to an offer contains additional or different terms, it's considered acceptance, as opposed to a counteroffer, and a contract is born, unless . . .

The "unless" near the end of subsection (1) gives the offeree a way to make its acceptance conditional upon the offeror's acceptance of the additional or different terms. In other words, if the offeree's form says there's no deal if the offeror doesn't agree to these new terms, that form is not an acceptance. *Offer and non-acceptance* is not a contract. Some disputes revolve around the language necessary to satisfy this requirement, but it's best to be very clear, expressly stating in effect, "If you don't agree to my terms, we don't have a deal."

If the language is clearly stated, then at this point, the offeror is free to walk away without being in breach. But because the offeror doesn't read the form, that rarely happens. Instead, the offeror files the form and proceeds with the transaction, leaving one to wonder what the terms are when the parties proceed without mutual assent.

The answer is in subsection (3), which essentially says that if the offeror makes acceptance conditional and the parties act as though they have a contract by accepting goods and paying for them, this is "conduct by both parties which recognizes the existence of a contract," so they've made a contract by their actions.

In such a case, follow the second sentence of subsection (3) to determine the terms of the contract:

✓ **Where the parties' forms agree on a term, that term is a part of their agreement.** For example, if both the buyer's and seller's forms state "The seller is excused from performance only if events A, B, and C occur," the terms match and are part of the contract.

✓ **Where they don't agree, the contradictory provisions aren't automatically part of the agreement.** For example, if the buyer's form states, "The seller is excused from performance only if events A, B, and C occur," and the seller's form states, "The seller is excused if events D, E, and F occur," the terms don't agree, so they're not part of the agreement. The term that becomes part of the agreement is supplied through the default rules provided by the Code or the common law.

✓ **Supplementary terms incorporated under any other provisions of the Code will then be included.** So, for example, if the terms relating to the seller's performance don't agree, then look for something in the Code to determine which events would excuse the seller's performance; this would be the rule from § 2-615 on Excuse by Failure of Presupposed Conditions. If the Code doesn't supply a rule, then as directed in § 1-103(b), use the common-law rule.

Dealing with additional or different terms

Assuming the offeror hasn't made acceptance conditional and that the offeree has accepted by responding with his own form, subsection (1) of UCC § 2-207 says that the parties have a contract. Now the question turns to which terms govern the contract, and that depends on whether the offeree's terms are additional or different, an important distinction drawn in subsection (1):

✓ **Additional terms:** By *additional,* the section probably means a term in the offeree's form that addresses a topic not addressed in the offeror's form. For example, if the offeror's form is silent on the method of dispute resolution, then the offeree's term stating that "all disputes go to arbitration" is an additional term.

✓ **Different terms:** By *different,* it probably means a term in the offeree's form that addresses the same topic addressed in the offeror's form in a different way. For example, if the offeror's form states, "All disputes go to arbitration in New York," and the offeree's form states, "All disputes go to arbitration in New Jersey," the terms are different.

With a clear understanding of the difference between additional and different terms, you're ready to determine which term is enforceable.

Choosing the term when additional terms exist

According to subsection (2), additional terms "are to be construed as propos-
als for addition to the contract." However, "between merchants such terms
become part of the contract." If both parties are merchants, then presumably the
offeree's proposed term becomes the contract term. For example, if the offeror's
terms were silent on dispute resolution and the offeree's form proposed arbitration, then the offeree's additional term presumably governs. But this is only a
presumption. The offeror has three chances to reject the proposal:

- ✔ Under subsection (2)(a), a rejection of the proposal exists if "the offer
  expressly limits acceptance to the terms of the offer." So the offeror has a
  chance to reject proposed terms by drafting that language in its contract.

- ✔ If the offeror didn't expressly limit acceptance to the terms of the offer,
  then under subsection (2)(c), a rejection of the proposed terms exists
  if "notification of objection to them has already been given or is given
  within a reasonable time after notice of them is received." In other
  words, the offeror has a chance to notify the offeree that it rejects the
  proposed term.

- ✔ If the offeror doesn't take advantage of that option, it gets a third bite at
  the apple. Under subsection (2)(b), the proposed terms are rejected if
  "they *materially alter* it," "it" being the contract.

The Code doesn't explain what "materially alter" means, but the drafters of
the Code provide some Official Comments as guidance:

- ✔ Official Comment 4 to this section of the UCC indicates that "materially
  alter" means that the terms "result in surprise or hardship if incorporated without express awareness by the other party." In the case of the
  arbitration clause example, most courts would reject the offeree's additional term stating that "all disputes go to arbitration," because it would
  result in surprise or hardship to the offeror.

- ✔ Comment 5 contains a list of clauses that would not involve "unreasonable surprise" — for example, "a clause fixing a reasonable time for complaints within customary limits."

Choosing the term when different terms exist

Unfortunately, subsection (2) provides no guidance on what to do with *different* terms in the offeree's form, so it's up to the courts to come up with a rule
to plug the gap. Courts in different jurisdictions have formulated three different rules to deal with this issue:

✔ **The knockout rule:** The knockout rule is the most popular approach (although it doesn't make a lot of sense to me). The court knocks out both terms that differ and reads in the default rule from the Code or common law. If the offeror's term states, "All disputes go to arbitration in New York," and the offeree's form states, "All disputes go to arbitration in New Jersey," the court knocks out both terms and reads in the common-law rule that supplements the Code, stating that the parties take their dispute to court.

✔ **Offeror's term prevails:** Some courts say that when different terms exist, the offeror's term prevails. If the offeror's form states, "All disputes go to arbitration in New York," and the offeree's form states, "All disputes go to arbitration in New Jersey," then the offeror's term prevails, and the contract term is "All disputes go to arbitration in New York."

Additional terms are handled very similarly according to subsection (2) (a): If the offeree proposes an additional term that the offeror objects to, that term is rejected. In this case, when the offeree proposes a different term, some courts take the view that the offeror has already objected to that term by having a different term in its form.

✔ **Same as additional term:** Some courts treat different terms the same way they treat additional terms (see the earlier section "Choosing the term when additional terms exist" for details). Because of the "materially alter" rule of (2)(b), only an offeree's term that doesn't differ substantially from the offeror's term becomes part of the contract. If the offeror's form states, "All disputes go to arbitration in New York" and the offeree's form states, "All disputes go to arbitration in New Jersey," a court would most likely not find the difference between the two terms material because it's no hardship for a New Yorker to cross over into New Jersey — the contract term would likely become "all disputes go to arbitration in New Jersey." However, if the offeror's form states, "All disputes go to arbitration in New York" and the offeree's form states, "All disputes go to arbitration in Hawaii," the offeree's different term most likely is material and the contract term would likely become "all disputes go to arbitration in New York."

Chapter 3

Sealing the Deal: The Doctrine of Consideration

. . . .

In This Chapter

▶ Detecting the presence or absence of consideration

▶ Distinguishing a bargained-for exchange from a gift promise

▶ Spotting promises that aren't (or look like they aren't) supported by consideration

▶ Knowing when contracts are enforceable even without consideration

. . . .

For centuries, societies have struggled to determine which promises to enforce. At one extreme, society could decide that promises are enforceable only if they're made with a great deal of formality, such as a promise accompanied by a ritual in which the parties cut their palms and shake hands, sealing their agreement in blood. A mere couple of centuries ago, people evidenced their promises in hot wax imprinted with their seals.

At the other extreme, society could declare *all* promises enforceable, but such a policy could result in mass confusion and chaos. An utterance of social politeness such as "My house is your house" or a bit of pillow talk like "I'll always take care of you" could prove disastrous, and the courts would soon tire of the lines of people seeking enforcement.

After centuries of groping for a solution, the Anglo-American legal system decided to enforce promises that comprise bargained-for exchanges. The something that's bargained for is *consideration* — what each party stands to gain.

Determining whether consideration is present seems straightforward enough — either the parties promise each other something, or they don't — but it's not always so obvious. This idea can work in your client's favor or against it, so you must be able to determine when consideration is or isn't present in an exchange. This chapter helps you make that determination and also discusses situations in which consideration isn't technically required.

Checking an Agreement for Consideration

You may need to look very closely to find consideration in an agreement. To determine whether consideration is present, try identifying the bargained-for exchange. In *bargained-for exchange,* one of the following situations occurs:

- ✔ Each party makes a promise to the other in order to get the other party to promise something in return.
- ✔ One party makes a promise to induce another party to perform, and the induced party performs to get that promise.
- ✔ Each party does something in order to get the other party to do something in return.

In a bargained-for exchange, to *bargain* doesn't mean to negotiate. It means that each party has the motive of getting something from the other in the exchange. Assume that I say to you, "I'm going to give you a bicycle for your birthday," and in response, you say to me, "That's great! And I'll give you some DVDs for yours." In this exchange, we each made a promise, but no bargain exists. I didn't make my promise to you with the *motive* of getting anything from you. This is an exchange of *gift promises,* meaning promises without consideration, so they aren't legally enforceable.

Using a simple Q&A

Because consideration requires a bargained-for exchange in which the motive for each party's promise or performance is to get a promise or performance from the other party, you can determine whether consideration is present through a brief Q&A. For example, assume that I offered to sell you my car for $10,000, and you agreed to purchase it. The Q&A might look like this:

Q: Why did I promise you the car?

A: To get the promise of $10,000.

Q: Why did you promise the $10,000?

A: To get the car.

Because the promises were made in order to induce the other to give a promise or performance, consideration is present. Famous American jurist Oliver Wendell Holmes would refer to a bargained-for exchange as *reciprocal inducement,* which establishes consideration. With my promise of the car, I'm inducing you to give me $10,000, and your promise of $10,000 induces me to give you the car.

Making a diagram

Consider diagramming the contract so you can see what each party bargained to receive from the other. In the agreement where I promise to sell my car and you promise to purchase it for $10,000, the bargained-for exchange diagram looks like Figure 3-1. If one of those arrows had nothing attached to it, then consideration would be absent. For example, if I promised to give you my car as a gift, consideration is absent because I didn't bargain to get anything in return.

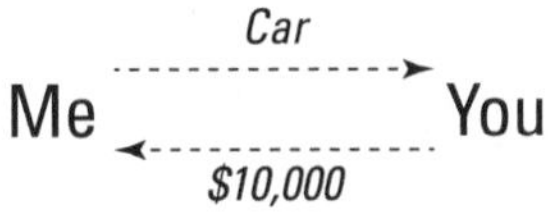

Figure 3-1:
A bargained-for exchange diagram.

```
              Car
    Me ------------------> You
       <------------------
             $10,000
```

In discussing an exchange, sometimes your instructor or a case may state that the *promisor* did such-and-such. This can be confusing, because contracts usually have *two* promisors, each promising something different. The trick is to figure out which promisor the speaker or author is referring to. In our hypothetical involving the sale of the car, if the instructor asks whether the promisor gave any consideration for *the car,* the instructor must be referring to you, because you're the promisor who bargained to get the car.

Although parties generally have freedom of contract, they don't have freedom to waive consideration. I may say to you, "I really, really want you to have my car, and I promise you can have it even without any consideration." But according to contract law, my promise would be unenforceable, because there's no consideration for it. However, I could accomplish my goal through means other than a contract, such as by making a gift. A gift is a property transaction, and after I transfer the property to you, it's yours.

Making and enforcing promises outside the courts

Individuals who make their own rules for enforceable promises are free to seek enforcement in a private dispute resolution system rather in a public court. In the wholesale diamond business, which is largely conducted by Orthodox Jews, parties traditionally close a contract by uttering the words "mazel and broche," meaning "luck and blessing." Can you imagine someone going to court and claiming, "This contract isn't enforceable because he didn't say 'mazel and broche'"? Not surprisingly, in this business, industry panels, rather than public courts, resolve disputes. See Chapter 18 for information on alternative dispute resolution (ADR).

Making Distinctions about Consideration

In some cases, a gift promise, which is insufficient for forming a contract, may look a lot like a bargained-for exchange. In addition, courts become concerned when what one party promised doesn't appear *adequate* to make the agreement enforceable.

As you evaluate cases, subtle distinctions may arise between what constitutes consideration and what doesn't. This section provides guidance to help you identify and analyze these distinctions.

Deciding whether it's a bargain or a gift promise

When examining a contract for consideration, consider whether the agreement functions as a bargain (enforceable) or merely a gift promise (unenforceable). Contract law provides two ways to make this determination:

- ✔ The Restatement of Contracts (see Chapter 1) asks whether a bargain exists — whether each party promised something in exchange for the promise of the other.

- ✔ Older cases ask whether the promisor sought either a *benefit* to the promisor or a *detriment* to the promisee. In other words, the promisor's receiving something *or* the promisee's giving up something is consideration. For example, as consideration for my promise to pay you $100, I may ask either that you give me your coat (a benefit to the promisor) or that you stop drinking soda (a detriment to the promisee). This method is useful in close cases in which what's being bargained isn't so obvious.

Samuel Williston, the early 20th-century expert in contract law, posed this challenging hypothetical situation:

A wealthy man tells a tramp that if the tramp goes around the corner to the clothing store, he'll buy him a new overcoat. [Figure 3-2 illustrates the exchange.] The tramp does so, and the wealthy man refuses to perform. Did the wealthy man bargain to get this performance (going around the corner) from the tramp, or did he merely tell the tramp that the clothing store was the place where he'd make a gift of a coat? If the former, then the wealthy man became bound when the tramp gave the performance; if the latter, then he was free to choose not to make the gift.

To answer this question, ask whether the promisor (the wealthy man) sought any benefit for himself or sought any detriment from the promisee (the tramp). If either condition is true, the wealthy man more likely bargained to get the performance, in which case consideration exists and the two parties have an enforceable contract; in short, the wealthy man would owe the tramp damages for not giving him a new overcoat.

Figure 3-2:
Exchange between the wealthy man and the tramp.

Wealthy Man ----New overcoat----> Tramp

<---Walk around the corner---

Williston maintained that a reasonable person would conclude that no bargain existed in this situation. The wealthy man doesn't benefit materially from having the tramp come to the store, and it's not a material detriment to the tramp to do so. Even if there is no bargained-for contract, a court may still provide relief to a party who acted on a promise by compensating that party on a *theory of reliance* — when a party acts or refrains from acting in response to a promise (see Chapter 4).

In the old case of *Hamer v. Sidway,* an uncle promised his nephew a large sum of money if the nephew didn't engage in a number of vices, including drinking and smoking, until he was 25. The nephew claimed he performed and sought payment, but the executor of the uncle's estate refused to pay, claiming no consideration existed because the agreement was of no benefit to the promisor, the uncle. In the old view, the promise is enforceable because the promisor (the uncle) did seek a detriment from the promisee (the nephew), who gave up something. The promise is also enforceable in the modern view, which downplays the importance of benefit and detriment, because the uncle got exactly the performance he bargained for under this unilateral contract: a contract where the offeror seeks acceptance by performance (see Chapter 2). The court properly held that the promise was enforceable.

Your instructor may spin some interesting hypothetical situations around the facts of this case. Here are a couple of hypotheticals to warm you up for the task:

✔ Suppose the uncle promised to give the nephew the money if he didn't smoke, and the nephew performed. Then the uncle claims absence of consideration because the nephew didn't smoke anyway. The uncle claims that he received no benefit and that the nephew suffered no detriment because he gave up nothing in return for the promise of the money.

In this case, the court would probably find that the nephew *did* do something: He refrained from taking up smoking, an activity he was perfectly free to engage in.

✔ Suppose the uncle promised to give the nephew money if he refrained from doing hard drugs. Because the nephew has a legal obligation not to do drugs, the uncle could argue that the nephew did nothing he wasn't already obligated to do.

Some courts would agree with that analysis, but others may say that this promise is enforceable because the duty not to do drugs is owed to society, and not to the uncle; therefore, there's consideration for avoiding drugs at the uncle's request. Others may say that the promise is enforceable because enforcing it is beneficial to provide another incentive to keep people from doing drugs. This is the kind of question that makes the Contracts class so interesting!

Don't look for a separate consideration for each promise in a contract. Although consideration must exist for each promise in a contract, a consideration can cover more than one promise. For example, suppose I promise you $1,000 if you promise to (1) perform certain research for me, (2) wash my car, and (3) walk across the Brooklyn Bridge. The fact that I promised you only one thing in exchange for three things from you doesn't matter as far as consideration is concerned, because I bargained for three things from you, and you bargained for only one thing from me.

Distinguishing between sufficient and adequate consideration

Although an enforceable contract requires a bargained-for exchange, contract law doesn't require that the exchange be equal. Courts generally don't place each party's consideration on the scales of justice to determine whether a contract exists. When disputes arise, courts may make a distinction between sufficient and adequate consideration:

✔ **Sufficient:** Consideration is sufficient if it satisfies the legal requirement that a bargained-for exchange exists.

✔ **Adequate:** Adequacy refers to the equivalency of the exchange — whether each party stood to receive something reasonably equivalent to what they promised.

Although consideration must be sufficient for a contract, the law generally doesn't inquire into the adequacy of consideration. I'm completely free to make a harebrained deal like selling my $10,000 car to you for $10, even though no reasonable person would consider $10 adequate. The fact that we each bargained for something is sufficient. People make bad bargains all the time.

Although a party can't claim lack of consideration to help her escape a contract when the exchange is lopsided, the court may scrutinize the deal more closely for other factors that may explain why a person agreed to such a bad deal. I discuss these defenses to contract formation, including fraud, duress, mistake, and lack of capacity, in Part II.

Detecting an Absence of Consideration

Not only do you need to be able to recognize consideration when you see it, but you also need to be able to detect a lack of consideration when you don't see it, which is often the greater challenge. To make your job even more difficult, some agreements contain promises that feign consideration — a party appears to offer something but really doesn't. This section describes three such situations — nominal consideration, pre-existing duty, and past consideration — so you're better equipped to spot a lack of consideration.

Spotting a phony: Nominal consideration

By definition, a *nominal consideration* is a consideration in name only — a phony consideration. For example, suppose I say to you, "I promise to give you my car." Knowing something about contract law you respond, "Wait a minute. That's a gift promise. To make it enforceable, I have to give you something for it." I agree, and I give you a dollar to hand back to me, which you do. I then give you the car.

If you come in at the end of the story, with a dollar being exchanged for a car, this would look like an enforceable contract, complete with consideration from both sides. But when you look at the whole transaction, you clearly see that no bargaining took place. You gave me a dollar to make it *appear* as though we had bargained. This constitutes nominal consideration, which is no consideration at all.

To qualify as consideration, we would need to make a genuine deal — one in which each of us bargained to get what we wanted. Even though courts don't require an exchange of equivalent values, they do require a bargain, and a deal as lopsided as a car for $1 doesn't look like a bargain.

In *Fischer v. Union Trust Co.*, a 1904 case (these nominal consideration cases tend to be rather old), a father gave his incompetent daughter a deed and promised to pay the mortgages on the property. As he gave her the deed on December 21, he said, "Here is a nice Christmas present." One of her brothers gave her a dollar, which she gave to her father, who took it. The father later died, and when his estate didn't pay the mortgages, she sued for breach of contract. The court reasoned:

> To say that the one dollar was the real, or such valuable consideration as would of itself sustain a deed of land worth several thousand dollars, is not in accord with reason or common sense. The passing of the dollar by

the brother to his sister, and by her to her father, was treated rather as a joke than as any actual consideration. The real and only consideration for the deed and the agreement, therein contained, to pay the mortgages, was the grantor's love and affection for his unfortunate daughter, and his parental desire to provide for her support after he was dead.

Could "love and affection" have been consideration if it had been bargained for? Under the Restatement view, which emphasizes bargain rather than economic value, it appears possible, but I suspect most judges are more flinty-eyed and will not enforce an exchange unless the thing bargained for has some economic value.

Don't confuse *nominal* with inadequate or small. The law doesn't inquire into the adequacy or amount of consideration. Any amount is sufficient, including, in old English history, something as insignificant as a peppercorn. But it has to be bargained-for — not trumped up.

Applying the pre-existing duty rule

According to the *pre-existing duty rule,* consideration is absent if a party merely promises to do what it's already bound to do. For example, as I explain earlier in "Deciding whether it's a bargain or a gift promise," a promisor can claim that avoiding drugs isn't consideration, because doing drugs is illegal anyway.

The pre-existing duty rule can be a problem when parties try to modify their existing contract. If I promise to sell you my car and you promise to buy it for $10,000 in 30 days, I'm bound to sell you the car, and you're bound to pay me $10,000 for it. We each obtained something of value — the binding promise of the other to perform — and we each provided something of value.

Now, suppose in 30 days, you show up with the $10,000 and I refuse to give you the car. I tell you I won't give it to you unless you give me another $500. You plead with me, but I won't budge. Desperate to get the car and move on, you hand me the $500, and I give you the car.

According to the pre-existing duty rule, I had no right to charge you another $500, because I was bound by the pre-existing contract to sell you the car for $10,000. I offered nothing for the extra $500. Because you received no consideration in return for that payment of $500, no contract existed, and you should get your money back.

For more information on the pre-existing duty rule, flip to Chapter 12, where I discuss it in greater detail in relation to contract modification.

Finding past consideration

Past consideration is a benefit that one party already received at the time he made his promise. As such, past consideration doesn't qualify as consideration if a person makes a promise in return for it. In fact, the term is a misnomer because past consideration is no consideration!

For example, if Joe says to Mary, "I'm so grateful for all you've done for me that I promise to give you $10,000," this promise is not enforceable. Assuming that Joe's speaking the truth, Joe already received some benefit from Mary *before* making his promise to give her $10,000. He doesn't bargain to get it.

The application of this concept has sometimes led to abuse. For example, after an employee begins working for an employer, the employer promises, "When you retire, I'll give you a pension." Many years later, the employee retires and the employer claims that the promise of the pension is not enforceable for the following reasons:

- ✔ The employer and employee never bargained for a pension.

- ✔ The fact that the employee performed services in the past was not consideration.

- ✔ Because the employee had a pre-existing duty to perform services in exchange for wages, the employer was getting no additional benefit for its promise.

Technically, the employer is right. (However, Chapter 4 explains that even though this isn't a bargained-for contract, the employee might recover on a theory of reliance.)

Similarly, a moral obligation rarely creates a legal obligation. In the old case of *Mills v. Wyman,* Mills found Wyman's ailing adult son and took care of him until the son died. Mills then submitted a bill for the expenses to Wyman, who promised to pay the bill. Wyman then changed his mind and refused to pay the bill. When Mills sued to enforce Wyman's promise, the court held that because the son was an adult, Wyman had no legal obligation to pay for his care. He may have a moral obligation to honor his promise, but such an obligation is enforceable in the forum of the conscience and not in the court system. Wyman didn't bargain for Mills's services because they'd been rendered already at the time he made his promise to pay for them. (Chapter 4 explains that even though this is not a bargained-for contract, Mills might recover from Wyman's son's estate on a theory of restitution.)

The rule of past consideration has one exception: If a legal obligation becomes unenforceable because the *statute of limitations* (the time within which a claim must be brought) expires, then a promise to pay the obligation becomes enforceable even though the promise to pay is for a benefit previously received and no legal obligation to pay exists under the original agreement.

For example, five years ago, Joe sold widgets to Mary for $5,000, but Mary never got around to paying for them. Tired of waiting, Joe sues Mary, and Mary raises the defense of the statute of limitations, claiming that the time to bring the suit has expired. In a fit of contrition, Mary writes Joe, "I feel bad about this, and I promise I'll pay you $3,000." She then fails to honor that promise, and Joe sues on it. The new promise is enforceable but only to the extent of the new promise, not to the extent of the original obligation. In other words, Joe can recover only $3,000, not $5,000.

Contract law used to have a similar rule that allowed debtors whose debts were discharged in bankruptcy to revive those debts by promising creditors they would pay them, but the Bankruptcy Code has ended that practice.

Tracking Down Illusory Promises

Sometimes you have to recognize a lack of consideration when you think you see consideration. Other times you have to do the opposite — recognize the presence of consideration when you think you don't see it.

Generally speaking, contracts are binding only if they bind both parties. If one party isn't bound to do anything, then consideration is absent — no consideration, no contract. If one party isn't bound by the agreement, then a party can raise a defense to enforcement of the contract by using the doctrine of *illusory promise*, also known as *lack of commitment* or *lack of mutuality*:

- *Illusory promise,* because in reality one party didn't promise the other anything that's legally meaningful

- *Lack of commitment,* because if a party isn't committed to doing anything, then he hasn't made a promise

- *Lack of mutuality,* because if one party isn't bound by the bargain, then neither is the other

The clearest example of an illusory promise would be if I e-mailed you, "For $10,000, I'll either sell you my car or I won't," and you e-mailed back, "It's a deal!" You now claim that we don't have a contract, so you don't have to buy the car. I claim that you made a promise to buy it for $10,000. You did, but I didn't make a promise to sell it. Because I'm not bound to do anything, you're not bound, either.

Recognizing an "imperfectly expressed" contract: How Judge Cardozo outsmarted Lady Duff-Gordon

One of the most famous examples of an alleged illusory promise arose in *Wood v. Lucy, Lady Duff-Gordon*. Lady Duff-Gordon (whom you may have seen in the movie *Titanic* having dinner with Jack and Rose) was a fashion designer who made a deal with Wood to get endorsement deals for her. The contract stated that he would have the exclusive use of her name (certainly sufficient consideration) and that in return, he would pay her 50 percent of the income from endorsements he secured.

Later, Lucy received a better offer from someone else and hired a lawyer to go over the Wood contract with a magnifying glass to find an escape hatch for her. Aha! The lawyer found something — although Wood promised to pay her 50 percent of the income from endorsements he got, he didn't actually promise to *get* endorsements. Therefore, the lawyer argued, Wood was free under the contract to do nothing, and if he wasn't

bound to do anything, then Lucy wasn't bound, either.

The Appellate Division, the intermediate appellate court in New York, actually bought this argument by a vote of 5-0. But fortunately the case went up to the highest court, the Court of Appeals, and fell into the hands of the great Benjamin Cardozo. Judge Cardozo stated that "the law has outgrown its primitive stage of formalism where the precise word was the sovereign talisman, and every slip was fatal." The parties were serious businesspeople who intended a serious business arrangement. The parties had formed a contract here — it was just "imperfectly expressed." So Cardozo expressed it more clearly — he found that the agreement implied that Wood had promised to use "reasonable efforts" to get endorsements. With that obligation imposed on Wood, there was consideration, so the contract was not illusory.

If a person is bound to do *anything,* then consideration exists. If I had written, "I'll sell my car to you for either $10,000 or $10," then I would be bound by your acceptance, because even though I have a choice, either alternative would be consideration. Both the sale of the car for $10,000 and the sale of the car for $10 are contracts with a bargained-for exchange.

The issue of illusory promises often arises in satisfaction clauses, output and requirements contracts, and settlement of claims, as I explain next.

Dealing with satisfaction clauses

The illusory contract issue often arises when the contract has a *satisfaction clause* — wording that makes a party's promise conditional upon that party's satisfaction with something. Suppose I agree to buy your house, subject to my satisfaction with (1) a structural report and (2) the interior painting. You then get a better offer on the house and claim that we don't have an enforceable contract, because nothing in the contract binds me. All I have to do is say, "I'm not satisfied," and the deal's off. And if nothing in the contract binds me, then you're not bound, either. But courts haven't gone for this argument.

Even though a satisfaction clause appears to be void of commitment, the courts read a commitment into it. The courts start the analysis by dividing satisfaction clauses into two types, objective and subjective:

- **Objective:** Objective satisfaction is measured in terms of mechanical utility or operative fitness, as would be reflected in a structural report. This type of satisfaction takes my discretion out of the equation. Because I must act as a reasonable person, I have a commitment to buy the home if the report shows that it's structurally sound.

- **Subjective:** Subjective satisfaction is measured in terms of personal taste, fancy, or judgment. You may think that a person would have unlimited discretion here, but the courts say that the person exercising satisfaction is bound to act in good faith, which means he must act honestly. For example, whether a paint job is up to my standards is a measure of subjective satisfaction. If my real reason for saying I'm not satisfied is that I found another house I want to buy instead, then I haven't acted honestly. I don't have complete discretion, and because I must act honestly, I have a commitment.

Satisfaction clauses don't make a contract or promise illusory. Both objective and subjective satisfaction clauses satisfy the consideration requirement.

Analyzing output and requirements contracts

Although the default rules can supply many missing contract terms (see Chapter 10 for details), contract law has no default rule for quantity. The general rule is that absence of a stated quantity is fatal to a contract, because without knowing how much the seller had promised, computing the buyer's remedy is impossible. The exception to this rule is that the quantity, even if not expressly stated, may be determined by the output of the seller or the requirements of the buyer.

For example, suppose a lumber mill promises its entire output of cedar shakes (roofing shingles) to a builder at a fixed price per bundle. Later, the market price of cedar shakes goes up, and the seller wants to sell them to other buyers for more money.

The seller claims that even though it had promised its entire output to the buyer, it didn't promise to *have* an output, and therefore the quantity is illusory — if the seller can either produce the shakes or not, then consideration is nonexistent.

According to the UCC, however, the contract is enforceable even though the quantity isn't stated as a certain amount but is rather measured by the output of the seller or the requirements of the buyer. Section 2-306(1), as enacted in North Carolina at 25-2-306(1) provides:

> § 25-2-306. Output, requirements and exclusive dealings.
>
> (1) A term which measures the quantity by the output of the seller or the requirements of the buyer means such actual output or requirements as may occur in good faith, except that no quantity unreasonably disproportionate to any stated estimate or in the absence of a stated estimate to any normal or otherwise comparable prior output or requirements may be tendered or demanded.

In the case of the cedar shakes and in accordance with this statute, the quantity is determined by the following:

- ✔ **Good faith:** The quantity of shakes should reflect the quantity the lumber mill is able to produce.

- ✔ **Comparable amounts from previous years:** If the price of shakes rises, the builder may, in good faith, require more of them, but the lumber mill may have historical demand that limits the number of shakes the builder can reasonably demand to purchase at that price.

Spotting illusory promises in settlements

A settlement is a type of contract referred to as a *release*. The "plaintiff" agrees to release his claim in exchange for something from the "defendant" — typically a promise of money. If you were to illustrate the agreement, this bargained-for exchange diagram for the release would look something like Figure 3-3.

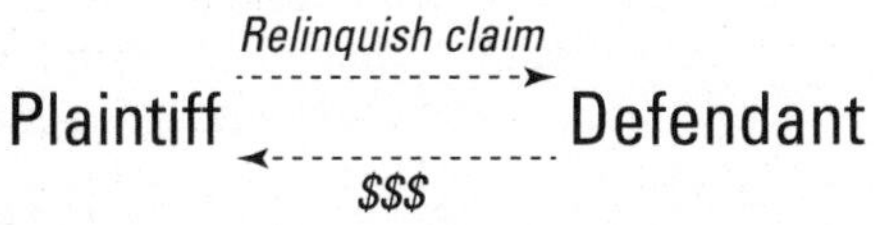

Figure 3-3:
Bargained-for exchange in a release (settlement).

But suppose that after the parties agree to the release, the defendant discovers that the plaintiff really didn't have a valid claim and, as a result, had offered nothing in exchange for the defendant's promise of money. Therefore, the defendant claims, the plaintiff's promise was illusory.

The courts usually resolve this problem by inquiring into the plaintiff's good faith, his motive for entering the settlement. If he honestly believed he had a claim, then he acted in good faith, which is sufficient consideration, and the court doesn't disturb the release agreement.

For example, in the notorious case of *Fiege v. Boehm,* Boehm claimed that Fiege was the father of her child. He entered into a release, agreeing to make support payments in return for her agreeing to give up claims against him. He then (a little late!) had a blood test done and found that he couldn't have fathered the child. He stopped making payments, claiming that the release was illusory: Because Boehm had no claim against him, no consideration existed for his promise. The court found that although Boehm had wrongly sought support from Fiege, the contract was enforceable because she brought the claim in good faith.

Too Many Blanks: Distinguishing Contracts from Agreements to Agree

After the parties have made what looks like a bargained-for exchange, you have to examine what they've exchanged to determine whether it's too *indefinite* to constitute consideration. If an agreement has too many indefinite terms, then a court can't determine what the parties promised each other, so it has to refuse to enforce the agreement. The parties might have made either of the following:

- **An agreement to agree:** The parties don't intend to have an agreement until they've made the terms definite.

- **An agreement with terms omitted:** The parties intend to have an agreement, and the court tries to fill in the missing terms if the parties don't. If the court can find an objective standard to use to determine the missing term, then there's an agreement.

For example, assume that I say to you, "I'll sell you my bicycle at a price to be determined later," and you say, "It's a deal." Apparently, we've exchanged promises, but what we've agreed to is unclear. We may be saying that we don't have a deal if we can't agree to the price, or we may be saying we have a deal and we expect that price term to be supplied.

Contract law doesn't have very good ways to determine whether the parties intended to make an agreement to agree. In the absence of language of the parties making it clear, look at the context for the degree of commitment and the number of missing terms.

For example, a motion picture company sued actress Pamela Anderson for agreeing to star in a movie called *Hello, She Lied* and then backing out. Pamela claimed that they had only an agreement to agree. The court found that because the parties had failed to complete the Nudity Rider that would spell out how much nudity would be in the movie, the parties had not committed themselves. No commitment = no consideration = no contract.

If a court has difficulty filling in what the parties would've agreed to, this fact often leads to the conclusion that the parties have an agreement to agree. For example, in our agreement for the sale of the bicycle, coming up with a reasonable price for the bicycle would be relatively easy, but coming up with the terms of Anderson's contract would've been difficult. In Chapter 10, I further explain how a court fills in the terms of the agreement after determining that the parties have an agreement.

Looking for Consideration Substitutes: Enforcing without Consideration

The fact that consideration is missing doesn't necessarily mean absence of contract. Occasionally, the legislature enacts a statute that makes certain promises enforceable without consideration. For example, the UCC *firm offer rule,* § 2-205, contains a narrow exception to the rule that an option contract requires consideration. (For info on option contracts, see Chapter 2.) As enacted in North Carolina as § 25-2-205, it provides the following:

> § 25-2-205. Firm offers.
>
> An offer by a merchant to buy or sell goods in a signed writing which by its terms gives assurance that it will be held open is not revocable, for lack of consideration, during the time stated or if no time is stated for a reasonable time, but in no event may such period of irrevocability exceed three months; but any such term of assurance on a form supplied by the offeree must be separately signed by the offeror.

Note that under this statute, the offeror can't revoke the offer even though no consideration is given for it. However, the statute stipulates a number of limitations on such an offer, including that it

- ✔ Applies only to an offer by a merchant
- ✔ Applies only to an offer to buy or sell goods
- ✔ Must be in a signed writing
- ✔ Must by its terms give assurance that it will be held open
- ✔ Is irrevocable for only a limited time (a reasonable time but no more than three months)

If an offeror jumps through these statutory hoops, then she's made an offer that's not revocable even though the offeree has provided no consideration. Why? Because the legislature says so. Why would the legislature say so? This UCC section is a good example of Uniform Commercial Code methodology. The Code doesn't want to regulate contracts; it wants to facilitate the process by reflecting what goes on in the commercial world. In the commercial world, merchants make offers that offerees expect them not to revoke, so the Code makes this practice the rule.

Sometimes courts use policies to plug the gaps when consideration is missing. They use the concept of *reliance,* or *promissory estoppel,* as an alternate theory for the enforcement of promises — consideration may be unnecessary if the promisee changes position in reliance on a promise. For info on the concept of reliance, turn to Chapter 4.

Evaluating the Recital of Consideration in a Contract Term

A *recital of consideration* is a statement in a contract that spells out a consideration. For example, the statement may say that "for $1 and other good and valuable consideration, the receipt of which is hereby acknowledged," one of the parties agrees to do something. Recital of consideration is neither necessary nor sufficient to establish consideration:

- ✓ **Not necessary:** A contract doesn't have to include a recital of consideration or even use the word "consideration." Consideration simply needs to exist for contract formation.

- ✓ **Not sufficient:** A contract may include a recital of consideration, but if the recital refers to a nominal consideration, it doesn't qualify as consideration (see the section "Spotting a phony: Nominal consideration," earlier in this chapter).

You may not be able to tell whether consideration is nominal just by looking at the recital of consideration in the contract, so investigate the background of how the transaction came about. In this inquiry, you must have a starting point for the analysis. The starting point, or default rule, is that the recital of consideration, even recital of $1, is presumed to be enforceable. For example, the California Civil Code provides in § 1614 that "A written instrument is presumptive evidence of a consideration."

But that presumption is rebuttable. The California Evidence Code § 622 provides

> The facts recited in a written instrument are conclusively presumed to be true as between the parties thereto, or their successors in interest; but this rule does not apply to the recital of a consideration.

In other words, the person attacking the contract has the burden to prove that the consideration was not real but nominal.

You may encounter an affirmative defense to contract called *failure of consideration,* which is really a misnomer. Either consideration is present or it's not, and if it's present, it can't fail. Therefore, "failure of consideration" is actually an issue of contract performance (see Chapter 16), not contract formation. (For additional details about contract defenses, including affirmative defenses, check out Chapter 5.)

Chapter 4

Noting Exceptions: Promises Enforceable without a Contract

In This Chapter

▶ Recognizing promises enforceable without a contract

▶ Understanding the doctrine of reliance and why it matters

▶ Sizing up cases that involve promissory estoppel

▶ Recognizing the role of restitution in enforceable promises

*T*he equation for contract formation looks something like this (see Chapters 2 and 3 for details):

Contract = Offer + Acceptance + Consideration

But contract law isn't always so formulaic. People have obligations to one another that extend beyond voluntary consent to enter agreements. As a result, contract law must address some exceptions to the equation. This chapter explores those exceptions so you can recognize situations in which enforceable obligations exist without the formality of a contract.

Examining Exceptions: When Contracts Aren't Necessary

The world of obligations encompasses more than just the obligations people voluntarily consent to by entering contracts. Obligations also arise from other sources. A party can also bring a claim based on tort, reliance, or restitution:

✔ **Tort:** A tort is a civil wrong unrelated to breach of contract. Society imposes tort obligations on its members, so everyone's required to honor these obligations regardless of whether they're willing to do so. Although you and I can't make a contract without our mutual consent, we're bound not to commit the tort of harming each other despite our lack of formal agreement.

Tort law is generally beyond the scope of this book, although occasionally a particular transaction gives rise to both tort and contract obligations. For example, if I contract with a lawyer to perform certain tasks for me, the lawyer's obligation to perform those tasks arises from our contract. If she doesn't perform them, she may be in breach of contract. In addition, tort law imposes an obligation on the lawyer not to harm me. If she fails to live up to that obligation, she may have committed the tort of malpractice.

✓ **Reliance:** Reliance occurs when a party acts or refrains from acting based on what someone else promises. For example, suppose a man tells his recently widowed sister that if she moves, he'll provide a place for her to live. This promise is probably not enforceable because he didn't bargain for her performance. However, if she incurs expense in moving and he then refuses to give her a place to live, the law of reliance kicks in. Even though his promise may not be enforceable as a contract, he may be legally obligated to pay the expenses she incurred in *relying* on his promise by moving.

✓ **Restitution:** Restitution is the act of making a party disgorge (relinquish) a benefit when one party has conferred a benefit on another. According to the doctrine of restitution, one party is not allowed to unjustly enrich himself at the expense of another. For example, in *Mills v. Wyman* (see Chapter 3), when Mills cared for Wyman's adult son, Wyman incurred no contractual obligation because Mills didn't bargain for anything in return for the services. But Mills is not out of luck — he has a claim against Wyman's son in restitution for the value of the benefit he conferred on him.

The following steps lead you through the process of determining whether two parties have a formal contract or are legally obligated by one of these fallback doctrines:

1. **Look for a bargained-for contract.**

   A bargained-for contract must meet all the following conditions (see Chapters 2 and 3 for details):

   - The offeror made the offer to induce acceptance.

   - The offeree gave acceptance to obtain what the offeror promised.

   - Each party offered something the other wanted (consideration).

   If a bargained-for contract exists and a party has breached the contract, then the injured party is entitled to the *expectancy* — the damages that put the injured party in the position she would've been in if the contract had been performed. (For info on expectancy, see Chapter 16.)

2. **Look for a claim based on reliance.**

   Even if there is no contact, if the promisee's change in position cost him something, then he may have a claim in *reliance* for compensation that puts him back in the position he was in before he relied on the promise. (Refer to the next section for details.)

3. Look for a claim based on restitution.

In the absence of a contract, restitution arises when one party confers a benefit on another without intending it as a gift or forcing it on the other party. If the person who received the benefit was unjustly enriched, then the law requires that she *disgorge* (relinquish) the benefit, returning each party to the position she was in before the benefit was conferred. (See "Deciding Cases That Test the Limits of Reliance: Promissory Estoppel," later in this chapter, for details.)

Reliance and restitution are not only stand-alone claims; they're also remedies for breach of contract, as I discuss in Part V.

The Doctrine of Reliance: Looking for a Promise That Induced Action

Reliance fits somewhat uncomfortably in the Restatement of Contracts, a compilation of rules based on past judicial decisions (see Chapter 1 for details). The Restatement begins by establishing the requirements for an enforceable promise through bargained-for contract. Then it says there's more to contract formation than that: You can have an enforceable promise even without a bargained-for contract. In other words, the Restatement accounts for the fact that courts have enforced promises in the absence of bargained-for contracts.

Restatement § 90(1) provides a good summary of the elements of claims that have led courts to enforce promises based on reliance, which is also known as *promissory estoppel.* It states the following:

> § 90. Promise Reasonably Inducing Action Or Forbearance
>
> (1) A promise which the promisor should reasonably expect to induce action or forbearance on the part of the promisee or a third person and which does induce such action or forbearance is binding if injustice can be avoided only by enforcement of the promise. The remedy granted for breach may be limited as justice requires.

Notice that § 90 is full of weasel words, including "reasonable," "justice," and "injustice." The purpose here is to remain flexible. The Restatement is intended to provide guidance, not set rigid rules.

Even if the situation meets all the conditions for reliance, the Restatement says that the remedy for breach may be limited. The following subsections explain the four conditions and the remedy limitation in detail.

The Restatement isn't a statute, so don't try to use it as a statute. Courts are not bound to follow it (though this particular section, Restatement § 90, may be more closely followed than many other sections). Furthermore, the outcome of any contract case depends not only on the rule but also on the facts, so outcomes may be very different depending on the facts involved. Think twice before you say with authority, "The Restatement says. . . ." A court is free to say, "We don't care. The Restatement is not the law in this jurisdiction. Please cite me some law I am bound to follow." Still, the Restatement is a useful tool for seeing the big picture and gaining a clearer understanding of how judges approach these cases, so you can use the Restatement as a short-cut to determine what courts tend to look for.

Determining whether reliance applies

Although Restatement § 90 is brief, it describes four conditions that must be present to form an obligation based on the doctrine of reliance:

- ✔ It must include a promise.
- ✔ The promisor must reasonably expect the promise to induce action or forbearance.
- ✔ The promise must be successful in inducing the expected action or forbearance.
- ✔ Enforcement of the promise must be the only way to avoid injustice.

This section covers these conditions in detail.

Finding a promise

Reliance always starts with a promise, so the first step toward determining whether reliance applies is to test the language for a promise (see Chapter 2). Does the language contain a commitment to do or not to do something with the expectation that the other party does something (action) or doesn't do something (forbearance)?

For example, if your rich uncle says, "I expect to be paying for your law school education someday," those words don't contain enough commitment to rise to the level of a promise; they merely express a hope. But if he says, "I'll set up a trust to cover your law school tuition and expenses," that's a promise intended to induce action (preparing to go to law school).

A promise isn't an offer if it doesn't ask for anything in return.

Asking whether the action or forbearance was reasonable to expect

Assuming the language contains a promise, the next step in finding out whether reliance applies is to determine whether the action or forbearance is reasonable to expect. Ask whether a reasonable person in the shoes of the promisor would've thought the promisee would do or not do what the promisor expected because of the promise. If you answer yes, then the language meets the second condition.

Suppose your 10-year-old brother is complaining that he doesn't have pocket money for ice cream, and your uncle tells him, "I'll give you $1,000." No reasonable person would expect your brother to take him seriously. On the other hand, if you were complaining that you didn't have enough money to get the supplies you needed for law school, a reasonable person would expect your uncle to follow through on a promise to give you $1,000 to cover the expenses.

Determining whether the promise really did induce action or forbearance

The next element of reliance is simple: Did the promisee act or refrain from acting because of the promise? This is especially important in terms of the remedy. You must determine what the promisee did or didn't do in reliance on the promise and at what cost to the promisee. (For more about remedy, see "Limiting the remedy for breach of the promise," later in this chapter.)

Asking whether injustice is avoided only by enforcing the promise

The final condition for reliance is that the promise is binding "if injustice can be avoided only by enforcement of the promise." Ask whether enforcing the promise is in the best interest of justice even though the parties fell short of forming a contract.

Look at the example of Williston's tramp, which I first present in Chapter 2. A wealthy man tells a tramp that if the tramp walks around the corner, the man will buy the tramp an overcoat. Williston concludes that consideration is absent, because the man was very unlikely to be bargaining for the tramp's performance. The tramp may use the fallback argument and say, "Okay, we had no bargained-for contract. Nevertheless, you made a promise and I took some action in reasonable reliance on it. So pay up."

The problem is that the tramp did very little — he just walked around the corner. But suppose your uncle told you, "I'm going to give you $3,000 so you don't have to spend your valuable time doing that work-study job while you're in school." If you've given up the job in reliance on that promise, then only by enforcing the promise is justice served.

Limiting the remedy for breach of the promise

In cases that involve an enforceable promise but no bargained-for contract, expect the courts to limit the remedy to whatever the injured party lost as a result of reasonable reliance on the promise. As the final sentence of Restatement § 90(1) states, "The remedy granted for breach may be limited as justice requires."

Suppose that your rich uncle says to you, "I hear you're going to law school! That's great! I'll give you $1,000 to help out." In reasonable reliance on his promise, you buy $200 worth of study aids, including, of course, *Contract Law For Dummies*. He then announces a change of mind and tells you that he's not going to pay you anything.

Clearly, you and your uncle don't have a bargained-for contract, because he didn't bargain for anything from you. You can fall back on reliance, however, because your uncle's promise induced you to do something — in this case, to purchase $200 worth of study aids. Therefore, his promise becomes enforceable.

How much is the remedy? Nowadays, courts generally limit recovery to the extent of the reliance. So you'd most likely recover $200 in your reliance claim against your uncle, not the $1,000 he promised.

Of course, in a situation where measuring the extent of the reliance is difficult, enforcing the promise may be the best option in terms of justice. For example, in a case where an employer promised an employee a pension of $200 per month when she retired, the employee retired and became virtually unemployable. The employer changed its mind and stopped paying the pension, claiming it had no contractual obligation. The court found that the parties had no bargained-for contract, but it also found that the employer should've reasonably expected her to rely on the promise. Although the court didn't discuss the extent of the reliance, measuring what the employee had done or not done in reliance would be difficult or impossible, so enforcing the promise to pay $200 per month seems just.

It wasn't always this way: Counting reliance as consideration

The final sentence of Restatement § 90(1), which mentions limits on the remedy when someone breaches an enforceable promise, is relatively new. It did not appear in the First Restatement, which was drafted in the 1920s. Apparently the principal author of the First Restatement, Samuel Williston, equated reliance with consideration. If a promisor was found in breach of an enforceable promise, the court would usually require the promisor to honor the promise in full; if your uncle promised to pay $1,000, that's what he owed you regardless of how much you spent in reliance.

When the Second Restatement appeared in 1981, the drafters added the final sentence to Subsection (1), reflecting the fact that courts now typically limit the remedy to the monetary value of whatever the injured party lost as a result of reliance on the promise.

Deciding Cases That Test the Limits of Reliance: Promissory Estoppel

Reliance is also called *promissory estoppel* — *promissory* because it deals with a promise and *estoppel* because the promisee's reliance on the promise prevents (estops) the promisor from denying the legal effect of that promise merely because consideration is absent.

The courts have struggled with numerous difficult cases to determine whether they should hold promisors liable on this theory. This section explains several types of common cases in which promissory estoppel comes into play.

Deciding whether a charitable pledge is enforceable

The question of whether a charitable pledge (promise) is enforceable has no easy answer. A wise dean may say, "If you promise $10,000 to the law school building fund, we'll put a plaque up in your honor." Assuming the prospective donor agrees, the two parties have a bargained-for contract, and the future donor is obviously bound by contract to follow through with the donation.

Most of the time, however, the narrative goes something like this: Someone at the not-for-profit sends a letter requesting a pledge. The prospective donor pledges a specific amount of money, say $10,000, to the law school building fund. On its surface, this doesn't qualify as a bargained-for contract, and the person who made the pledge may refuse to perform.

Nevertheless, courts are sympathetic to enforcing a charitable promise, and they look for some basis to enforce it. The dean may claim, for example, that by committing to have construction begin, he reasonably relied on the promise.

Restatement § 90 even has a special subsection devoted to charitable promises. Subsection (2) states that "A charitable subscription . . . is binding under Subsection (1) without proof that the promise induced action or forbearance." In other words, the court doesn't care whether consideration or reliance exists — it's going to enforce the charitable pledge because it considers doing so good policy.

The Restatement is not the law. A court is free to refuse to enforce a charitable pledge in the absence of reliance on it.

The death and resurrection of contracts: Is consideration required?

In his book *The Death of Contract,* Grant Gilmore explains how the drafters of the First Restatement of Contracts in the 1920s came to include two rules in it: one saying that consideration was required for an enforceable contract and one saying that consideration was not required:

> A good many years ago Professor Corbin gave me his version of how this unlikely combination came about. When the Restaters and their advisors came to the definition of consideration, Williston proposed in substance what became § 75. Corbin submitted a quite different proposal. . . . Corbin, who had been deeply influenced by Cardozo, proposed to the Restaters what might be called a Cardozoean definition of consideration — broad, vague and, essentially, meaningless — a common-law equivalent of *causa,* or cause. In the debate Corbin and the Cardozoeans lost out to Williston and the

Holmesians. In Williston's view, that should have been the end of the matter. . . .

> Instead, Corbin returned to the attack. At the next meeting of the Restatement group, he addressed them more or less in the following manner: Gentlemen, you are engaged in restating the common law of contracts. You have recently adopted a definition of consideration. I now submit to you a list of cases — hundreds, perhaps or thousands? — in which courts have imposed contractual liability under circumstances in which, according to your definition, there would be no consideration and therefore no liability. Gentlemen, what do you intend to do about these cases?

The answer is that the drafters of the Restatement embodied in that work the concept of reliance, or promissory estoppel, as an alternate theory for the enforcement of promises.

Deciding whether a sophisticated party can claim reliance

Most reliance cases involve a person who's not very sophisticated in distinguishing the subtle differences between contracts and gift promises. Assuming that the promisee relies on a promise, the law turns what would otherwise be a gift promise into an enforceable promise. Courts are much less likely to find reliance in cases involving sophisticated parties, such as two people in business. These parties ought to know better than to rely on a promise, so the promisor wouldn't reasonably expect the promisee to rely on the promise.

For example, if a franchisor says to a franchisee, "We're going to give you a franchise," the promisee should know that businesses don't give away franchises for nothing; they expect something in return. In the famous case of *Hoffman v. Red Owl,* however, the franchisees kept being told they would get the franchise, but they had to do just one more thing first. After they jumped through a series of hoops, the franchisor said, "Sorry, no franchise for you."

The court found that although no contract was formed, the franchisees had acted in reasonable reliance on these promises and were able to recover for their losses. Note, however, that even though setting up a franchise is a business deal with a lot of money at stake, the franchisee has very little bargaining power and may, for this purpose, be considered an unsophisticated party.

Remembering that reliance doesn't usually qualify as acceptance

Reliance isn't a viable fallback option when an offeree fails to accept an offer. You have to accept an offer, not simply rely on it, to make it enforceable.

For example, suppose I offer you 10,000 pens for $10,000, and you don't express acceptance. Minutes later, you decide to open a pen store. You rent space at the local mall and sink some money into advertising. You show up at my door, and before you have a chance to utter a word, I say, "I revoke my offer."

I successfully exercised my right to revoke the offer at any time before acceptance. You may say, "But I *relied* on your offer," as evidenced by renting office space and taking out advertising, but I would assert, and the courts would agree, that you shouldn't have relied on the offer; you should've accepted it by promising to pay me the $10,000 I had requested.

Note the difference between a promise and an offer. By presenting an offer I made a promise, but as an offer, it called for acceptance and consideration — in this case, your promise to pay me $10,000. You knew you had to accept the offer, not rely on it, to make it enforceable. If you wanted some time to think it over, you should've entered into an option contract by paying me a consideration to keep my offer open (see Chapter 2 for details).

The Doctrine of Restitution: Creating an Obligation to Prevent Unjust Enrichment

Contract law is always on the watch for anything that seems unfair, including *unjust enrichment* — when one party unfairly gains a benefit at another party's expense. To prevent or mitigate unjust enrichment, the courts rely on the doctrine of *restitution,* doing whatever's required to compensate both parties fairly or return them to their original positions prior to their dispute. This section reveals how the courts use restitution to deal with unjust enrichment.

Battling unjust enrichment with the implied-in-law contract

One tool the courts use to prevent unjust enrichment is the *implied-in-law contract,* or *quasi (pseudo) contract* — an obligation the law imposes on the parties when the parties haven't entered into a formal agreement.

An implied-in-law contract must meet the following three conditions:

- ✔ Services must not be performed as a gift.
- ✔ Services cannot be forced on a party.
- ✔ The obligation formed by the implied-in-law contract must prevent unjust enrichment.

 Don't confuse the *implied-in-law* contract with the *implied-in-fact* contract. An implied-in-fact contract is a real contract (that is, a bargained-for contract) found in the conduct of the parties rather than in their words (see Chapter 2). An implied-in-law contract is not a bargained-for contract but an obligation based on restitution.

 The classic example of an implied-in-law contract occurs when a doctor renders emergency medical services to a comatose patient and then bills the patient for those services. The patient may emerge from the coma and say something like, "Too bad, but I never agreed to pay for those services." However, contract law would likely side with the doctor to prevent unjust enrichment — the patient's receiving medical treatment without giving the doctor anything in return. Someone may claim that the treatment was forced on the patient, but the courts would argue otherwise, stating that any reasonable person in the doctor's shoes would've concluded that had the patient been conscious, he would've requested the services and is therefore obligated to pay.

On the other hand, if I mow your lawn without your asking me to do so and then claim that I conferred a benefit on you for which you should compensate me, the law would say that my act was *officious* — performed without your consent — in which case you're not obligated to pay for it. Society doesn't want businesses to go around forcing people to accept services and then demanding payment.

 Although the reasonable value of services in a particular situation is not always clear, reasonable value of the benefit conferred is always the starting point for measuring the recovery in restitution.

EXAMPLE

Awarding restitution for saving a life?

A restitution issue arises when one person claims that another has a "moral obligation" to pay for a benefit conferred. Today people try to stick to looking at legal obligations, but the legacy of past cases remains. In *Webb v. McGowin,* a 1923 Alabama case, Webb, an employee of McGowin, was in the process of throwing a block and tackle (rope and pulley system) from a loft when he saw his employer, McGowin, moving directly into the path of the falling object. To save McGowin from injury, Webb threw himself at the falling block and tackle, diverting it so it missed McGowin, but severely injuring himself in the process. In those days workers' compensation was non-existent, but McGowin promised to pay Webb $15 every two weeks for the rest of Webb's life. McGowin made the payments until he died five years later. When the executor of his estate refused to continue the payments, claiming the estate had no contractual obligation to make them, Webb sued.

Webb had a lot of sympathy going for him but not a lot of law. Obviously McGowin and Webb had no bargained-for contract. Nor did Webb rely on the promise by McGowin; he had already acted before the promise was made. What about "moral obligation" — does McGowin have an obligation to pay Webb for a benefit conferred, even though the law didn't require it? Today the courts would say no, because they're concerned only with legal obligations.

But what about restitution — didn't Webb confer a benefit on McGowin? One problem with the restitution claim in this case is that society generally thinks that a person who saves someone's life or commits a similar heroic act has conferred a gift on the person and is not entitled to compensation. Society honors heroes for their courage and sacrifice but doesn't allow them to recover from the person they saved. In this case, however, McGowin promised to pay Webb. Does a promise by the person saved take what was otherwise a gift and change it into an enforceable promise? Maybe. For one thing, the promise makes the act appear less like a gift, because people generally don't offer to pay for gifts. For another, because the recovery in restitution is the value of the benefit conferred, the promise puts a value on the act that otherwise would be difficult to determine.

In this case, the court held that a contract was formed. That seems like nonsense to me, but it may make sense to say that a promise in a situation like this is enforced as a kind of restitution where the value of the benefit conferred can't be determined. The result of the case has been captured in Restatement § 86, the principles of which can be summarized in the context of restitution as the following:

✔ If a benefit conferred is not a gift and not officious, then the party who was unjustly enriched must pay the value of the benefit conferred. If the party who received the benefit made a subsequent promise to pay, the amount promised is irrelevant because the claim is in restitution, not contract.

✔ If a benefit is conferred as a gift, as in the case of most rescues, then neither claim in restitution nor promise to enforce in contract is present.

✔ If a benefit is conferred and the person who received the benefit made a subsequent promise to pay, even if no claim in restitution would exist, the promise may be enforceable in contract to the extent necessary to prevent injustice.

Apparently in the good old days, doctors commonly set fees based on each patient's ability to pay. In one particular case, after rendering services on an unconscious person, a doctor discovered that the person was very wealthy and sent him an inflated bill. The court held that the doctor and patient could've contracted for that amount, but when the claim is based on an implied-in-law contract, the measure of the recovery is the value of the benefit conferred rather than what the contract price would've been.

Determining when a court is likely to find unjust enrichment

Whenever one party confers a benefit on another that's not a gift and not offi-cious (forced upon the recipient), then look to a claim based in restitution. Courts commonly award restitution when parties enter a contract and then one of the parties successfully asserts a contract defense that destroys the claim that the parties made a bargain (see Part II for info on contract defenses); the court then tries to restore the parties to their positions prior to contract formation. In doing so, the court employs the principle of restitution.

For example, if I orally agree to buy your house for $100,000 and give you a down payment of $5,000, you may correctly claim that our contract is not enforceable because it was oral. (As I explain in Chapter 7, all real estate con-tracts must be evidenced by a writing.) You win that particular battle, but now you have $5,000 of my money that I didn't hand you as a gift nor confer on you officiously, so I ought to get it back. Because we have no contract, the proper claim is in restitution — you keep your house, and I get my $5,000 back.

Sorting out restitution in a material breach

The restitution issue arises when a party can't make a contract claim because she's materially breached the contract. (A *material breach* is any failure by the breaching party that's significant enough to give the injured party the right not to perform his part of the contract.) In such cases, the court may compel the injured party to provide restitution in an amount equal to the benefit that the breaching party conferred on the injured party. (See Chapter 14 for more about material breach.)

For example, suppose I hire a contractor to build a house for me for $200,000. The contractor builds 40 percent of the house and then stops. Obviously, the contractor can't recover from me on the contract because he's completed so little of the project. That's a material breach.

But I did receive a benefit. Hiring another contractor to finish building the house may cost me only $120,000. Should I get to keep the benefit conferred by the dirty contract-breaker without paying for it? Authority is split on this question, but the modern view is to allow the party who breaches a contract to recover in restitution for the benefit conferred. In this case, the courts would likely order me to pay the first contractor $80,000. The contrary view is that he has committed a wrong, and a wrongdoer should not be able to make an equitable claim.

Of course, because the contractor is in the wrong, my recovering my expectancy damages (putting me where I would've been had the contract been performed) takes priority over his getting restitution. If he claimed that he spent $100,000 building the house before he quit and completing it cost me $120,000, he gets only $80,000 in restitution because I'm entitled to get what I bargained for — the house for $200,000.

Part II

Determining Whether a Contract Is Void, Voidable, or Unenforceable

The 5th Wave   By Rich Tennant

"I'd like to see how he plans to enforce a contract written on a baseball bat. It's not even notarized."

In this part . . .

Freedom of contract is the most basic principle governing contract law. It gives everyone of legal age and sound mind the freedom to bargain fairly for contracts allowable by law. In certain situations, however, a person may appear to have freely entered into a contract when she really didn't. In such cases, the person can challenge contract formation or try to avoid the contract by launching a contract defense.

The chapters in this part explore common contract defenses, which arise from illegal contracts, contracts contrary to public policy, unconscionable terms, lack of capacity, fraud, duress and undue influence, mistake, and the statute of frauds.

Chapter 5

Introducing Contract Defenses

A contract defense is a challenge to a contract's formation and enforce-ability. For example, suppose you're a plaintiff trying to get a court to enforce a contract you think I've breached. You present your case and prove we formed a contract through offer, acceptance, and consideration (see Part I of the book for details). Even so, the contract isn't necessarily valid or enforceable. I have the opportunity to present a contract defense — to offer proof claiming that certain facts undermine the contract's formation and destroy its enforceability.

These facts typically have less to do with the three elements of contract for-mation (offer, acceptance, and consideration) and more to do with policies adopted by courts and regulations enacted by federal or state legislatures. This chapter introduces and explains these policies and regulations so you're better equipped to challenge a contract's validity or defeat that challenge. The remaining chapters in this part focus on specific policies and regulations that influence decisions in contract cases.

Leveraging the Power of Policies

Contract law has four key policies that guide the courts in deciding whether contracts or terms are enforceable by law:

- ✔ Freedom of contract
- ✔ Efficiency
- ✔ Fairness
- ✔ Predictability

No single policy takes precedence over another in all cases. In fact, contract law is often an attempt to reconcile competing policies. As an attorney, you can use this idea to your client's advantage, as long as you understand the different policies and how the courts are likely to reconcile competing policies.

Freedom of contract

Freedom of contract is the most basic principle governing contract law. It gives everyone of legal age and ability the freedom to bargain fairly for contracts allowable by law.

All other things being equal, freedom of contract rules the roost. If two parties agree to a deal that passes the formation requirements (which I outline in Part I), it's enforceable in a court of law. However, the law has the power to scrutinize the agreement to make sure that nothing about it is illegal or unfair. If a deal is lopsided enough, a court may inquire into it based on the principle of fairness.

As you explore the various devices courts use to overturn agreements, remember that freedom of contract includes the freedom to make a bad deal. If nothing's wrong with the transaction other than the fact that one party agreed to sell something for a lot less than it's worth, the law should let the agreement stand.

Efficiency

The principle of efficiency facilitates the free and fair exchange of goods and services. Generally, freedom of contract ensures economic efficiency, because parties freely bargain for what they want to get out of the transaction. The assumption is that each party agrees only to what's in her best interest. But if one party engages in certain conduct that takes advantage of the other party (unfair conduct), the efficiency of the transaction may be impaired, both in terms of economics and justice.

You need to look at efficiency both in terms of freedom of contract and fairness. If I have a car worth $10,000 and I agree to sell it to you for $100, an economist may say the deal was efficient because $100 had more utility than the car had for me and obviously the car had more efficiency than your $100 had for you. On the other hand, inquiring minds want to know whether such a deal is fair: Something seems fishy about the transaction. Why would I sell a $10,000 car for $100? Was something illegal going on? Did you hold a gun to my head and make me agree? Was I out of my mind at the time? These facts would show that the agreement wasn't economically efficient because I wasn't able to maximize my interests.

Fairness

The principle of fairness is designed to keep one party from making a sucker of the other, perhaps by slipping terms into the contract that are unfavorable to the other party or that the other party is unlikely to read or understand.

Of course, you can't merely claim that a contract or term is unfair; you must fashion a legal argument that indicates precisely what's offensive about the transaction. Chapter 6 exposes you to contract practices and terms deemed illegal or unfair to assist you in gauging the legality, fairness, and enforceability of a contract and its terms.

Predictability

The principle of predictability facilitates contract planning. It provides everyone involved in contract law with the secure knowledge that if you enter into a transaction in a particular way or use certain words, then the outcome is the same as it has been in the past. Courts generally follow this rule, which goes by the Latin name of *stare decisis,* which means "let the decision stand."

But different contract cases arise under different facts, and a court may apply a rule to one set of facts that it doesn't apply to another set of facts. As a result, contract law isn't always as predictable as most people want it to be.

For example, what level of quality can the buyer of a used car expect? Assume an automobile wholesaler sells a car to a used-car lot, the used-car dealer sells that car to a consumer, and the buyer sells the car to a friend. The transactions involve the sale of the same car, but in the first transaction, the parties are sophisticated commercial parties; in the second, they're a sophisticated commercial party and a consumer; and in the third, they're two unsophisticated parties. In these different circumstances, you can't assume that a court will apply the same rule in the same way.

Making the Most of Statutes

Contract law has two layers: common law and statutes. *Common law* is any collection of laws established by prior judicial decisions (precedents). *Statutes,* which federal and state legislatures have the power to pass, govern particular transactions. These statutes may clarify, reinforce, or override the common law, so when you're dealing with a contract defense, you need to be aware of statutes that may be relevant to the defense.

In this section, I explain how the authority of federal and state statutes differ and provide general guidance on how to make strategic use of these statutes to bring a contract claim.

Protecting consumers with state and federal statutes

Contract law is traditionally state law. The federal government may get involved, however, because Congress has the authority under the Constitution to regulate interstate commerce, and many contracts involve interstate transactions.

Both federal and state legislatures have been active in enacting statutes that apply to a *consumer transaction* — a transaction that an individual enters into with a business for personal, family, or household purposes. Here are a few example transactions to help you tell whether you're dealing with a consumer transaction or something else:

- **Consumer transaction:** You buy a car from a dealer. The dealer is a business, and you're a consumer.

- **Business-to-business transaction:** A used-car dealer buys a car from a distributor. No consumer is involved, so it's not a consumer transaction.

- **Peer-to-peer transaction:** I buy a used car from you. In most jurisdictions, this doesn't constitute a consumer transaction because neither party is a business.

Federal and state statutes are primarily for consumer protection, but they differ in the types of protection they afford consumers, as I explain next.

The Federal Trade Commission (FTC) Act

The United States Congress passed the Federal Trade Commission (FTC) Act in 1914. The FTC Act very broadly forbids "unfair or deceptive acts or practices" in interstate trade and commerce. Over the years, the FTC has adopted rules and guidelines that list the acts and practices the FTC considers unfair or deceptive for various industries.

For example, the FTC discovered that used-car dealers frequently made false or misleading statements about the condition of the cars they were selling and the warranties buyers were getting. As a result, the FTC now requires used-car dealers to put a sticker on the window of each car that clearly discloses whether any warranty is provided, and if so, what it covers.

The FTC is primarily a consumer protection agency. Consumers may file complaints with the FTC to seek justice, but the FTC is likely to pursue only the most significant claims. For individual recovery, consumers may need to pursue a claim under the state law.

State statutes

Although the FTC can bring a complaint on behalf of a consumer, an individual doesn't have a *private right of action,* meaning that he can't bring his own claim under the FTC Act. Every state has solved this problem by enacting its own Consumer Protection Act that operates like a mini–FTC Act. Under the state statutes, both a state agency and the consumer can bring a complaint. In fact, in most jurisdictions, attorneys have an incentive to help consumers bring these claims, because if they're successful, they can collect attorney's fees from the losing defendant. (You may not appreciate that now, but you will when you get into practice!)

The principal statute you encounter in contract law is Uniform Commercial Code (UCC) Article 2, which applies to the sales of goods. Most UCC provisions are not regulatory; they're *default rules* that apply in the absence of rules in the parties' agreement.

Most of the provisions of UCC Article 2 apply to transactions involving the sale of goods, regardless of whether the parties are merchants. Nevertheless, a court may well apply a section differently depending on whether the transaction involves two sophisticated parties, a sophisticated party and an unsophisticated party, or two unsophisticated parties.

Contract law in the U.S. Constitution

The United States Constitution has little to say about contracts. The Contract Clause — Article I, Section 10, Clause 1 — provides that "No state shall . . . pass any . . . Law Impairing the Obligation of Contracts." Although that may sound like the law should let people contract as they please, courts have applied the clause much more narrowly. The drafters were apparently concerned about a widespread practice under the old Articles of Confederation whereby states would relieve individuals of their obligation to pay debts, particularly debts to foreign creditors.

In modern times, parties to contracts have challenged the constitutionality of state regulations that affect their contracts. The Supreme Court laid out a three-part test for whether a law violates the Contract Clause in *Energy Reserves Group v. Kansas Power & Light,* 459 U.S. 400 (1983). It allows the state to interfere with freedom of contract if

✔ The state regulation does not substantially impair a contractual relationship.

✔ The state has "a significant and legitimate purpose behind the regulation, such as the remedying of a broad and general social or economic problem."

✔ The law is reasonable and appropriate for its intended purpose.

Most regulations have no problem overcoming these hurdles and trump freedom of contract.

Tapping the power of statutes to bring a contract claim

As an attorney, you need to be well versed in both federal and state statutes. If a statute addresses a particular transaction or a particular term in the contract, check whether you can bring a claim under the statute in addition to or rather than the common law.

For example, an advertisement is not an offer (see Chapter 2 for details). If an ad induces you to go to a store and the store tells you it doesn't have the advertised goods and tries to steer you to other goods, you have no claim in common-law contracts. But this practice — called *bait and switch* — is likely to be a violation of a state Consumer Protection Act statute. And under that statute, you may be entitled to enhanced remedies such as punitive damages and attorney's fees.

Before bringing a common-law contract claim, check the following to see whether you can bring a claim under a statute instead:

- ✔ Does the transaction involve a consumer?
- ✔ Does a statute or regulation apply to this particular agreement?

If your claim meets either of these conditions, you have a good chance of being able to bring a claim under a statute. Some consumer protection statutes allow individuals to bring statutory claims on their own, whereas others allow only the state or federal consumer protection agencies to bring claims on behalf of affected consumers. Of course, a statute often needs to be interpreted, so researching any cases on point is also important.

For example, suppose an attorney in Montana has a disabled client whose wheelchair doesn't work properly. The attorney finds no cases on point but knows that UCC Article 2 applies because the transaction involves the sale of goods. The seller has complied with the Code statutes on the exclusion of warranty, so the client appears to be out of luck. The attorney digs deeper and discovers that the Montana legislature has enacted a Wheelchair Warranty Act that may provide relief for a consumer in this situation.

Examining the Courts' Role in Policing Contracts

In the United States, a government agency doesn't need to approve a contract in advance, and most of the time no statute regulates the contract. Assuming that nobody broke the law, as soon as the parties agree through offer, acceptance, and consideration, a contract is formed. The courts get involved only if one of the parties challenges the contract in court.

Even if both parties concede that the contract was formed through offer, acceptance, and consideration, one party may challenge the contract by claiming that certain facts undermine its formation and destroy its enforceability. In England, this is called *vitiating* (taking the life out of) the contract. In the U.S., we just call it establishing a defense to the contract.

The general rule is that assuming the plaintiff has proven the formation of a contract, it's *presumed* valid, but a presumption is just a starting point. If the presumption is *rebuttable,* meaning capable of being proven invalid, then the defendant has an opportunity to show that additional facts provide a *defense to the contract,* as I explain next.

Checking into Affirmative Defenses

According to the Rules of Civil Procedure, the defendant must prove an *affirmative defense* — proof that effectively challenges the contract or its terms. Rule 8(c) provides in part

> (c) Affirmative Defenses. In pleading to a preceding pleading, a party shall set forth affirmatively accord and satisfaction, arbitration and award, assumption of risk, contributory negligence, discharge in bankruptcy, duress, estoppel, failure of consideration, fraud, illegality, injury by fellow servant, laches, license, payment, release, res judicata, statute of frauds, statute of limitations, waiver, and any other matter constituting an avoidance or affirmative defense.

Note that although the rule lists a number of defenses, it also states that a party can prove "any other matter" that would be a defense to the contract.

UCC Article 2 doesn't state any rules that allow a party to assert a defense to the formation of a contract for the sale of goods. Nevertheless, those rules are in the Code! Article 1, which applies to the other articles of the Code, provides the following in § 1-103(b), as enacted in North Carolina at § 25-1-103(b):

> (b) Unless displaced by the particular provisions of [the Uniform Commercial Code], the principles of law and equity, including the law merchant and the law relative to capacity to contract, principal and agent, estoppel, fraud, misrepresentation, duress, coercion, mistake, bankruptcy, and other validating or invalidating cause supplement its provisions.

Section 1-103(b) is one of the most important provisions of the UCC. It specifies that in a contract for the sale of goods under Article 2, where the Code doesn't supply a rule, you must read in "the principles of law and equity" — the rules from the common law. So when dealing with an Article 2 (sale of goods) transaction, take the following steps:

1. **Look for the rules in the Code.**
2. **If you can't find a rule that applies, look to a statute that addresses the particular transaction.**
3. **If you can't find a statute, then look to the common law.**

In this section, I provide general guidance for examining defenses to contract formation.

Distinguishing valid, void, and voidable contracts

Depending on the outcome after applying an affirmative defense, a contract falls into one of the following three categories:

- ✔ **Valid:** Initially, a contract is presumed to be *valid,* meaning that it's enforceable under law.

- ✔ **Void:** A contract is void if the affirmative defense provides sufficient evidence that no contract was formed due to additional facts. If a contract is void, it never was and never will be a valid contract. For example, suppose you used *fraud in the factum* (Latin for "fraud in the making") to trick me into signing a document I didn't realize was a contract and then claimed that I had agreed to buy your house. In such a case, the contract is void and we're restored to our pre-contract positions; you get the house, and I get my money.

- ✔ **Voidable:** Most of the time, a contract that's formed is *voidable* if an affirmative defense is proven. This means that it was valid when formed, but a party has the power to avoid or affirm the contract. For example, if you used the more common form of fraud, called *fraud in the inducement,* to get me to buy your house by representing that it had two working bathrooms when it had only one, I'd have the option of avoiding or affirming the contract:

  - • **Avoid:** If I were to avoid the contract, I would render it ineffective by proving a defense to contract. The court restores us to our pre-contract positions; you get the house, and I get my money.

  - • **Affirm:** My other option is to affirm the contract, waiving my defense. In that case, the contract is valid, and I may have a claim against you in tort for damages.

Separating matters of law and matters of fact

Courts may determine that contracts are void or voidable based on matters of law or matters of fact:

- **Matters of law:** If a contract is void or voidable *as a matter of law,* the party doesn't have to prove any facts to show that the contract was vitiated, because it never was a contract. The law covers it. As a matter of law, a contract may be either void or voidable:

  - **Void:** An example of a contract that's void as a matter of law arises when a person has gone through a court proceeding that determines the individual is mentally incompetent, called an *adjudication of incompetence.* Because the legal system has decided that the person is incapable of entering contracts, any contract he enters into is void as a matter of law.

  - **Voidable:** An example of a contract that's voidable as a matter of law is one that a minor enters into. If you're under 18, any contracts you enter into are valid, but you can avoid them without having to present a contract defense.

- **Matters of fact:** If a contract is voidable as a *matter of fact,* it starts as a valid contract, and the party must prove the facts that vitiate it. If a person hasn't been adjudicated incompetent but claims she lacked the mental competence to enter a particular contract, then she must prove as a matter of fact that she wasn't competent at the time she entered the contract. For example, if Britney goes to Las Vegas, gets drunk out of her mind, and gets married, then after she sobers up, she can avoid the marriage contract by proving facts that show she was mentally incompetent at the time she entered it. If she had previously been adjudicated incompetent, the contract would be void without need for further proof.

As you consider specific contract defenses (which I cover in Chapters 6, 7, and 8), ask yourself the following:

- Is the person claiming the defense trying to prove that the contract is *void* or *voidable?*

- Is the case proven *as a matter of law,* or does the person have to prove it *as a matter of fact?*

Chapter 6

Considering Whether an Agreement Is Unenforceable Due to Illegality or Unfairness

. . . .

In This Chapter

▶ Analyzing the degree of illegality in an agreement

▶ Applying the concept of defenses based on public policy

▶ Policing agreements with the doctrine of unconscionability

▶ Checking contract terms against the doctrine of reasonable expectations

. . . .

*C*ontract law has a number of competing policies. One important policy is *freedom of contract,* which grants parties the right to make binding agreements. But another important policy is the *police power* of the legislature and the courts — the power to determine whether the entire agreement or a term in an agreement is enforceable. To make that determination, courts must consider these two policies and others.

This chapter reveals the most important considerations courts use to determine the enforceability of an agreement or a term within the agreement:

✔ The legality of the agreement itself or more subtle violations of law that may affect the enforceability of the agreement

✔ Whether the agreement or a term in it violates public policy

✔ Whether the agreement or a term in it is unconscionable (shocks the conscience of the court)

In examining these considerations, this chapter shows you what to be aware of when planning an agreement or deciding whether to challenge an existing agreement.

Determining Enforceability When the Legislature Has Spoken

Legislatures may make certain agreements illegal to discourage undesirable conduct, but they must weigh the necessity of discouraging certain conduct against the parties' right to form a contract. This section enables you to weigh the two for yourself and your clients.

Recognizing illegal agreements that are unenforceable

Sometimes determining enforceability is easy: A particular agreement isn't enforceable because the legislature says very clearly, "Don't do this!" In such cases, society discourages undesirable conduct by making it illegal for the parties to enter an agreement. The legal system has the power to challenge agreements in three ways:

- ✔ **Civil:** The agreement is void as a matter of law, so nobody can base a contract claim on it.
- ✔ **Criminal:** Parties may face a penalty for making the agreement.
- ✔ **Procedural:** Using the courts to enforce such agreements is inappropriate.

For example, consider a state statute that makes distribution of methamphetamine illegal. Suppose Walter agrees to sell Tuco a pound of meth for $40,000. Tuco takes the meth but refuses to pay Walter, so Walter sues. Do the parties have freedom of contract to make this agreement? Clearly not. Public policy against distributing dangerous drugs outweighs any interest in enforcing the contract. You can find that policy in the fact that the legislature made it a crime. On the civil side, the agreement is void, and on the criminal side, the parties may face charges for making the agreement. Furthermore, the courts would look foolish if they supported Walter's claim, so they'd likely toss him out of court on his ear.

Most law students and lawyers carelessly use the words *agreement* and *contract* interchangeably, but note the difference:

- ✔ An *agreement* is what parties agree to, whether enforceable or not.
- ✔ A *contract* is an enforceable agreement.

An agreement can be enforceable or not, but a contract by definition is enforceable. The Code makes this distinction in the definitions of *agreement* and *contract* in UCC § 1-201. Section 1-201(b)(3) as codified in North Carolina provides the following:

"Agreement," as distinguished from "contract," means the bargain of the parties in fact, as found in their language or inferred from other circumstances, including course of performance, course of dealing, or usage of trade as provided in G.S. 25-1-303.

Section 1-201(b)(12) as codified in North Carolina provides

"Contract," as distinguished from "agreement," means the total legal obligation that results from the parties' agreement as determined by this Chapter [the Uniform Commercial Code] as supplemented by any other applicable laws.

So using these words in this sense, parties can make an agreement in fact to sell drugs or to restrain trade, but they're not making a contract because in law these obligations are not enforceable.

Consider a business accused of making an agreement with another business in violation of the antitrust law, which prohibits agreements that restrain trade. The defense claims that because the agreement was void, they didn't make an agreement, so no violation! Of course, this defense doesn't hold up in court, because of the difference between an *agreement* and a *contract*. The parties, in fact, made an agreement.

Noting exceptions: Illegal but enforceable agreements

Not every agreement that involves illegality is unenforceable. Recall that society is trying to balance two interests: the freedom-of-contract interest in enforcement of the agreement and the public policy interest against enforcement. The policy behind making agreements illegal is to discourage undesirable conduct. But sometimes the interest in enforcing the bargain, either in whole or in part, outweighs the interest in discouraging the conduct.

To determine which interest — freedom of contract or public policy — carries more weight, courts typically consider the following factors:

- ✔ The expectations of the parties; that is, what they had hoped to gain by entering into the agreement

- ✔ Whether failure to enforce the agreement would result in *forfeiture* — an out-of-pocket loss — by the party seeking enforcement

- ✔ Any public interest in enforcement

This section describes situations in which agreements may be enforceable according to one, two, or all three of these factors, despite being illegal.

When one party is innocent

A court may decide that the interest in enforcement of an agreement out-weighs the interest in non-enforcement when non-enforcement would harm the person the policy of the law was designed to protect. Sometimes one of the parties to an illegal agreement is innocent of any wrongdoing. Failing to enforce the agreement may harm that person more than it would harm the wrongdoer. Courts like to invoke Latin expressions when they're trying to do the right thing, so in this case, the court may say that the parties are not *in pari delicto,* meaning not "in equal fault."

Suppose a state statute regulates life insurance and requires that a life insur-ance policy include certain statements. An insurance company issues a life insurance policy on John, omitting the required statements. The life insurance company and John have entered into an agreement that violates the statute. Sometime later, John dies and Mary, his beneficiary, seeks enforcement of the policy. The insurance company states that because the agreement violated the law, the agreement to insure John is not enforceable.

Balance the factors for and against enforcement. Even though John is dead, you can still consider his interest as a party to the agreement. He entered the agreement with the expectation that Mary would benefit from its purchase. If it were not enforced, he would suffer forfeiture, because he would've paid the premiums in exchange for nothing. And the public would not benefit if enforce-ment were denied. Although the regulation may be important to enforce as a matter of principle, its enforcement in this case would not harm (and would actually benefit) the wrongdoer, the insurance company, but would harm John and Mary — the innocent parties. Therefore, in this type of situation, the agree-ment would be found enforceable even though it's in violation of the law.

When the crime is not serious

Enforceability may hinge on the degree of illegality. Obviously, some crimes, such as drug dealing, are more serious than others, such as operating a busi-ness without a license. When determining the enforceability of agreements that involve illegality, the degree of illegality is an essential consideration. When making the determination, the courts consider the following factors:

- ✔ **The strength of the policy as reflected in statutes or case law:** How much interest does society have in enforcement?

- ✔ **Whether refusal to enforce the agreement furthers the policy:** Will enforcement encourage parties to disobey the law?

- ✔ **The seriousness of the misconduct:** Was the misconduct serious enough to challenge enforcement of the contract?

- ✔ **The connection between the misconduct and the agreement:** Did the mis-conduct go to the heart of the parties' agreement, or was it just incidental?

For example, if you hold yourself out as an attorney and enter into agreements with clients without having a license to practice law, any agreement you enter into is illegal, and you're not allowed to keep any of your fees. That's because in the interest of protecting the public, practicing law without a license is illegal. On the other hand, suppose in a jurisdiction that licenses contractors, an unlicensed contractor renovated a house for $100,000, and then the homeowner refused to pay on grounds that the agreement was illegal. The court would likely be torn. Non-enforcement would put teeth in the licensing provision, but it would also do the following:

✔ Give the homeowner a windfall, because she would keep the improvements for free.

✔ Encourage homeowners to hire unlicensed contractors to receive free renovations.

A court may therefore decide that protection of the public was a less-important factor in this situation than in the situation of the unlicensed attorney. If the primary purpose of a licensing statute is to raise money, courts usually find that the agreement made by the unlicensed party is enforceable.

Look for techniques courts use to enforce the agreement (or part of it) that don't involve a balancing test. Here are two such techniques:

✔ **Using the concept of *divisibility of contract* to enforce the agreement in part:** The court separates the parts of the agreement that are illegal from the parts that are not and then enforces the legal parts. For example, in the case of the unlicensed contractor, the court may divide the agreement into the *services* rendered by the contractor and the *supplies* used by the contractor. The court could then say that the services portion was unenforceable but the supplies portion was not.

✔ **Not enforcing the agreement but allowing restitution:** Another technique a court may use would be to declare the agreement void, barring enforcement under contract law, but then let the contractor recover in restitution the value of the services and supplies. In *restitution,* even if no contract exists, a person may recover the reasonable value of goods and services supplied. (See Chapter 4 for info on restitution.)

When the connection to illegality is iffy

When illegality is involved in an agreement, the balance swings in favor of non-enforcement. But if the illegal aspect isn't closely connected to the agreement, then the balance may swing the other way. It all depends on the facts.

Suppose a company owns a business on a busy street where parking is illegal and subject to a $50 fine. The company orders $10,000 worth of goods for delivery and agrees to reimburse the seller $50 if it has to pay a parking fine. The company obtains the goods and then refuses to pay for them because the seller parked illegally when it delivered the goods.

Most courts would have no problem enforcing this agreement for the following reasons:

- ✔ A parking violation doesn't constitute serious misconduct (as you may have discovered when you had to disclose criminal acts in order to apply to law school!).
- ✔ The misconduct isn't closely connected to the agreement. This is an agreement to buy/sell goods, not to commit a crime.
- ✔ The seller would suffer a serious loss if the buyer were allowed to keep the goods without paying for them.

In this case, the factors weigh in favor of enforcing the agreement in spite of the fact that an illegal act was committed during its performance.

Making a Public Policy Argument

Most of the time, no law tells the parties ahead of time (called *a priori* in Latin) that they can't make a certain agreement. Nevertheless, one of the parties may ask the court to declare after the fact (called *ex post* in Latin) that their agreement isn't enforceable based on *public policy,* the need to protect some aspect of the public welfare. In such a case, the agreement is presumptively (assumed to be) valid but is subject to a defense that *vitiates* (nullifies) it, making it a *voidable* contract. If the court agrees with the party, the court often justifies its decision to avoid the contract by stating that the agreement "violates public policy."

Unfortunately, courts rarely explain what "violating public policy" means. What they usually mean is that some other public policy carries more weight in this particular case than the public policy of freedom of contract. Courts often invoke public policy when the contract meets any of the following criteria:

- ✔ It restrains trade.
- ✔ It interferes with family relationships.
- ✔ It encourages *torts* (wrongful acts for which victims may claim damages).

This section explains how to evaluate enforceability based on public policy and, in the process, formulate a more articulate public policy argument.

Riding the unruly horse of public policy

In a very old case, an English judge wrote that "public policy is a very unruly horse, and once you get astride it you never know where it will carry you." All too often, "public policy" is a conclusion rather than a reasoned argument, so determining exactly why the court objected to the agreement may be very difficult.

An old lawyer's joke offers some sage advice: "If the facts are in your favor, argue the facts. If the law is in your favor, argue the law. If neither is in your favor, argue public policy."

Examining enforceability in agreements that restrain trade

An agreement with the sole purpose of restraining trade is illegal under antitrust laws. When an agreement's purpose is not exclusively to restrain trade, however, the courts must consider several factors to determine whether a term in the agreement is enforceable:

- ✔ The interests of the party who requested the term
- ✔ The reasonableness of the trade restraint
- ✔ The hardship of the party who agreed to it
- ✔ The public interest

A good example of such a term is a *restrictive covenant* — a term in an employment contract that forbids the employee from accepting certain employment opportunities after employment is terminated for whatever reason.

For example, the contract of an employee of a software company in Silicon Valley provides that when her employment terminates, she agrees not to work for another software company in Silicon Valley or in the State of Washington for a certain period of time. This term restrains the employee from practicing her trade, but because it's only one term in an otherwise reasonable employment contract, the entire purpose of the contract is not the restraint of trade.

In deciding whether to enforce a restrictive covenant, a court weighs both sides. On one hand, people should be able to work for whomever they please. On the other hand, the employer has an interest in protecting its trade secrets and competitive advantage. Most courts balance these interests by considering the extent of the restriction in respect to

> ✔ **The scope of employment:** What kind of employment does it restrict?
>
> ✔ **The geographical area:** Does the restriction prevent the employee from finding other work anywhere or only where that employment is likely to interfere with the employer?
>
> ✔ **The time:** Does the restriction last only a reasonable period of time?

If the court concludes that these factors favor the employee's arguments against enforcement, it will not enforce the term. It then faces the further question of which remedy to employ. Courts may strike the offending term entirely, rewrite it to make it more reasonable, or revise it by using the *blue pencil test* to strike certain words. For example, from the term "not work for another software company in Silicon Valley or in the State of Washington," a court may use the blue pencil to strike the words "or in the State of Washington," limiting the geographical area of the restrictive covenant to Silicon Valley.

Examining enforceability in agreements that interfere with family relationships

The area of family relationships is one in which courts often use the doctrine of public policy to discourage undesirable conduct. In such cases, the court tries to balance freedom of contract against other policies.

A good example is the case of *In the Matter of Baby M,* which arose in the mid-1980s, when assisted reproduction techniques were still a novelty. A married couple, William and Elizabeth Stern, was unable to have children because of Elizabeth's medical condition. With the help of an attorney who specialized in such matters, they entered into an agreement with a woman named Mary Beth Whitehead. The agreement provided that Whitehead would be a surrogate mother, bearing William's baby by artificial insemination and then giving it to the Sterns in a private adoption. After she gave the child, known as Baby M, to the Sterns, Whitehead had a change of heart and wanted to get her back. The Sterns sued to enforce the agreement.

The trial court thought that this was a matter of freedom of contract and enforced the agreement, but the Supreme Court of New Jersey vigorously disagreed. The court found that it was a case of illegal baby-selling and added that even if it weren't, it wasn't the kind of agreement the court thought people should be making. It declared the agreement to be against public policy and unenforceable, saying, "[H]er consent is irrelevant. There are, in a civilized society, some things that money cannot buy."

Examining enforceability in agreements that encourage torts

A *tort* is a civil wrong, such as negligence, for which victims may claim damages. The obligations people have to not commit torts arise from the law, but their obligations in contract arise only from their voluntary agreements. Contract law and tort law intersect when the agreement contains an *exculpatory clause* stating that one party agrees not to hold the other party liable for negligent acts he commits after they make the agreement. The word *exculpatory* comes from the Latin *ex,* meaning "not," and *culpa,* meaning "guilt." If a person is exculpated from his acts of negligence, then he's not guilty of committing a tort.

Exculpatory clauses used to be common in residential leases, but you can easily imagine why courts were concerned about them. Suppose a tenant agrees not to hold the landlord liable for negligent acts, such as failing to repair common areas. If the tenant trips and falls, injuring herself, the landlord could say, "Ha-ha! You don't have any tort claim against me because you agreed to an exculpatory clause."

Evaluating exculpatory clauses

Courts have struggled with the question of whether to enforce exculpatory clauses. They want to uphold freedom of contract, but they also want to discourage acts of negligence.

To make a strong public policy argument, begin by asking, "Exactly which aspects of an exculpatory clause make it offensive and therefore contrary to public policy?" Here's a list of common concerns about exculpatory clauses:

- ✔ **How broad is it?** Does it exculpate the party not only from acts of simple negligence but also from more-serious acts like intentional torts? Of course, a party can draft the clause narrowly to address this concern.

- ✔ **Does it give adequate notice?** If the clause is found in fine print, the other party may not have known it was in the contract. To address this concern, the exculpatory clause can be presented in bold print on the front page of the contract or on its own page to be signed separately.

- ✔ **Did the other party lack bargaining power?** If housing is scarce, for example, tenants may agree to almost anything to obtain housing. A landlord can do little to address such a concern, but courts would have to decide on a case-by-case basis whether the tenant had any bargaining power.

- ✔ **What are the economics of the situation?** Who should bear the risk of loss? Who has the most control over avoiding the cost of injury? In the case of a tenant-landlord contract, making the landlords responsible for this loss would give them an incentive to keep the premises repaired. Moreover, they could obtain insurance to cover any claims and could pass the cost of the insurance to their tenants through the rent.

Determining the present state of the law regarding exculpatory clauses

A number of state legislatures have enacted statutes that make exculpatory clauses in residential leases illegal before the fact — that is, they make it illegal to include the term in an agreement. In other states, the courts have ruled that the terms are unenforceable after the fact. In such a jurisdiction, lawyers face an ethical dilemma when deciding whether to include an exculpatory clause in a lease. On the one hand, drafting it in the agreement isn't illegal. On the other hand, the other party probably doesn't know it's likely to be unenforceable and may be misled by its presence in the agreement.

The question of the enforceability of exculpatory clauses in transactions other than residential leases is very much up in the air. You can safely say that the answer is "It depends on the jurisdiction!" Most courts have found transactions that don't involve much public interest, such as commercial leases, to be an appropriate area for freedom of contract, leaving it to the parties to allocate the risk. But in transactions that do involve public interest, where a member of the public has little opportunity to bargain, most courts have refused to enforce exculpatory clauses. Examples include exculpatory clauses in agreements for public conveyance and for hospital services.

Not knowing whether a term is going to be enforced isn't desirable in contract law. Knowing the rules of the game ahead of time improves efficiency in planning transactions and makes it easier for everyone to stay out of court.

Testing an Agreement against the Doctrine of Unconscionability

Everyone agrees that courts have the power to determine that an agreement or a term in an agreement is *unconscionable* and refuse to enforce it even if the agreement or the term isn't illegal. What they don't agree on is when courts should use that power.

Part of the problem is that *unconscionable* is a vague word. For example, UCC § 2-302 gives courts this power, but it doesn't define *unconscionability*. The Official Comment states that "the basic test is whether [. . .] the clauses involved are so one-sided as to be unconscionable." Thanks a lot! The Code's failure to define the term is no doubt intentional, because to define is to limit, and the law wants the concept to be flexible.

Think of *unconscionable* as meaning that the agreement or the term shocks the conscience of the court. But one person's meat is another's poison, so don't expect consensus on which terms are shocking enough to be unconscionable.

Applying the doctrine of unconscionability in the UCC

A party may ask the court to strike not an entire agreement but just the offensive term as unconscionable. This power is given to courts in cases involving the sale of goods by UCC § 2-302, which provides the following in subsection (1) as enacted in North Carolina:

> § 25-2-302. Unconscionable contract or clause.
>
> (1) If the court as a matter of law finds the contract or any clause of the contract to have been unconscionable at the time it was made the court may refuse to enforce the contract, or it may enforce the remainder of the contract without the unconscionable clause, or it may so limit the application of any unconscionable clause as to avoid any unconscionable result.

Note how flexible the unconscionable-contract-or-clause statute is. It starts with the words "If the court *as a matter of law* finds." Judges decide matters of law, and juries decide matters of fact. Because this statute says that the court has to find unconscionability as a matter of law, the determination of unconscionability is up to the judge, not the jury. The courts wouldn't want juries to get carried away by sympathy for the plaintiff! The judge has the power to determine whether the agreement or a term of the agreement is unconscionable. Having found it unconscionable, the judge is then free to fashion an appropriate remedy. The judge may throw out just the term, throw out the entire agreement, or limit the application of the term.

The classic example of application of the concept of unconscionability is the case of *Williams v. Walker-Thomas Furniture Co.* Williams, a mother on welfare, purchased a number of goods from the defendant's store on credit. Each time she did so, she signed a new agreement. After a number of years, when she was unable to make a payment on a record player, the store demanded that she return everything she had ever purchased from the store on credit. It turned out that a clause buried in the agreement, called a *cross-collateralization clause,* stated (in a lot more words than this) that if she defaulted on one agreement, the store could take back not just the item she bought under that agreement but everything she had ever purchased from them on credit. With the help of Legal Aid, she sued to have the clause stricken from the agreement.

The trial court judge condemned the practice of the store but found that he lacked the power to do anything about it because the jurisdiction had not enacted the UCC at the time the agreements were entered into. The appellate court reversed, holding that it didn't matter that the UCC had not been enacted, because the doctrine of unconscionability was found in the common law. Therefore, judges can decide that a term is unconscionable even if no statute authorizes them to do so. Although that was the holding of the case, the judge *in dicta* (language of a court opinion addressing an issue that did not need to be resolved to decide the case) indicated how courts could analyze an agreement to determine whether unconscionability was present. The next section explains how to make that analysis.

Distinguishing procedural and substantive unconscionability

For a term or contract to be found unconscionable, it must pass a two-part test to meet the conditions of procedural unconscionability and substantive unconscionability:

- ✔ **Procedural unconscionability:** This point concerns the procedure by which the parties entered into the contract. Did one of the parties have an absence of meaningful choice?

- ✔ **Substantive unconscionability:** This point concerns the fairness of the contract or term being contested. Is the contract or any term it contains unreasonably favorable to one of the parties?

This section helps you examine these two conditions of unconscionability and develop a clearer understanding of them.

Examining procedural unconscionability: Take-it-or-leave-it deals

Procedural unconscionability occurs most commonly in a *contract of adhesion*. With a contract of adhesion, the parties don't engage in back-and-forth negotiation and then give their final assent to the terms they've both agreed to. One party dictates the terms, and the other party either accepts or walks away. Contracts of adhesion account for a huge majority of all contracts, including those for leasing an apartment, taking out a student loan, or purchasing just about anything online.

Although negotiation is absent in most contracts of adhesion, they're still enforceable because the parties give their assent to be bound. Under the doctrine of *objective manifestation of intent,* you're bound by a contract even if you didn't read it or understand it (see Chapter 2). Nevertheless, courts often scrutinize a contract of adhesion more closely because of the procedure by which it was formed. Therefore, when analyzing a transaction, always ask whether it involves a contract of adhesion.

Procedural unconscionability may occur in other types of contracts as well. Situations in which courts find procedural unconscionability include the following:

- ✔ One party pressured the other to sign without providing any opportunity to read the contract.

- ✔ The contract is unreadable because it's full of complex language or terms written in fine print.

However, procedural unconscionability isn't sufficient grounds for finding a term or a contract unconscionable. The contract or term must satisfy *both* parts of the two-part test. It must show evidence of substantive unconscionability, too, as I explain next.

Examining substantive unconscionability: Unfair terms

Courts tend to scrutinize contracts of adhesion closely because courts are concerned that the party who prepares the contract, knowing that the other party must sign it as written, may be tempted to slip in some very harsh terms. After all, if negotiation is not an option and the other party probably won't even read the contract, the drafter has plenty of motivation and little deterrent in setting terms.

This is where substantive unconscionability — the second condition necessary to find a contract or any of its terms unconscionable — comes into play. But what does it mean that a term is substantively unfair, and how do you prove it to a court? The plaintiff may allege that the term

- ✔ Was unfairly oppressive
- ✔ Took the plaintiff by surprise
- ✔ Allocated most of the risks to the plaintiff

In *Williams v. Walker-Thomas Furniture Co.,* for example, the plaintiff's claim was that the cross-collateralization clause was overly protective of the seller's interests and caused out-of-proportion harm to the buyer. (See the earlier section "Applying the doctrine of unconscionability in the UCC" for details on this case.)

However, the party who drafted the contract has the opportunity to challenge that allegation. Subsection (2) of UCC § 2-302 says that the party who slipped the unfair term into the contract should be given an opportunity to prove that in its commercial context, the term wasn't so bad after all. As enacted in North Carolina, § 25-2-302(2) provides:

Seeing the economist's perspective on unconscionability

Our economist friends, such as Judge Richard Posner of the United States Court of Appeals for the 7th Circuit, look skeptically at the doctrine of unconscionability. They think that a person always has the choice not to enter a contract. If a contract contains outrageous terms, people can refuse to sign it, and the market may counter with someone who offers better terms. An economist may argue that if the court denies a furniture store its cross-collateralization clause (which allows the store to repossess all items a customer ever purchased from it on credit if the buyer defaults on one agreement), the store either must raise its prices or go out of business, neither of which is a helpful outcome for the furniture buyer.

(2) When it is claimed or appears to the court that the contract or any clause thereof may be unconscionable the parties shall be afforded a reasonable opportunity to present evidence as to its commercial setting, purpose and effect to aid the court in making the determination.

In other words, even if a contract or clause looks shocking at first glance, the drafter has the opportunity to explain why it makes sense in its context, which often involves the economics of the situation.

To qualify as unconscionable, a term must pass the two-part test, so the fact that a term is unfair is not sufficient. The procedure must be unfair as well. If the parties negotiated, they had the opportunity to protect themselves from unfair terms. If a party agreed to an unfair term, she probably got something she wanted in return.

If I buy for $1,000 a TV that regularly sells for $700, the deal may seem substantively unfair, but because the price term was obvious and I knew exactly what I was getting into, the term appears to be free of procedural unconscionability. This is why courts rarely find unconscionability when the only issue is the price.

The concept of unconscionability is most common when a consumer enters a contract with a business for personal, family, or household purposes, because consumer transactions usually involve an unsophisticated party who lacks bargaining power. It's less common in contracts between two commercial parties. Exceptions exist, but they usually arise when a commercial party, like a consumer, has no bargaining power, as in the case of a *franchise agreement* — a contract to license the sale of a trademarked product, like a brand of burger or taco. Even though this commercial contract may involve a lot of money and sophisticated parties, it may still be a contract of adhesion that a court is willing to scrutinize. In fact, some jurisdictions have enacted statutes to regulate this type of contract.

Challenging Enforceability with the Doctrine of Reasonable Expectations

One doctrine that courts increasingly use to police contracts is the *doctrine of reasonable expectations*. The defense is that the offending term may not be so bad as to be unconscionable, but a reasonable person probably wouldn't have agreed to it if he or she had known it was in the contract. The doctrine of reasonable expectations is based on three assumptions:

✔ Parties don't read contracts of adhesion.

✔ Parties assume that they know the essential terms of the transaction.

✔ Parties can't negotiate the terms even if they do read and understand them.

Therefore, the drafter has a duty to call unusual terms to the attention of the other party.

For example, some car rental companies in California were hitting drivers with a substantial additional charge when they took the car to Las Vegas. A number of drivers were abandoning the cars in Las Vegas, and the charge was intended to discourage that practice. Therefore, the company may have had a reasonable commercial reason for putting the term in the contract. The problem was that customers were taken by surprise and didn't know the term was in the contract until after they had violated it.

The car rental agency may maintain that under the doctrine of objective manifestation of assent, renters are responsible for the terms of the contract whether they read them or not. On the other hand, that's not realistic for the three reasons I mention previously:

✔ Renters don't read their contracts.

✔ Renters *think* that they know what terms the contract contains.

✔ Renters can't negotiate the terms anyway.

The solution for the drafter who wants to make an unusual term enforceable is to call it to the attention of the other party. They can do this by making it conspicuous — calling it to your attention by putting it in bold print at the top of the contract or having you separately sign that term. This is why when you enter into a contract of adhesion to buy something online, instead of just checking that you've read the terms and conditions, sometimes the seller calls a few of the terms to your attention to be individually acknowledged. The company is probably trying to comply with the doctrine of reasonable expectations to prevent you from claiming you didn't know that those terms were included in the contract.

Chapter 7

Evaluating the Parties' Ability to Make the Contract

In This Chapter

▶ Determining whether a party was capable of making a contract

▶ Checking whether a party was tricked or coerced into making a contract

▶ Challenging a contract formed by mutual or unilateral mistake

*I*n forming a contract, parties express themselves as autonomous individuals, freely committing to bargains that may have serious consequences. Contract law wants to be sure that the parties know what they're doing when they undertake this important task, and it provides a defense if a person doesn't act in his own best interests because he's unable to, the other party does something to coerce or mislead him, or one or both parties make a mistake.

This chapter reveals how contract law makes these determinations so you're better able to evaluate contracts in disputes that involve your clients.

Recognizing Who Can Legally Make a Contract

Although the United States Constitution doesn't expressly mention the freedom to make contracts, it's an important individual freedom that contract law wants to protect. However, contract law must also protect individuals who lack the capacity to act in their own best interests from entering into agreements that take unfair advantage of them. You can call this protection freedom *from* contract. It protects individuals who

✔ Have a mental incapacity due to

- Mental illness or other brain disorders
- Being under the influence of alcohol or other substances that may negatively affect judgment

✔ Are minors (under the age of 18)

This section explains each of these conditions in detail.

Passing the mental capacity check

Contract law presumes that each party has the mental capacity to make a contract. This capacity is a given unless an *adjudication of incompetency* proceeding determines that the person is incompetent. After a person is ruled legally incompetent, she's incapable of entering into contracts *as a matter of law,* and any contracts she makes are void from the beginning.

An incompetency ruling can prevent problems for the person's family; for example, it can prevent an individual from improvidently contracting away the family's assets. On the other hand, because taking freedom of contract away is so serious, the court doesn't do it lightly.

Lacking mental capacity as a matter of fact

If a person hasn't been ruled incompetent, she may still be considered legally *incompetent as a matter of fact* at the time she entered into the contract. In other words, even though no formal legal proceeding determined incompetence before the person entered into the contract, evidence that the person was incompetent at the time she entered the contract can be shown after the fact. If the proof is successful, then the presumptively valid contract is *avoided* (declared to be of no legal effect).

To determine incompetence as a matter of fact, the courts rely on one of the following types of tests:

✔ **Cognitive:** Traditionally, courts have used a *cognitive test* to determine whether the person understood the nature and consequences of the transaction at the time. A reasonable person should be able to tell from someone's outward manifestations whether she has sufficient understanding.

✔ **Motivational:** A number of courts have adopted a *motivational test* that goes beyond determining whether a person understands the situation. This test also looks at

- Whether mental illness renders the person unable to act in accordance with that understanding, and
- Whether the other party knows or has reason to know of the other's lack of capacity

For example, in the case of *Ortelere v. Teachers' Retirement Board,* Mrs. Ortelere had suffered a "nervous breakdown" that a psychiatrist diagnosed as involuntary psychosis. She also suffered from cerebral arteriosclerosis. Her teacher's retirement plan provided that she would receive $375 per month, and if she died, the remainder of her account would go to her husband. Later, she entered into a contract to change that benefit to a plan in which she would receive $450 per month, and if she died, nothing would go to her husband, who had quit work to care for her. Two months later, she died. Her husband sued on her behalf, asking the court to determine that because she was mentally incompetent at the time she entered the transaction, the contract should be avoided.

The problem for the court was to determine which test to use to determine mental incompetence. The trial court had used the cognitive test. Unfortunately for Mr. Ortelere, Mrs. Ortelere showed a great deal of cognitive understanding — she had written a letter to the Board clearly indicating that she understood the consequences of her choice — and the court had found her competent. Mr. Ortelere's attorney persuaded the appellate court to allow a new trial in which the trial court would use the motivational test, allowing the contract to be avoided even if she understood it, as long as the fact that she couldn't act in accordance with that understanding was proven.

The dissent went ballistic, making the point that the policy of the law was to prevent people from taking advantage of someone deemed incompetent. The strength of the cognitive test was that a reasonable person ought to be able to see whether the person claiming incompetence understood the transaction, and if the person did, the contract was binding. But under the motivational test, a person apparently demonstrating full understanding could come back and say, "Let me out of the contract because I couldn't act in accordance with that understanding!" According to the dissenters, this would upset the sanctity of contract.

The majority backed off a bit, saying that the court would apply the new test to avoid the contract of the incompetent party only when

- ✔ The other party knew of the mental illness.
- ✔ The mental illness was serious.
- ✔ The other party didn't rely on the contract (see Chapter 4 for details on reliance).

In Mrs. Ortelere's case, her mental illness was in the records of the Teachers' Retirement Board, it was a serious mental illness, and the retirement fund had many contributors, so the fund was not seriously impacted by a change on the part of one individual. Therefore, it was an appropriate case for application of the motivational test.

Making contracts under the influence of drugs or alcohol

The principle that applies to mental incompetence (see the preceding section) applies when a person is under the influence of drugs or alcohol, because that individual probably lacks the ability to understand the nature and consequences of the transaction. The court expects the other party not to make contracts with individuals who exhibit signs of so much intoxication that they don't understand the transaction.

If the other party does make a contract, it is voidable by the intoxicated person. For example, if Britney goes to Las Vegas, gets drunk, and gets married on impulse, she can avoid the marriage contract after she sobers up and realizes what she did.

In *Lucy v. Zehmer,* a farmer sold his farm at a Christmas party at which alcohol was flowing. Although he claimed he was "high as a Georgia pine," the court found from the evidence that he wasn't so drunk that he couldn't understand the nature and consequences of the contract. He was stuck with the deal he made.

Enforcing the obligation of the incompetent through restitution

Because people who lack capacity as a matter of law can't make valid contracts, and people who lack capacity as a matter of fact can make only voidable contracts, businesses might understandably be reluctant to contract with them. It could produce undesirable results. A hotel clerk, for example, might deny a room to a person who's had too much to drink, because the clerk may fear a court would later determine the person was incompetent and therefore would not be obligated to pay anything for the room.

If someone lacks the mental capacity to enter into an enforceable contract, that person may still be liable for necessities such as food, shelter, and clothing under the *doctrine of restitution* (see Chapter 4). Restitution protects both parties:

- ✔ **Provider:** The person providing the benefit is due compensation for the value of that benefit. Even if the contract isn't enforceable, the person who provided a necessity should get restitution for the reasonable value of the benefit.

- ✔ **Recipient:** The person who received the benefit is obligated to compensate the provider only for the value of the benefit and not necessarily for the amount agreed upon at contract formation. For example, if a hotel clerk takes advantage of a patron who's drunk by selling a $100-a-night room for $1,000, the patron could claim that the contract to pay $1,000 was voidable, but he'd be liable in restitution for the reasonable value of $100.

Child's play? Making contracts with minors

A *minor,* sometimes referred to in cases as an *infant,* is anyone under the age of 18 years. A minor is capable of entering into only *voidable contracts* — contracts the minor can choose to get out of.

Don't consider contracts with minors void or unenforceable. Voidable contracts are presumed to be valid. A contract is ineffective only if the minor affirmatively and timely avoids it. The following rules apply to most contract cases involving a minor:

- ✔ The minor can avoid the contract at any time before he turns 18 or within a reasonable time thereafter.

- ✔ The minor can *affirm* (decide to stay in) the contract only after he turns 18.

Only the minor has the power to avoid the contract. If a person over the age of 18 enters into a contract with a minor, that person can't seek to avoid it on the grounds of the other party's being a minor.

Although all the states agree that minors may avoid their contracts, states disagree on many issues that arise in connection with the minor's avoiding the contract, such as the following considerations:

- ✔ **When a minor is considered *emancipated* (able to enter contracts in spite of being under the age of 18):** A state may consider minors emancipated if they're married or in business. In some states, however, a minor must go through an emancipation proceeding. You may have heard of entertainers and athletes, including actress Drew Barrymore and gymnast Dominique Moceanu, doing this.

- ✔ **What minors must give back if they avoid a contract:** In many jurisdictions, minors must give back only what remains of the consideration they received, regardless of any decline in the value of the consideration. That is, if the minor avoids a contract, he doesn't have to make restitution. If a minor buys a car and totals it, in most jurisdictions, the minor need only return the totaled car to get his money back.

- ✔ **Which exceptions bind the minor to the contract:** Many states create exceptions in some situations and require the minor to return the value received. These exceptions include situations in which the minor convincingly misrepresented his age or paid in cash instead of buying on credit. And — sorry, folks — most states have statutes stating that minors can't avoid contracts for student loans.

  Restitution also applies when the minor buys necessities, such as food, shelter, and clothing. The policy behind the general rule clearly tells people that they deal with minors at their own risk, but they shouldn't have to take a risk if they're providing necessities.

Basing a Contract Defense on One Party's Bad Actions

Even if both parties are capable of making a contract based on age and competence, Party A could do something to coerce or mislead Party B into making a contract that doesn't serve Party B's best interests. To discourage this kind of behavior and enable victims to escape such agreements, contract law provides for defenses based on fraud, duress, and undue influence, as I explain in this section.

Saying things that aren't true: The fraud defense

The *fraud defense* arises when one party is misled to a point at which she can't appreciate the actual consequences of entering into the contract. Misleading actions or deeds may result in one of the following types of fraud:

- ✔ **Fraud in the factum (making [of the contract]):** This type of fraud involves misleading a person to the point at which he doesn't even realize he's entering into a contract. In these cases, the parties haven't formed a contract. For example, suppose I hand you a piece of paper that's folded over to reveal only a space for a signature. I say, "This is my new will. I would like you to sign it." You sign it, and then I say, "Ha-ha! You just signed a contract to sell me your house for $100,000."

- ✔ **Fraud in the inducement:** Fraud in the inducement involves making a false representation to get a person to enter into a contract. In this case, both parties are well aware that they're entering into a contract, but one party provides misleading information to the other concerning an important term of the agreement. For example, assume that you and I are negotiating the sale of my house. Knowing my house has termites, I say, "This house has no termites." I've just committed fraud in the inducement. If you later discover that the statement is false, you can avoid the contract.

Proving fraud in the inducement may be quite a challenge because the plaintiff (the party claiming fraud) must prove that the other party (the defendant) made a misrepresentation of fact, that the defendant knew it was false, that it was material, and that the plaintiff reasonably relied on it. This section explains these issues in greater depth and explores the victim's option of seeking a claim in contract or in tort.

Recognizing misrepresentations that constitute fraud

To constitute fraud, a misrepresentation must be *of fact* — something that can be verified or disproven.

To determine whether a misrepresentation is one of fact, ask whether an objective standard is available for measuring its truth or falseness. For example, if I claim that the car I'm selling is rust-free, and the floor is rusted out, the rust is objective proof that my assertion is false.

Non-fact misrepresentations may be opinions or puffing. If in the course of selling you my car, I say things like "you won't get a better deal in all of the town" or "this baby runs like a dream," those are probably not the kind of statements that give rise to fraud, because someone would have a tough time digging up evidence to disprove them.

One of the most difficult problems in fraud is deciding when a failure to disclose a fact is the equivalent of making an affirmative misrepresentation (coming right out and saying it). When disclosure is required, the two are equivalent, but deciding what the parties must disclose is a moving target. To determine whether the law requires disclosure, consider factors such as the following:

- ✔ **The jurisdiction:** Check the statutes and case law for the jurisdiction that governs the terms of the contract to determine what each party must disclose in a certain type of transaction.

- ✔ **The nature of the item for sale:** Different rules may govern the sale of different items such as a house, car, appliance, or collectible.

- ✔ **Whether the party is the buyer or the seller:** Different rules may apply to the buyer and seller.

For example, in most jurisdictions, the seller of residential real estate must disclose to the buyer any material problem that is *latent* (hidden from view). On the other hand, if the buyer knows that the property is or soon will be worth a lot more than the seller thinks it is, the buyer is not required to divulge this nugget of information. Sellers of used cars usually don't have to disclose defects even if they're aware of the problems. In recent years, many jurisdictions have enacted statutes addressing whether sellers of homes must disclose murders or deaths from AIDS on the premises.

Acts such as concealment and telling a half-truth to prevent the discovery of a problem also may be the equivalent of making an affirmative misrepresentation. If I cover up the termite holes in my house to prevent you from seeing them, that's fraud. If you ask me about termites and I say, "We used to have them" but don't tell you that we still do, that's fraud, too.

Relying on the misrepresentation: What does the contract say?

The defrauded party has to prove that he relied on the fraud. Proving reliance can be a problem when the contract shifts responsibility from one party to the other by stating that one party did not rely on any statements or is solely responsible for obtaining that information.

For example, a buyer claims that after he purchased a property, he discovered that the basement contained water damage that the seller had failed to disclose. The seller says that the damage was *not latent* (that it was plainly visible) and the buyer should've seen it when inspecting the basement. The buyer says that he didn't inspect the basement because the seller told him there was nothing to see down there. As if that weren't problem enough, the contract contains a provision that says

> The buyer has fully inspected the premises and is satisfied with their condition. No statements about the condition of the premises have been made to the buyer other that what is contained in this agreement. The buyer accepts the premises as is in their present condition.

Under such circumstances, proving that the buyer relied on any statement would be tough. However, if the seller has a duty to disclose, none of this evidence that appears to work against the buyer matters. The seller should've disclosed the damage.

Furthermore, some courts may say that if one party fraudulently induced the other to enter into the contract, then what the contract says doesn't matter because a fraudulent act voided the contract.

When you're writing a contract, if your client is relying on a certain representation or promise by the other party, include that representation or promise in the contract so your client has an easier time of proving reliance or breach if a dispute arises.

Choosing a remedy: Contract fraud or tort fraud

If the victim of fraud can prove that the other party intentionally misled her, she can decide which remedy she wants to pursue:

- ✔ **Contract fraud:** Avoid the contract and be put back in the pre-contract position.
- ✔ **Tort fraud:** Affirm the contract (stay in it) and make a claim to recover damages, which may include punitive damages that aren't allowed in contract law.

The tort option is available only if the misrepresentation is intentional. If the party making a statement doesn't know it's false, then you have an innocent misrepresentation, not fraud. If, not knowing the house has termites, I say, "This house has no termites," I haven't intentionally misled you, so a tort remedy is not an option. However, you're just as misled as if I did know, so in most jurisdictions you can still avoid the contract on grounds called *constructive fraud* — fraud lacking the intent to deceive.

In contract planning, think ahead to which remedy your client wants in the event that fraud occurs. Will she want out of the contract, or will she want to keep the contract and pursue damages? Include language in the contract that enables your client to pursue that remedy.

Suppose Business A is buying Business B, and Business B has stated that it has assets worth $300,000. Business A must decide whether, if that statement is not true, it wants damages for breach of contract to get what it was promised or whether it wants to get out of the contract. If the contract says, "Business B *warrants* that it has assets worth $300,000," then Business A can get damages if the warranty is not true. If the contract says, "Business B *represents* that it has assets worth $300,000," then Business A can avoid the contract if the representation is not true. Many drafters use the phrase "warrants and represents" to preserve a choice of remedies.

Making an offer they can't refuse: The duress defense

In contract law, *duress* occurs when one party makes an unlawful threat to the other party that gives the person no reasonable alternative but to enter into the contract. In duress, the victim acts against his own will and enters into the contract involuntarily. To qualify for a duress defense, the plaintiff must prove the following:

- ✔ One party threatened the other with a serious and unlawful threat, such as bodily harm, death, or financial hardship.

- ✔ The threatened party had no reasonable alternative but to accept the terms being offered.

- ✔ The threat induced the contract formation.

- ✔ The party presenting the threat caused or threatened to cause the duress instead of simply taking advantage of it.

Claims for duress more commonly arise from financial (economic) rather than physical threats. For example, a web developer may hold a client's website hostage two days prior to its highly promoted unveiling to force the client to renegotiate the contract and pay $10,000 more than the total price they originally agreed to. Having invested considerable resources and with insufficient time to hire a replacement, the client has no recourse but to pay the extra $10,000.

In an economic duress case, determining whether the threat is improper and whether the party had a reasonable alternative may be more difficult than with a physical duress case. Furthermore, merely taking advantage of a situation is unlikely to constitute duress.

Suppose I owe you $10,000, and I hear that you really need the money. I offer you a car worth $6,000 to settle the debt and inform you that if you don't accept, I'll resist your claims to recover any money from me. You take the car. I clearly took advantage of your situation, but I didn't make an unlawful threat or cause the duress (the reason you needed the money so badly). And you had the reasonable alternative of bringing legal proceedings to recover the $10,000 from me. (For more about settlement of debts, head to Chapter 12.)

Taking unfair advantage: The undue influence defense

Undue influence is any inappropriate method of persuasion that a dominant party uses to convince a weaker or more vulnerable party to enter into a contract against his better judgment. One old case described it as "persuasion which overcomes the will without convincing the judgment." Using undue influence to take advantage of a situation results in a voidable contract.

When evaluating for undue influence, look for the following common signs:

- ✔ The victim was weaker or more vulnerable, typically due to dependency, age (very old or very young), mental or physical disability, illness, social isolation, depression, anxiety, and so on.

- ✔ The dominant party initiated the transaction and attempted to prevent the other party from seeking independent advice.

- ✔ The transaction appears suspicious — for example, elderly homeowners sell their property for significantly less than market value, even though they owe practically nothing on the mortgage.

Undue influence plays a major role in deeds, trusts, wills, real estate transactions, investments, and stock purchases and sales.

Whoops! The Mistake Defense

In contract law, a *mistake* is a belief that's not in accord with the facts. A mistake may be *mutual* (both parties were mistaken) or *unilateral* (only one party was mistaken). This section explains how to evaluate a mutual mistake defense, use the mutual mistake defense to get out of a *release* (a contract in which one party relinquishes all claims in return for something, usually money), and evaluate a unilateral mistake defense.

A mistake may make a contract voidable, but the mistake defense is limited. People are always claiming that they made a mistake in entering a contract; for example, they think that something is worth more or less than it really is. But a bad financial or business decision doesn't constitute the kind of mistake that can avoid a contract.

Evaluating a mutual mistake defense

To avoid a contract for mutual mistake, a party must show that the mistake is mutual, goes to a basic assumption, and is material. In addition, the party claiming the defense must not bear the risk of being mistaken — something I get to in a moment.

To evaluate a mutual mistake defense, take the following steps:

1. **Identify the mistaken belief.**

   What did one or both parties believe that was not in accord with the facts?

2. **Determine whether the mistake is mutual.**

   Did both parties believe the same information? If I think your house would make a great rental property and buy it for that purpose, but you have no opinion on the matter, and then I find that no one wants to rent it, then I made a mistake, but you didn't. The mistake isn't mutual. I have no claim for mutual mistake.

3. **Determine whether the mistake relates to a basic assumption.**

   A *basic assumption* is something the contract hinges on. Would this mistake reasonably discharge a party from the contract? For example, if we agree that your house would make a great rental property, and then it turns out to have no value as a rental, the assumption of its being a good rental property is a basic assumption.

4. **Determine whether the mistake has a material effect on the transaction.**

   Material means significant — usually that the financial impact is significant. If you're looking at a $20,000 transaction, $1,000 may not be material, whereas $10,000 certainly is.

5. **Determine whether the party seeking to avoid the contract carried the risk of being mistaken.**

   A party may assume the risk of being mistaken in either of the following ways:

   - **Expressly:** The contract states which party carries the risk. For example, the contract may state, "The buyer has conducted his own investigation of the property as a rental and accepts it in its present condition."

   - **As the business norm:** Subject to some exceptions, the buyer normally bears the risk that the goods are worth the price.

Contract law properly places the burden on a party to investigate the facts — he shouldn't treat his assumptions as sufficient. If a person is unwilling to take the risk, then he can bargain for a promise or representation from the other party. For example, instead of taking the risk that your house is a good rental property, I could bargain for a contract term that stated something like the following:

Seller warrants and represents that the house will generate monthly rentals of at least $2,000.

The fact that most sellers are unwilling to agree to such a term should induce buyers to do their own investigating.

Using the mutual mistake defense to escape a release

Mutual mistake is one of the most common defenses raised to avoid a *release* — a contract in which one party gives up all claims against the other in return for a consideration, usually the payment of money. Both parties enter into the release believing that a set amount of money is sufficient to cover damages. Later, the party who received payment discovers that the payment was insufficient and claims a mistake defense to avoid the release so she can pursue her original claim.

For example, if you crash into me on your skateboard and injure my leg, I have a negligence claim against you. My doctor believes that the leg is broken and will heal completely. On that basis, you offer and I accept $10,000 for my release. Later, I find out that the doctor was wrong. Not only is the leg injury worse than we'd thought, but I also have an arm injury the doctor overlooked. I try to pursue my claim against you, and you wave the release at me, claiming that it bars any further action. I now have to avoid the release in order to pursue my claim against you.

According to the step-by-step evaluation process, the situation qualifies as a mutual mistake because it meets all the required conditions:

- ✔ **The release was based on a mistaken belief.** The extent of the leg injuries and the undiagnosed arm injury are much more serious than the contract reflects.

- ✔ **The belief was mutual.** Both you and I contracted for the release based on the same information from the doctor.

- ✔ **The mistaken belief goes to a basic assumption of the contract.** The release hinges on the assumption that $10,000 will cover the injuries.

- ✔ **The mistaken belief has a material effect on the transaction.** Additional treatments along with other losses are likely to cost significantly more than $10,000, so the effect is material.

- ✔ **The injured party doesn't bear the risk of the mistake.** The case will likely turn on this factor. I was in a position to evaluate the facts. On the other hand, a court may find that we did not intend the release to be binding if there was a mistake as to (1) the unknown consequences of a known injury, such as the leg injury, or (2) an unknown injury, such as the arm injury.

In this example, the release is likely to contain language stating the extent to which I bore the risk. However, the courts will scrutinize that language carefully to see whether they can interpret it in my favor. Even if I released you from both the extent of the leg injuries and other injuries, including the arm injury, courts don't like to uphold releases in situations like these. This is especially true when the injured party is an unsophisticated party who wasn't represented by an attorney and the other party is an insurance company or a workers' compensation system. Courts are human, and they often consider factors, such as fairness, that aren't within the elements of mutual mistake.

Finding relief when the mistake is unilateral

A *unilateral mistake* is an erroneous belief that only one of the parties holds. When evaluating a unilateral mistake defense, follow the same steps you'd take for evaluating a mutual mistake defense (see the earlier section "Evaluating a mutual mistake defense"), with a slight change in Step 2:

1. **Identify the mistaken belief.**

2. **Check for evidence showing that the circumstances meet the following conditions:**

    • **Only the party seeking to avoid the contract was mistaken.**

    • **The other party should've known about the mistake, or enforcing the contract would be unconscionable.**

3. **Determine whether the mistake relates to a basic assumption.**

4. **Determine whether the mistake has a material effect on the transaction.**

5. **Determine whether the party seeking to avoid the contract carried the risk of being mistaken.**

The typical situation in which the unilateral mistake arises is a bid by a subcontractor. Suppose a contractor seeks bids for a job, and a subcontractor makes a bid (offer) of $10,000. The contractor accepts it. The subcontractor now says, "Wait a minute. We put the decimal point in the wrong place. We meant to bid $100,000." This mistake is unilateral. If the contractor should've known about the mistake because the other bids were coming in at around $100,000, then the court will allow the subcontractor to avoid the contract.

If, however, the subcontractor bid $90,000 and the other bids were coming in at around $100,000, then a contractor may reasonably think this was just a low bid and not a mistake. Also, binding the subcontractor to its promise to do a $100,000 job for $90,000 would not be unconscionable, although binding him to do the job for $10,000 would be unconscionable.

Chapter 8

Assessing the Enforceability of Oral Agreements

. . . .

In This Chapter

▶ Evaluating contract formation in oral agreements

▶ Knowing which types of agreements must be in writing

▶ Determining whether a writing is sufficient proof of an agreement

▶ Recognizing exceptions to the rules

. . . .

*T*he aim of contract law is to give individuals as much freedom as possible to form contracts, so the general rule is that oral contacts are just as valid and binding as written contracts. Questions sometimes arise with oral agreements, however, over *contract formation* (whether the parties intended to enter into a binding agreement without a written contract) and *contract defense* (whether the contract is enforceable).

For example, even when the law allows oral agreements, parties may discuss the terms of an agreement with the intent to make a later written contract. Problems may arise, however, if the written contract never happens and one party claims that the discussion constitutes a contract. In such a situation, the challenge is to determine the parties' intent. If the parties intended to make a binding agreement but made it orally, contract law says that in general, oral agreements are enforceable. The exceptions to this rule are laid out in the *statute of frauds* — the collective name for statutes that require written evidence of a contract.

This chapter tackles both contract formation and contract defense of oral agreements. Here, you discover how to evaluate the parties' intent to form a binding contract, how to identify a contract that's within the statute of frauds, and how to satisfy the requirement of a signed writing or prove that an exception makes a signed writing unnecessary. (A *writing* is any sufficient written proof of an agreement, such as a handwritten note by one party.)

Oral means spoken as opposed to written. Some people mistakenly refer to oral contracts as *verbal* when they say something like, "That was just a verbal agreement!" *Verbal* means *using words,* so oral and written contracts are both verbal. *Nonverbal* is communicating without words, such as by nodding or shaking one's head. This chapter focuses on oral agreements — spoken, not written.

Asking Whether the Parties Intended to Orally Form a Contract

When parties enter into an oral agreement with the intention to reduce their agreement to a writing later, a problem often arises. Did they intend to form a binding contract solely through their oral agreement, or did they intend not to have a binding contract until they executed the signed writing? The intent of the parties determines whether that oral agreement results in a contract.

Proving something that's as subjective as intent can be difficult. Contract law meets the challenge by examining objective factors, including the following:

- ✔ **Whether that particular type of contract is usually found in writing:** If the type of deal is typically executed with a written, signed contract and no such contract exists, then the parties' discussion probably doesn't prove intent to form a contract.

- ✔ **Whether the contract requires a formal writing for its full expression:** If the agreement demands precise wording that spoken language is unlikely to produce, then discussion of the transaction probably doesn't show intent to form a contract.

- ✔ **The level of detail:** A simple oral agreement with few terms may show intent to form a contract. But in a complex deal with numerous terms, parties typically expect the agreement to be binding only upon signing a written contract.

- ✔ **The amount involved:** Parties often enter into oral agreements for transactions of only a few hundred dollars. When parties discuss high-value transactions, they typically intend to be bound only by a contract in writing.

- ✔ **The uniqueness of the deal:** A discussion may show intent to form a contract in common transactions, such as purchasing goods or hiring someone to perform a job. But if the parties are engaged in an unusual deal, an oral exchange probably doesn't show that intent.

- ✔ **Whether the negotiations indicate that a final signed writing is required:** If during their discussion one or both parties indicate that their agreement is valid only upon the signing of a written contract, then they have expressed intent not to form an oral agreement.

For example, the president of BigCo runs into the president of SmallCo at a trade show. The BigCo president says, "We're interested in acquiring your company for $10 million. Will you sell?" The SmallCo president says, "It's a deal." The BigCo president says, "Great! I'll have our lawyers get together and draw up the papers," and they shake hands. Later, when the lawyers are drawing up the papers, the parties encounter a number of problems that they're unable to resolve, and BigCo says it's not buying SmallCo after all. SmallCo responds, "But we have a contract."

The decision on this case could go either way. On the one hand, the oral agreement appears binding because

- ✔ No rule requires a writing for the purchase of a business.

- ✔ It's foggy whether the parties intended for the agreement to be enforceable only after the agreement had been written up and signed. The parties seemed to view the written contract as a mere formality.

On the other hand, the oral agreement doesn't seem binding because

- ✔ The consideration of $10 million is substantial. People wouldn't normally execute such a transaction without a written agreement.

- ✔ The details of an agreement to sell a $10 million business are considerable. This isn't the type of simple transaction to be sealed with a handshake.

The parties in this transaction should've made clear at the outset that any agreements weren't binding until written and signed by both parties.

Often, the parties to a complex deal proceed in stages, securing agreement at each stage, with an understanding that they have no binding agreement until they reach the final stage. To avoid misunderstandings, parties involved in such transactions should make their intent clear in initial documents. Many parties use an initial transaction called a *Letter of Intent* or *Memorandum of Understanding* that indicates they're not bound until they enter into a final, signed agreement.

Challenging Oral Agreements with the Statute of Frauds

A transaction is within the *statute of frauds* when a statute requires that the transaction be evidenced by a *writing* (written proof of the agreement). This requirement exists largely for historical reasons, but it arguably serves four functions:

- ✔ **Fraud prevention:** As its name suggests, the main purpose of the statute of frauds is to prevent fraud. The statute prevents a person from claiming that someone entered into a contract when he really didn't. For example, if you claim that I agreed to sell you a certain baseball card for $500 when I really didn't, the statute of frauds says that the agreement isn't enforceable unless you can prove that a writing exists.

- ✔ **Cautionary:** The cautionary function serves as a warning to reflect on what you're doing — this is serious business, so you had better take the trouble to put the agreement in writing.

- ✔ **Channeling:** The statute channels behavior, encouraging parties to get certain types of agreements in writing. If you fear that your oral agreement won't be enforced, you have an incentive to put it in writing, thus making it easier for courts to find the agreement.

- ✔ **Evidentiary:** Having the agreement in writing provides a valuable piece of evidence to prove that the parties entered into a contract and specifies its terms.

The transactions that are within the statute of frauds developed historically and seem somewhat arbitrary. In this section, you discover which kinds of transactions fall under this statute and how the statute can render oral agreements unenforceable.

Determining whether a transaction is within the statute of frauds

To determine whether a transaction is within the statute of frauds, check whether the transaction is any of the following:

- ✔ An agreement concerning real estate
- ✔ An agreement to rent real property for longer than a year
- ✔ An agreement that can't be performed within a year from the making
- ✔ An agreement to answer for the duty of another
- ✔ An agreement for the sale of goods for $500 or more

This section examines each of these types of transactions, which must be evidenced by a writing to be enforceable.

Although contract law refers to *the* statute of frauds, each state has its own statute of frauds, so check the statute in your jurisdiction for specifics. (Historically, English law had a *Statute of Frauds,* enacted in 1677, that listed various transactions. American jurisdictions copied the law, but individual jurisdictions aren't required to enact the same law. Curiously, the English largely repealed their statue in 1954!)

Real estate transactions

A *real estate transaction* is any transaction involving the sale of land and improvements (houses, buildings, and other structures) on that land. Applying the statute to real estate transactions probably serves the statute's cautionary function because real estate transactions often involve a lot of money and require a clear understanding of how the buyer is to pay and take possession.

Leasing property for longer than a year

If a party is leasing a property for more than one year, the agreement must be in writing, but shorter leases are an exception. The reasoning behind this seems to be that short-term rentals don't necessarily involve a lot of money. If Joe agrees to rent Mary an apartment for $500 per month for three months, that transaction is relatively insignificant both in duration and dollar amount. In most jurisdictions, an oral lease of real property for one year or less isn't within the statute of frauds, so it's enforceable.

Agreements that can't be performed within a year from the making

An agreement is within the statute if it can't by its terms be performed within a year from the making. The phrase *by its terms* is key here. If for $2 billion, a contractor orally agrees to build a nuclear power plant in six months, that agreement can *by its terms* be performed within a year because the terms give the contractor six months to build it. The agreement isn't within the statute of frauds, so this particular oral agreement is enforceable.

If the oral agreement *can* be performed within a year, regardless of that likelihood, then it's enforceable. For example, if you orally agree to take care of a 20-year-old for the rest of her life, the term "the rest of her life" could end up meaning six months. Because the 20-year-old could die before the year is up, the oral agreement isn't within the statute of frauds. If the 20-year-old lives 60 more years, that oral agreement is still enforceable over those 60 years.

This provision presumably serves the cautionary function (because a person is entering into a long-term commitment) and the evidentiary function (because evidence becomes stale over time); however, this provision can bar enforcement of an oral agreement even when the evidence is fresh.

For example, assume that Joe orally hires Mary to provide housecleaning services for him for two years. A week later, he terminates the contract without cause, claiming that the agreement isn't enforceable because it couldn't be performed within a year from its making. Even though the agreement is only a week old, Mary would have to produce a writing that Joe signed to make it enforceable.

If they'd made the same agreement for services for 11 months and Joe tried to terminate it 6 months later, the agreement would fall outside the statute of frauds. Mary would have to prove only that they had an oral agreement even though the evidence is now six months old.

Agreements to answer for the duty of another

When a third party (a person not a party to the contract) — who often gets no benefit from the transaction — agrees with a creditor to perform if someone else doesn't (often called a *suretyship agreement*), the agreement is typically within the statute of frauds. This probably serves the cautionary function of the statute, ensuring that the third party understands the seriousness of what may be an informal agreement.

For example, Tom agrees to buy goods from Dick on credit. Dick's concerned that Tom may not be able to pay, so Harry agrees to pay Dick if Tom doesn't. Harry's agreement to answer for Tom's duty must be evidenced by a writing. In this example, the promise is made by the surety (Harry) to the creditor (Dick), not to the debtor (Tom).

The situation would be different if the surety instead makes the promise to the debtor. If Tom says to Harry, "I have this debt to Dick, and I'm worried that I won't be able to pay it," and Harry tells Tom, "Don't worry, if you can't pay, I'll cover you," then Harry's promise doesn't have to be in writing because it was made to Tom (the debtor), not Dick (the creditor).

Agreements that involve the sale of goods for $500 or more

Under the UCC, transactions for the sale of goods for $500 or more are within the statute. UCC § 2-201(1), as enacted in North Carolina, provides:

> § 25-2-201. Formal requirements; statute of frauds.
>
> (1) Except as otherwise provided in this section a contract for the sale of goods for the price of five hundred dollars ($500.00) or more is not enforceable by way of action or defense unless there is some writing sufficient to indicate that a contract for sale has been made between the parties and signed by the party against whom enforcement is sought or by his authorized agent or broker. A writing is not insufficient because it omits or incorrectly states a term agreed upon but the contract is not enforceable under this paragraph beyond the quantity of goods shown in such writing.

This statute probably serves the cautionary function (though $500 isn't what it used to be in the 1950s, when the statute was first enacted).

Note that the writing only has to be signed by one of the parties — "the party against whom enforcement is sought." If I orally agree to sell a baseball card to you for $500 and you claim the statute of frauds defense, then I'd have to prove the contract with a writing you had signed; if I claim the defense, then you'd have to produce a writing I had signed.

Looking at criticism of the statute of frauds

Critics challenge the statute of frauds on a few grounds:

✔ **The transactions within the statute seem arbitrary.** The sale of a $10 million business isn't within the statute, but the sale of a $500 baseball card is. Moreover, the statute covers the sale of a baseball card for $500, but it doesn't cover the sale of the same card for $499.

✔ **The statute is unfair.** Critics of the rule think it's unfair for people to avoid agreements they made merely because they didn't sign a written agreement. For example, if I agree to sell you a baseball card for $500, I shouldn't be able to use the statute of frauds to get out of the contract by saying, "Sure, I agreed to sell you the baseball card for $500, but you can't enforce it because I didn't sign anything saying I would."

For these reasons, courts are wary of enforcing the statute and often look for ways to get around its strict application.

Distinguishing between voidable and unenforceable agreements

Sometimes courts say that an oral agreement within the statute of frauds is *void* or *invalid*. That statement isn't accurate, because like a voidable contract, the oral agreement is perfectly good unless one party offers proof that *vitiates* it (destroys its legal validity). Saying it's *unenforceable* is better, because the statute may affect only one party and not the entire agreement. Here's the difference:

✔ **Voidable:** If a party claims an agreement is voidable, then that party may present evidence that no contract was formed. If the evidence is successful, then the parties don't have a contract and are returned to their pre-contract positions. (Chapter 6 provides examples of voidable contracts.)

When a contract is within the statute of frauds, the issue isn't whether the contract was in fact made. People are sometimes concerned that without a writing, they won't be able to prove they made a contract — they say, "It's just his word against mine!" But that's why society has courts and trials. If you state something as a fact in court or present credible witnesses to say it and a court believes it, then it's proven.

✔ **Unenforceable:** If a party claims that a contract is within the statute of frauds, he may present evidence that he didn't sign any writing. That may make the contract unenforceable against him, but it doesn't *avoid* the contract (return the parties to their pre-contract positions). The contract may still be enforceable against the other party if that party signed a writing.

A contract within the statute of frauds isn't enforceable unless there's a writing signed by the party against whom enforcement is sought. If you signed a writing and the other party didn't, then the other party can enforce the contract against you, but you can't enforce it against the other party.

Finding a Writing That Satisfies the Statute

UCC § 2-201(1) — the UCC statute I quote earlier in "Agreements that involve the sale of goods for $500 or more" — is typical of other statutes of frauds in stating that the contract isn't enforceable "unless there is some writing sufficient to indicate that a contract for sale has been made between the parties and signed by the party against whom enforcement is sought."

Under the statute of frauds, the contract doesn't have to *be* in writing; it just has to be *evidenced by* a writing. Don't make the writing do too much work. Courts often show that they disfavor the statute by accepting informal writings to satisfy it. Whether that writing is good enough to satisfy the statute depends on whether it satisfies both of the following conditions:

- ✔ Sufficiently describes the contract
- ✔ Is signed by the party against whom enforcement is sought

For example, Tom orally agrees to sell his house to Mary for $300,000. Tom then goes to his lawyer's office and, finding that she's not there, leaves a note on her desk that says "Just sold my house to Mary for $300,000. Please draw up the papers. —*Tom*." Tom then gets a better offer on the house and refuses to sell it to Mary, claiming that their contract is within the statute of frauds. If Mary discovers the note that Tom left for his lawyer, then she can produce it as evidence of a writing that satisfies the statute, because the note (1) sufficiently describes their contract and (2) is signed by Tom.

This section explains the two conditions necessary to satisfy the statute of frauds in greater detail.

Does it describe the contract?

Although the writing must indicate that the parties entered into a contract, the writing doesn't have to *be* the contract — it only needs to serve as evidence that the oral contract exists by identifying the parties, the subject matter, and the essential terms of the contract. The UCC statute of frauds specifically says that a "writing is not insufficient because it omits or incorrectly states a term agreed upon." The court may fill in the details of the agreement with the parties' testimony or with gap fillers (as I discuss in Chapter 3).

Although the writing doesn't need to include all the contract terms, for the writing to be sufficient under the UCC, it must include the quantity sold. If Tom Smith buys widgets and produces a signed memo from the seller stating, "Just sold Tom Smith Type X widgets," that writing would be insufficient to prove the contract because even though it identifies the parties and the subject matter, it fails to state a quantity. If the signed writing stated, "Just sold Tom Smith 100 Type X widgets," the buyer would be able to enforce a contract for the sale of 100 widgets. If the seller actually had agreed to sell 200 widgets, however, the writing couldn't prove that.

Is it signed by the party against whom enforcement is sought?

Although the statute requires a writing signed by the party against whom enforcement is sought, courts are generally very lenient when determining what constitutes a writing and whether it's signed. The UCC includes the following definitions, as enacted in North Carolina 25-1-201(b)(37) and (43):

> (37) "Signed" includes using any symbol executed or adopted with present intention to adopt or accept a writing.

> (43) "Writing" includes printing, typewriting, or any other intentional reduction to tangible form. "Written" has a corresponding meaning.

Under these definitions, a memo on the letterhead of a business could constitute a signed writing. The name of the business on the letterhead is a symbol "adopted with the present intention to adopt" the writing as coming from that business. Many courts have brought the concept into the electronic age by finding that an e-mail is a signed writing. The sender or signature line indicates the intention of the sender to adopt it. Even though the e-mail exists only in cyberspace, printing reduces it to tangible form.

Finding Exceptions to the Statute

As a matter of policy, courts tend to treat agreements as enforceable unless presented with good evidence to the contrary. A court may narrow the scope of the statute of frauds so fewer transactions fall within it and liberally interpret the requirement of a signed writing to make an agreement enforceable. In addition, the court may find exceptions to the statute of frauds in reliance, main purpose, restitution, and statutory exceptions in the UCC. The following sections explain these exceptions.

KEY CASE

McIntosh v. Murphy: Taking multiple views of the statute of frauds

The case of *McIntosh v. Murphy* shows how divided courts are about the statute of frauds. According to the facts found by the jury, on Saturday, April 25, Murphy, who ran a car dealership in Hawaii, telephoned McIntosh, who was in California, to tell him that a job was open and work would begin on Monday. McIntosh moved to Hawaii and began work on Monday, April 27. Less than three months later, Murphy fired McIntosh. McIntosh sued for breach of contract. Murphy claimed that the employment was "at will," meaning McIntosh could be discharged at any time. The jury, however, found that the contract was for a year's duration, that Murphy was in breach for letting him go during that time, and that McIntosh was entitled to damages in the amount of some $12,000.

Murphy appealed on the grounds that the jury hadn't been asked to determine whether the contract had been formed on Saturday or on Monday. The contract could've been formed by McIntosh's promise to perform on Saturday or by his performance of showing up on Monday. What difference would that make? If the oral contract was formed on Monday, then it would've been fully performed a year later. That scenario would present no problem with the statute of frauds. But if it was formed on Saturday, it would not be fully performed until a year from Monday, which is a total of a year and two days. Under that scenario, the parties would have an oral contract that by its terms couldn't be performed within a year from its making, so it would need to be in writing to be enforceable — no writing, no enforceability, and Murphy's off the hook!

The trial judge, the majority in the appellate court, and the dissent in the appellate court all took different views of the statute of frauds:

- The trial judge said that applying the statute of frauds made the law look ridiculous, so he essentially said that weekends don't count when computing time.

- The majority in the appellate court worked around the statute of frauds by creating an exception based on reliance. Even if the agreement was within the statute of frauds, McIntosh had reasonably relied on Murphy's promise, so the court let the decision stand. (According to this view, McIntosh should've recovered only what he spent in reliance — the cost of relocating to Hawaii to take the job. However, the jury based McIntosh's damages on the expectancy — what he would've earned had the contract been completed.)

- The dissent thought that the role of the court was to follow the dictates of the legislature, and if the legislature had enacted a statute of frauds, then the courts should carry out the law regardless of the hardship that would cause. In other words, if the contract was formed on Saturday, McIntosh shouldn't be entitled to damages, because the oral agreement was unenforceable.

This variety of views isn't surprising, given that the statute of frauds is so controversial.

Revisiting reliance

If a contract is within the statute of frauds and isn't evidenced by a writing, a court may nevertheless enforce the promise because of *reliance* (a party changes her position in response to another party's promise). For example, although real estate transactions are within the statute of frauds, an oral agreement may be enforceable if a party relies on it. (For more about reliance, see Chapter 4.)

Assume that Joe orally agrees to sell a tract of land to Mary for $300,000. With Joe's consent, Mary takes possession of the land and builds a house on it. Joe then refuses to sell the land to Mary, raising the statute of frauds as a defense. A court would likely find that Mary's reasonable and substantial reliance on Joe's promise bars him from raising the statute of frauds as a defense.

Finding an exception in the main purpose rule

The main purpose rule applies to suretyship agreements, in which a third party agrees to perform if another party doesn't. The *main purpose rule* arises if the main purpose of the third party's agreement is for his own financial advantage. In such a case, contract law has less reason to caution the third party because the party recognizes the potential risks and benefits of entering into the agreement. Therefore, the statute of frauds doesn't apply and the agreement is enforceable.

Suppose Tom is building a house for Harry, and Tom has a duty to pay for materials. Tom fails to pay Dick's Lumber, and Dick refuses to provide more materials. To get the house built, Harry calls and tells Dick he'll pay for the materials Tom ordered. That oral agreement isn't within the statute of frauds, because the main purpose of the promise Harry made was to benefit himself.

Examining part performance and restitution

Whether *part performance* (partial performance of the contract terms) creates an exception under the statute of frauds is under debate. Some performances are not performances of the contract but may serve as evidence of reliance and function as an exception to the statute of frauds. However, if the court doesn't accept the part performance as evidence that makes the contract enforceable, then a party may recover the value of that performance in restitution.

For example, if Tom orally agrees to buy Mary's house for $300,000, she may ask for $3,000 as a down payment. If Tom signs a check with a notation on it indicating what it's for, that check may be enough to constitute a writing Tom signed, evidencing the agreement. If Mary endorses the check, that may constitute a writing she signed. Mary's acceptance of $3,000 in cash, however, may be part performance, but it isn't evidence of the agreement. If a court finds the agreement unenforceable, then John has conferred a benefit on Mary that wasn't a gift and wasn't officious. In restitution, Tom should have a claim for the recovery of the $3,000.

Finding exceptions in UCC § 2-201

The UCC statute of frauds contains a number of unique exceptions that result in the enforcement of an agreement that's otherwise unenforceable under the UCC's statute of frauds. These exceptions include the merchants' confirmation, specially manufactured goods, performance, and admission, as I discuss in the following sections.

Confirming the contract by sending a writing

The *confirmation exception,* which applies only between merchants, states that confirmation of an oral agreement sent by one party is binding on the receiving party if that party doesn't object to it in a reasonable amount of time. UCC § 2-201(2), as enacted in North Carolina at 25-2-201(2), provides the following:

> (2) Between merchants if within a reasonable time a writing in confirmation of the contract and sufficient against the sender is received and the party receiving it has reason to know its contents, it satisfies the requirements of subsection (1) against such party unless written notice of objection to its contents is given within ten days after it is received.

For example, a grain buyer from Minneapolis sweeps across the northern plains, making oral agreements to buy wheat from farmers. The buyer records the orders in his books and then sends confirmations to the farmers when he returns to the office. At harvest time, a farmer discovers that he could get a better price elsewhere and claims he's not bound by the oral agreement. The buyer raises the confirmation defense.

Some farmers have eluded this exception to the statute by claiming that they're not merchants. This seems to be a poor argument in an era when farmers are savvy about market prices, but it has persuaded a few sympathetic courts.

Specially manufacturing the goods

The UCC's statute of frauds doesn't apply to *specially manufactured* goods —
when a seller begins to manufacture goods for a buyer under an oral agreement.
UCC § 2-201(3)(a), as enacted in North Carolina at 25-2-201(3)(a), provides:

> (3) A contract which does not satisfy the requirements of subsection (1)
> but which is valid in other respects is enforceable
>
>> (a) if the goods are to be specially manufactured for the buyer
>> and are not suitable for sale to others in the ordinary course of
>> the seller's business and the seller, before notice of repudiation is
>> received and under circumstances which reasonably indicate that
>> the goods are for the buyer, has made either a substantial begin-
>> ning of their manufacture or commitments for their procurement.

For example, for a business I'm planning, I order a neon sign that says "Scott's
Kontracts Krafted Kwik." I lose interest and cancel the order. The seller says,
"We're nearly done making it." I say, "I don't care. The agreement was oral, so
it's unenforceable." I'll lose that argument because the seller reasonably relied
on my request for the specially manufactured goods and is unlikely to find
another buyer for the sign.

Performing the contract

After the parties have performed the contract, it's too late to claim that
the contract is unenforceable based on the UCC's statute of frauds. This
is because of the doctrine of *waiver:* Each party had the right to raise the
defense but gave it up. Mutual performance proves that both parties went
along with the agreement, so neither party could've been defrauded. This
rule is found both in the common law and in the UCC. UCC § 2-201(3)(c), as
enacted in North Carolina at 25-2-201(3)(c), provides

> (3) A contract which does not satisfy the requirements of subsection
> (1) but which is valid in other respects is enforceable [. . .]
>
>> (c) with respect to goods for which payment has been made and
>> accepted or which have been received and accepted

Admitting making the contract

Under the *admission* exception to the statute of frauds, if a party admits
under oath to making an oral contract, the contract is enforceable despite
the absence of a writing. UCC § 2-201(3)(b), as enacted in North Carolina at
25-2-201(3)(b), provides

(3) A contract which does not satisfy the requirements of subsection (1) but which is valid in other respects is enforceable [. . .]

> (b) if the party against whom enforcement is sought admits in his pleading, testimony or otherwise in court that a contract for sale was made, but the contract is not enforceable under this provision beyond the quantity of goods admitted.

This exception to the signed writing requirement is the most interesting and reveals concerns with the policies behind the statute of frauds. The exception discourages parties from making agreements and then claiming that they don't have to honor them.

Suppose I agreed to sell you a certain baseball card for $500 and then tried to weasel out of it in court by saying, "Sure, I agreed to sell you that baseball card for $500, but you can't produce a signed writing that evidences the agreement, so you're out of luck." Under the admission exception to the statute, I wouldn't be able to get away with that. By admitting that we made the agreement, I lose the benefit of the statute!

Looking for a statute of frauds that didn't exist

A fascinating case in the Oregon Court of Appeals involved the sale of cedar shakes from a Canadian corporation to an American corporation. The agreement was oral, and the seller had sent a written confirmation to the buyer, but the parties differed in their opinion as to whether the document constituted a confirmation that would satisfy the Oregon UCC, which the parties had assumed governed the agreement. They spent a great deal of time and money arguing about whether the confirmation was sufficient to satisfy the statute of frauds.

Then a judge on the court woke up and realized that the parties had made a mistake: The contract lacked a choice-of-law provision, so the United Nations Convention on Contracts for the International Sale of Goods (CISG) governed the agreement. The CISG is like an inter-national UCC that applies to businesses located in countries that have signed onto it — and both the United States and Canada are signatories. Therefore, the CISG should've provided the applicable law. The punch line is that the CISG provides that no statute of frauds applies to international agreements for the sale of goods! Article 11 states in full:

> A contract of sale need not be concluded in or evidenced by writing and is not subject to any other requirement as to form. It may be proved by any means, including witnesses.

The moral of the story: Carefully scrutinize all contracts, especially international contracts, to determine the rules that govern them either by default or by a choice-of-law provision in the contract.

Note, however, that the admission defense is available only in a case arising under Article 2 of the UCC, meaning that the agreement involves the sale of goods, and it applies only to an admission made under oath.

Don't make the common mistake of thinking that the UCC doesn't apply to the sale of goods for less than $500. The UCC applies to *all* sales of goods. If the sale is for less than $500, then the UCC *statute of frauds* doesn't apply to the transaction.

Finding a big exception in international contracts

When writing or evaluating international contracts, be aware that different statutes may come into play and, along with them, you may encounter a different or nonexistent statute of frauds. The United Nations Convention on Contracts for the International Sale of Goods (CISG), for example, has no statute of frauds — oral contracts need not be evidenced by a writing and may be proven by any means, including witnesses.

Part III
Analyzing Contract Terms and Their Meaning

The 5th Wave   By Rich Tennant

"I guess you should have read the fine print on that tag before you ripped it off the mattress."

In this part . . .

No contract ever contains everything the parties agreed to, and no contract can address all possible future events that might affect how the parties perform (or fail to perform) their duties under the contract. As a result, parties often disagree over what the terms of the contract are or what those terms mean. When disputes arise, contract law must step in and sort things out.

The chapters in this part explain several strategies the courts use to find the contract, plug the gaps in the contract, and interpret what the language really means (or at least what it would mean to reasonable people in the parties' place). By understanding how the courts plug gaps and interpret the language of contracts, you develop the knowledge and skills to draft better contracts and predict the outcome of cases that come your way.

Chapter 9

Evaluating Unwritten Terms with the Parol Evidence Rule

As parties form agreements, they often discuss terms that fail to make their way into the written agreement. In such cases, one party may later claim that the parties agreed to a term that's not in the writing, saying something like, "Just before I signed the contract, you told me you'd do such and such." This party believes that the agreement goes beyond the writing and includes all the terms in the written contract plus other agreed-upon terms that don't appear in the written contract.

The other party, looking at the written contract, says, "I don't see that term in the contract." In other words, that party believes that because the term's not in the written contract, it's not part of the agreement and shouldn't be enforced.

Who's right? This situation is where the parol evidence rule comes into play. Courts use the parol evidence rule to determine whether evidence presented for the purpose of adding a term to a written, signed contract is admissible. This chapter explains the parol evidence rule and how to use it along with other relevant information to determine whether a term the parties agreed to outside the written contract is actually part of their agreement.

Introducing the Parol Evidence Rule

The *parol evidence rule* resolves the problem of whether a term that's not in the written contract is part of the agreement between the parties. The rule states the following:

Once the parties have reduced their agreement to a writing that they intend to contain the final and complete statement of their agreement, then evidence of terms that would supplement or contradict it are not admissible.

At first glance, the parol evidence rule appears to say that if the term is not in the written contract, it's not part of the agreement. However, the rule is not that simple. Read the rule closely, and you find references to issues that can be argued in court:

✔ Whether the parties *intended* the writing to contain the final and complete statement of their agreement

✔ Whether the writing was *final*

✔ Whether the writing was *complete*

In addition, courts must determine whether the parol evidence rule even applies to a specific contract or term based on the party's purpose in presenting that evidence.

Oral contracts are generally enforceable, subject only to the statute of frauds (see Chapter 8). If you can prove that the parties formed an oral contract, then proving its terms becomes a question of fact. That is, if you can prove to a court that both parties agreed to a term, then that term becomes part of the contract, regardless of whether it's in writing.

However, as a practical matter and to avoid future disputes, most parties should and do document the terms of the agreement in a written, signed contract.

Identifying Parol Evidence: The Stuff outside the Writing

Whenever a party claims that the parties agreed to a term that's not in the written contract, the first step is to identify the *parol evidence,* evidence that's not included in (that's extrinsic to) the written contract. Parol evidence often takes the following forms:

✔ **Spoken term:** Parol evidence usually takes the form of a promise one party made or a term that the parties agreed to orally. The word *parol* comes from the French word meaning "speech," but parol evidence doesn't have to be oral.

✔ **Another document:** Written evidence may show that the parties' agreement is found in more than one place.

✔ **Custom and usage:** Parties often exclude terms supplied by *trade usage* (standard usage in a particular industry or business) from their written agreements. See Chapter 11 for details on trade usage.

Whatever form the parol evidence takes, your first job is to identify it.

In the famous case of *Mitchill v. Lath,* the buyer of a house claimed that the seller had orally promised to tear down an unsightly ice house (a shed used to store ice for year-round use) on property across the street. The parol evidence in this case is the seller's oral promise to tear down the ice house. The seller claimed that, under the parol evidence rule, evidence of the promise wasn't admissible because it wasn't contained in the written contract. (Later, in "Recognizing the difference between subjective and objective intent," you see how the courts applied the parol evidence rule in this particular case.)

Don't confuse *parol evidence* with the *parol evidence rule. Parol evidence* is pretty much synonymous with *extrinsic evidence.* However, not all parol evidence invokes the parol evidence rule. To invoke the rule, the evidence must be presented as proof that a term not in the written contract needs to be added to it. After identifying the parol evidence, the next step is to determine whether that evidence invokes the parol evidence rule.

Asking Why the Evidence Is Being Offered

Parties have different reasons for presenting parol evidence. Your job is to identify the reason so you can begin to determine whether it invokes the parol evidence rule. Ask, "What's the purpose of this evidence?" The answer determines whether the parol evidence rule applies and how the court is likely to apply it.

Only parol evidence presented to prove a term of the contract invokes the parol evidence rule. Parol evidence presented for one of the following reasons usually doesn't invoke the parol evidence rule:

- ✔ To prove a modification
- ✔ To prove a defense to formation
- ✔ To prove an unfulfilled condition
- ✔ To prove the meaning of a term

This section explains each of these reasons and helps you determine whether the parol evidence invokes the parol evidence rule.

The question "What's the purpose of this evidence?" often comes up in court. Assume, for example, that the seller in *Mitchill* has refused to tear down the ice house as promised (see the preceding section for more about *Mitchill*). The buyer sues for breach of contract. At trial, the buyer testifies, "The seller promised us that he would—" Before he can complete his sentence, the seller's lawyer jumps out of her seat and says, "Objection." At this point, the judge may excuse the jury so he can decide a matter of law in order to rule on the objection. He would then ask the buyer's lawyer, "For what purpose are you offering this evidence?" If you're that lawyer, you'd better have a good answer. This section provides the guidance you need.

To prove a modification

After parties make an agreement, they're free to change its terms through modification (see Chapter 12). The parol evidence rule doesn't apply to changes made after signing. To determine whether the parol evidence rule applies to a term, find out when the parties agreed to it:

- ✔ **Before signing the agreement:** If a party offering proof of a term not found in the writing says that the parties agreed to the term before they signed the agreement, then the parol evidence rule applies.

- ✔ **After signing the agreement:** If the parties agreed to the term after they signed the agreement, then the parol evidence rule doesn't apply, and you're dealing with a modification issue.

In the *Mitchill* case, for example, if the buyer told the judge, "Before we signed the agreement, while we were still negotiating, the seller promised me that he would remove the ice house," then you'd have a parol evidence rule issue. But if he told the judge, "After we signed the agreement, I asked him if he would remove the ice house and he said he would," then you're looking at a modification issue.

To prove a defense to formation

If one party presents parol evidence to support a defense to formation (claiming the parties didn't actually form a contract), then the parol evidence rule usually doesn't apply. In such cases, you're probably dealing with an issue of contract formation, as discussed in Part II.

In general, the parol evidence rule doesn't bar evidence of factors that may invalidate a contract, such as fraud, mutual mistake, lack of capacity, or duress. For example, if a buyer wants to testify, "Before we signed the agreement, the seller threatened me to sign it or else, so I signed it," then you're dealing with a contract formation issue, namely duress, and not with a parol evidence rule issue.

The purpose of the parol evidence rule is to find the terms of the agreement, not to question whether the parties formed an enforceable contract.

Using parol evidence to prove a contract defense may work against your client, voiding the contract when what your client really wants is to keep the contract and add a term. If, in the *Mitchill* case, the buyer proves a formation defense, then he may be out of the contract, but that's not what he wants. He wants to buy the house and have the seller remove the ugly ice house across the street. He wants to keep the contract and prove that the term was part of it.

To prove an unfulfilled condition

In agreements that contain conditional terms outside the written contract, the parol evidence rule doesn't apply. For example, suppose a buyer agrees to purchase a seller's car on condition that the seller has the muffler and brakes replaced. They draw up and sign a contract to document the sale of the car but omit the part about replacing the muffler and brakes.

In most jurisdictions, the parol evidence rule doesn't apply to cases in which a party presents evidence to prove a condition that's not in the written agreement. As with evidence to prove a formation issue, the court will admit evidence that shows the parties agreed that performance was subject to a condition. If performance is subject to a condition, then a party doesn't have to perform if the condition doesn't occur, as I explain in Chapter 14.

The problem with offering parol evidence to prove a condition is that it may not get the party what she wants. The buyer wants this car with a new muffler and brakes. If the buyer successfully proves that getting the muffler and brakes was a condition to performance of the contract, then she doesn't have to perform if that condition didn't occur; in this case, she doesn't have to buy the car. But that doesn't get her what she wants.

To prove the meaning of a term

If the parties disagree over the meaning of language in the contract, as they often do, the court doesn't apply the parol evidence rule to clarify the meaning. Chapter 11 reveals how the courts deal with questions of interpretation.

In *Mitchill v. Lath,* for example, suppose the written contract contained the seller's promise to "make the ice house more attractive-looking." The seller does some work on it, but the buyer thinks it's still ugly. The seller refuses to do any more. In order to resolve the dispute, the court would have to determine the meaning of "more attractive-looking." That's not a parol evidence rule issue because the disputed term is in the writing.

To add a term to the agreement

When a party presents evidence to add a term to the agreement, the parol evidence rule comes into play, assuming that *both* of the following are true:

✔ **The promise was made before signing.** If a party made a certain promise before signing, you may be looking at a parol evidence rule issue. If the promise was made after signing, you're dealing with a modification.

✔ **The promise and the bargained-for consideration are not part of a separate agreement.** A party may offer consideration in exchange for several promises from the other party. If the consideration in the writing is what the party offered in exchange for the alleged promise, then you may be looking at a parol evidence issue. If the other party offered separate consideration for the alleged promise, then you're looking at two separate contracts, and the parol evidence rule doesn't apply.

For example, suppose the buyer claims, "Just before we signed the agreement, the seller promised he would remove the ugly ice house across the street." This evidence fulfills the first condition because the promise was made *before* signing. Now you must determine whether the bargained-for consideration for that promise is found in the written agreement or in a separate agreement:

✔ **Written agreement:** The buyer may claim that he promised to pay a sum of money in exchange for the seller's promises to (1) sell the house and (2) tear down the ice house. This claim is perfectly legitimate *if the seller's two promises are both part of the agreement.* If they're both part of the agreement, then the bargained-for consideration (the sum of money the buyer offered) presented in the written contract applies to both promises by the seller. Now you have a true parol rule evidence problem.

✔ **Separate agreement:** If the buyer promised the seller something specific in exchange for that particular promise (for example, offering the seller $50 in exchange for tearing down the ice house), then you're dealing with two separate contracts: a written contract for the sale of the house for a sum of money and an oral contract to tear down an ice house for $50. The statute of frauds (see Chapter 8) requires the first contract to be in writing because it's a real estate transaction, but it doesn't require the second contract to be in writing. Evidence of the oral contract is admissible, and the parol evidence rule doesn't apply in this case.

Assuming that the promise meets both conditions, you're looking at a true parol rule evidence problem. You can now use the parol evidence rule to determine whether the term is part of the agreement.

Deciding Whether the Agreement Is Final and Complete

After a party presents parol evidence, offers that evidence for the purpose of adding a term to the agreement, and can't prove that the term is part of a separate enforceable agreement, the next step is to decide whether the parties intended the written agreement to be final and complete. This is the hardest part of the rule because you need to assess the parties' intent.

The parol evidence rule directs the court to refuse to admit evidence "once the parties have reduced their agreement to a writing *that they intend to contain the final and complete statement of their agreement.*" If the parties didn't consider the written contract final or complete, then the court is free to admit evidence of terms that would supplement the contract. So determining whether the parties intended the written agreement to be final and complete is a crucial step.

Recognizing the difference between subjective and objective intent

Courts draw a distinction between two types of intent:

- ✔ **Subjective intent:** Subjective intent is what's in each party's mind. Determining subjective intent may require having a trial and taking each party's testimony.
- ✔ **Objective intent:** Objective intent is what a reasonable person would've intended. A judge can determine objective intent without hearing the parties' testimony.

When deciding whether the parties intended their entire agreement to be found in the writing, authorities are divided into two camps. In the subjective camp are Arthur Corbin and the Restatement, which are interested in what the parties actually intended. In the objective camp are authorities like Samuel Williston and many modern courts, which are interested in what reasonable parties would've intended. Note that one advantage of the objective approach is judicial efficiency: A court can make this determination more efficiently if it doesn't have to hear from the parties. (For info on Corbin, Williston, and other major players in contract law, see Chapter 22.)

In *Mitchill,* authorities favoring the objective view wouldn't ask Mitchill and Lath what they'd intended. Instead, these authorities would ask whether reasonable parties in that situation would've put this understanding in the writing. *Mitchill* was decided on summary judgment without the need for a trial. The majority ruled that because it was a contract for the sale of real estate, reasonable parties would've included every detail of the sale, including the promise to remove the ice house, in the written contract.

Figuring out whether the agreement is final

To determine whether the parties intended the agreement to be final, examine the negotiation process. If the parties kicked several drafts back and forth before signing a final draft, that's a pretty good indication that they intended the signed agreement to be final.

Think of the parol evidence rule as the "prior negotiation" rule. As parties hammer out the terms of the agreement, they may discuss numerous different terms. Signing of the agreement signals an end to negotiations and the parties' final agreement to those terms. As soon as the parties sign off on the agreement, it's considered final for purposes of the parol evidence rule.

Checking whether the agreement is complete

A writing is *complete* if all the terms the parties agreed to are found in the writing. You can determine whether the parties intended the written contract to be complete in a few ways.

- ✔ Look for a merger clause in the contract stating that the contract is complete. I discuss this clause in the next section.

- ✔ Look for a written agreement that appears to be very comprehensive and detailed.

- ✔ Look for a type of contract where all the terms would normally be included in the final writing. For example, a separation agreement between husband and wife should be complete because it's intended to wrap up all the loose ends of their relationship.

An agreement that's partly written and partly oral is fine *unless* the parties intended the written contract to be not only the final statement of their agreement but also the complete statement of their agreement. (A writing that the parties intended to be complete is often referred to as an *integrated agreement* — all the terms are integrated or merged in the writing.)

In *Mitchill v. Lath,* the majority said, *Look, this is a real estate deal involving a lot of money. When reasonable people make such an agreement, they put all the terms they agreed to in the writing.* Notice that this reasoning references objective intent; nobody asked the buyer or seller what they actually intended — what matters to the court is what reasonable parties would've intended.

The dissent made a good point, however: The ice house was not on the land that was being purchased but on land located across the street. Therefore, reasonable people might put all their understandings with respect to the land being sold in the writing but put their other understandings in an oral agreement.

Dealing with a merger clause that says the contract is final and complete

Because the outcome of a parol evidence rule issue depends on intention, a drafter often states that intention in the agreement by including a *merger clause,* such as the following:

> This writing constitutes a final written expression of the terms of this agreement and is a complete and exclusive statement of those terms.

Most courts find that although the merger clause may offer some evidence of the parties' intentions, it's not conclusive.

How much weight the court is likely to give a merger clause often hinges on the type of contract:

✔ **More weight in a negotiated contract:** The *negotiated contract* comes about when the parties bang their heads together to work out the terms. One party may draft a proposed contract that proceeds through a series of revisions. Finally, both parties sign it. This act indicates that they've finished their negotiations and reached an agreement that they can both live with and, more important, intend to be final and complete.

✔ **Less weight in a contract of adhesion:** The *contract of adhesion* results when the more powerful of two parties presents its boilerplate contract and the other party agrees to it, sometimes by signing, sometimes by an act such as clicking a button on a web page or tearing the shrink wrap off a package. The merger clause is usually at the end of a boilerplate contract that consumers probably aren't going to read, so it doesn't indicate much about the parties' intentions. (See Chapter 6 for more about contracts of adhesion.)

Even if the agreement lacks a merger clause, a court can still find that the parties intended it to be final and complete. For example, a court may recognize a detailed contract in an area where the purpose of the agreement is to wrap up all the details of the transaction as a final and complete contract.

Considering Evidence That Supplements or Contradicts the Agreement

If a court decides that the writing is final but not complete (only *partially integrated*), the court admits parol evidence to supplement the contract but not to contradict it. A court is not about to step in and undo what the parties agreed to in writing. In a parol evidence rule issue, the court looks for evidence to prove that something not in the written contract needs to be added.

For example, suppose that the written agreement in *Mitchill* set a closing date of March 1. Just before the parties signed the agreement, they orally agreed to change the closing date to April 1 and that the seller would tear down the ice house across the street. If the court found that the writing was only a partial integration of the parties' agreement, the court would admit evidence of one of these oral agreements but not the other:

- ✔ **Not admissible:** Evidence of the closing date, because that evidence *contradicts* a term in the written contract — the oral agreement of the April 1 date contradicts the written agreement of the March 1 date.

- ✔ **Admissible:** Evidence of the promise to remove the ice house, because that evidence *supplements* the agreement — it adds a term not in the written agreement.

Just because a court admits evidence for the purpose of adding a term to the contract, that doesn't mean the term automatically becomes part of the contract. The parol evidence rule is intended to determine whether evidence may be admitted to supplement the written contract *as a matter of law.* A jury still has to decide *as a matter of fact* whether the evidence presented proves that the parties really agreed to that term. A party objecting to the admissibility of the evidence is perfectly free to say something like, "Yes, I said that, but I said a lot of other things that didn't end up in the agreement. The terms we intended to make part of our agreement we wrote down and signed."

Here's how these decisions concerning parol evidence could've played out in *Mitchill v. Lath:*

- ✔ **Matter of law:** The court first decides whether the writing is complete as a matter of law:

    - • **Complete integration:** If the court decides that the writing is a complete integration of the parties' written agreement, it won't admit evidence that supplements or contradicts the writing.

    - • **Partial integration:** If the court decides that the writing is only a partial integration, then the court would admit evidence that supplements the written contract but not evidence that contradicts it.

- ✔ **Matter of fact:** If the court decides to admit evidence that supplements the partially integrated contract, then the jury or the judge (in a case heard without a jury) would decide as a matter of fact whether the parties had in fact made that oral agreement. So even if the court admits the buyer's testimony that the seller promised to tear down the ice house, the finder of fact could determine that the seller had said no such thing.

Contrasting the Common Law with the UCC Parol Evidence Rule

The UCC parol evidence rule is very similar to the common-law rule. However, the UCC rule provides a few exceptions in which evidence that supplements a complete and final writing is admissible.

As enacted in North Carolina at 25-2-202, the UCC parol evidence rule provides the following:

> § 25-2-202. Final written expression; parol or extrinsic evidence.
>
> Terms with respect to which the confirmatory memoranda of the parties agree or which are otherwise set forth in a writing intended by the parties as a final expression of their agreement with respect to such terms as are included therein may not be contradicted by evidence of any prior agreement or of a contemporaneous oral agreement but may be explained or supplemented
>
> > (a) by course of dealing or usage of trade or by course of performance; and
> >
> > (b) by evidence of consistent additional terms unless the court finds the writing to have been intended also as a complete and exclusive statement of the terms of the agreement.

The first paragraph states that if the parties intended the writing to be a "final expression of their agreement," then the evidence may not contradict a term in the writing. Subsection (b) states that the writing can be supplemented by additional terms unless the writing is intended to be complete and exclusive. In other words, if the written contract is fully integrated, it can't be supplemented or contradicted.

Subsection (a), however, adds something to the common-law rule: It states that even if it the writing is final, it can be explained or supplemented "by course of dealing or usage of trade or by course of performance." (See Chapters 10 and 11 for more about these important aspects of commercial law.) Note that the language from subsection (b) — "unless the court finds the writing to have been intended also as a complete and exclusive statement of the terms of the agreement" — doesn't apply to subsection (a). So even if the parties intended the writing to be a final and complete agreement, evidence of the following is admissible to supplement or explain the writing:

✔ Course of dealing

✔ Usage of trade

✔ Course of performance

Finding an exception in international contracts

When drafting an international contract for the sale of goods, many U.S. companies include a *choice-of-law clause* providing that the UCC of a particular state governs the agreement. If they don't do this and both parties' countries have signed the United Nations Convention on Contracts for the International Sale of Goods (UNCISG), then the contract is governed by the UNCISG.

The CISG doesn't have a parol evidence rule. Article 8(1) of the CISG instructs courts to interpret the "statements [. . .] and other conduct of a party [. . .] according to his intent" as long as the other party "knew or could not have been unaware" of that intent. The language of the Convention, therefore, makes it a question of fact whether an understanding was reached that didn't end up in the writing.

In one case, an American company purchased marble from an Italian company. The buyer complained about the quality of the marble, but the seller defended on the grounds that the buyer hadn't complied with the method for making complaints stated on the back of the form the parties had signed. The buyer claimed that before they signed the agreement, the parties had agreed that the terms written on the back of the form wouldn't be part of their agreement.

If the UCC governed, the buyer would've been laughed out of court. But the court found that under the CISG, if the seller was aware of the buyer's intent not to be bound by those terms, then that evidence would be admissible under Article 8(1).

For example, assume that a seller sells a widget to a buyer. The parties sign a fully integrated writing that states that the sale price is $1,000 payable 30 days after delivery. Seven days after delivery, the buyer sends the seller $950 in full payment for the widget. The seller claims breach, but the buyer offers evidence that in all the other contracts the parties had agreed to, they had an understanding that paying within ten days earned the buyer a 5 percent discount. The seller says, "I don't see that in the writing." The buyer says, "This is evidence of a course of dealing (what we did under previous contracts between us) that is admissible even though the writing is fully integrated."

You may think that the buyer's evidence contradicts the writing because the writing says that the price of the widget is $1,000, not $950. Most authorities, however, say that the question of contradiction doesn't turn on whether the offered term directly negates what's in the contract but on whether it can live in harmony with what's in the contract. In other words, if the contract included a term that said "5 percent discount for payment within ten days," would that contradict the term that states the price of the widget? Most authorities would say no. The additional term could live in harmony with the $1,000 price term, so it doesn't contradict.

You can defang subsection (a) of UCC § 2-202 by including a term in the written contract that makes such evidence inadmissible; for example, "Evidence of course of dealing is not admissible to supplement or contradict this agreement." But watch out — that term could bite you back if you want to admit the evidence!

Getting Terms in Writing to Avoid the Parol Evidence Rule Quagmire

To avoid the parol evidence rule quagmire, encourage your clients to get all promises in writing. Prior to having your client sign any contract, ask, "Did they promise you anything that's not in this writing?" If the answer is yes, then instruct your client to get all those promises in writing before signing anything.

If everyone would write fully integrated contracts, contract law wouldn't need a parol evidence rule. Until that day comes, you had better study up on it!

Listening to the FTC

A number of years ago, the Federal Trade Commission (FTC) discovered that used-car dealers were making a lot of promises to buyers that didn't end up in the written contract and that the dealers later refused to honor. The FTC solution was to require used-car dealers to put a sticker on the side window of the car that tells the customer exactly what they're getting. The first thing the form says is this: "Spoken promises are difficult to enforce. Ask the dealer to put all promises in writing." The FTC's mission is to protect consumer interests. Protect your clients' interests by offering them the same advice.

Chapter 10

Finding Unwritten Terms That Complete the Contract

- -

In This Chapter

▶ Understanding how contract law fills gaps in contracts

▶ Ensuring that parties act in good faith — honestly and reasonably

▶ Recognizing default rules and using freedom of contract to override them

▶ Understanding express and implied warranties

▶ Shifting and limiting risk with warranty disclaimers

- -

*E*ven if the parties believe they've formed a contract that's final and complete, their contract has gaps where the parties either assumed that they were in agreement or failed to foresee an issue that arose only during performance.

To fill many of these gaps, contract law supplies terms. Some of those terms are based on what contract law concludes reasonable parties would've agreed to; some are based on the parties' previous experience, as determined by their course of dealing; and others are based on rules, such as implied warranties.

When drafting contracts for your clients or evaluating contracts in dispute, you need to be aware of the terms implied in a contract and how the courts use these terms and other approaches to fill the gaps and resolve disputes, as this chapter explains.

Finding the Terms of an Incomplete Contract

One of the jobs of contract law is to find the terms of a contract. A good starting point is the terms the parties expressly agreed to in writing. The parol evidence rule (see Chapter 9) can help determine whether a contract contains additional terms, either in speech or in writing. Even after the court identifies the terms that the parties expressly agreed to, however, the contract may still be incomplete. The contract may also include terms that the law supplies when the parties don't expressly include them in the contract. In other words, if the drafter didn't include a particular term in the contract, the law may supply it.

In this way, a contract differs from other types of documents, such as books and newspapers. If a mystery writer omits a passage that's essential for the reader to solve the mystery, no mystery novel law tells the reader what to plug in. With contracts, however, the law is often able to supply a term that's missing from the contract.

Furthermore, contract performance generally takes place in the future, and no one can foresee everything that might happen. If, somewhere down the line, the parties need to deal with an unforeseen issue, they're free to come up with a term on their own. If they can't do it themselves, contract law does it for them.

Terminology used to describe the gap-filling process varies. Some refer to it as adding *implied terms,* but that's not very accurate because contracts often contain nothing that implies a certain missing term. Others refer to gap-fillers as *constructive terms,* indicating more accurately that the court constructs something where there's nothing. I generally refer to the court's *supplying* terms, but contract law often calls these terms *implied* terms. Whatever you call them, this section describes the process that contract law uses to fill these gaps.

Using contract rules to fill the gaps

When a court needs to fill a gap, it goes to a contract rule. Typically, the rule tells the court to determine the term that reasonable parties in the shoes of the parties to the contract would've agreed to if they had thought about it.

The court follows the same approach when a contract doesn't address a future event. For example, if an unforeseen event prevents a party from honoring his end of the bargain, contract law determines whether the party's nonperformance is excused. It does so by asking under what circumstances reasonable parties would've decided to excuse nonperformance if they'd thought about it when drafting their contract. I discuss excuses for nonperformance in Chapter 13.

The UCC provides a number of devices available to plug the gaps and enforce contracts for the sale of goods. What the courts typically do in such cases is fall back on what's considered *reasonable:*

- ✔ **Price:** The price must be *reasonable*.

- ✔ **Time of delivery:** The item must be delivered in a *reasonable* amount of time. The courts may look at what's customary.

- ✔ **Location:** The item must be delivered at the seller's place of business or residence, which is the usual practice.

- ✔ **Order of the exchange:** The parties must make the exchange simultaneously.

- ✔ **Quality:** The quality of the promised item is determined by warranty law (as I explain in the later section "Protecting Buyers through Warranties").

The reasonable terms are exclusively for plugging gaps when the parties failed to agree on a term. For example, if I agree to sell you my $10,000 car for $5,000, I couldn't complain that I should be able to avoid the contract because the price was not reasonable. The price only has to be reasonable, according to UCC § 2-305, when the contract fails to specify a price. In that event, the court may consult the Kelley Blue Book to determine the car's reasonable market value.

Suppose I offer to sell you my pen, and you agree to buy it. We each committed to do something, but we omitted numerous details, including price, time of delivery, destination, who goes first, and the pen's condition. Using the list of gap-fillers, the courts can fill in the blanks and enforce the contract according to those terms.

One gap the court usually can't fill in is the quantity term. If I agree to sell you pens and then I refuse to perform, filling the gap isn't possible, because the court has no way of knowing with any certainty how many pens I promised to sell you. The court may be able to establish a reasonable quantity based on either of the following:

- ✔ **Course of dealing:** The court may look at quantities specified in previous contracts between the two parties. In this case, the court looks at the number of pens I sold you under previous contracts. For example, if for each of the preceding three years, I had sold you ten pens, the court could reasonably conclude that I was agreeing to sell you ten pens this time, too.

- ✔ **Seller output or buyer requirements:** Even though no specific quantity is stated, the parties may measure the quantity in terms of output or requirements, as I explain in Chapter 3.

Understanding types of gap-filling rules

Contract law uses two varieties of rules to fill gaps in contracts:

✔ **Default rules:** These terms are supplied unless the parties contract around them. Think of them as the default settings in your word-processing program; unless you change a particular setting, the program uses the default. Examples of default rules include the price gap-filler — if the parties don't specify a price, the default rule sets a price at what's considered "reasonable."

✔ **Immutable rules:** These terms are always supplied and the parties are not free to change them. A good example is the covenant of good faith and fair dealing, which I discuss later in this chapter in the next section.

Although parties are free, within certain limits, to change the terms of default rules, they're not free to change the immutable rules, which include the rules of contract law — including offer, acceptance, and consideration — that determine whether parties have a contract.

Reading In the Duty of Good Faith

One of the terms that the law supplies in every contract is the duty of good faith. This is an immutable rule that the parties aren't allowed to disclaim. Both the UCC and the Restatement state that every contract contains a duty of good faith:

✔ **UCC:** The UCC contains a definition of good faith. Section 1-201(b)(20), as enacted in North Carolina at 25-1-201(b)(20), provides that "Good faith, except as otherwise provided in Article 5 of this Chapter, means honesty in fact and the observance of reasonable commercial standards of fair dealing." This definition specifies two requirements of good faith — the objective and subjective standards — as I discuss in this section.

✔ **Restatement:** The Restatement is more vague. It doesn't define "good faith," leaving the courts to decide what it means in different contexts. Some of the situations identified in the Comment to Restatement § 205, where courts have found bad faith, involve "evasion of the spirit of the bargain, lack of diligence and slacking off, willful rendering of imperfect performance, abuse of a power to specify terms, and interference with or failure to cooperate in the other party's performance."

Under the UCC, good faith requires that a person both be honest and observe reasonable standards; failing to live up to either of those standards shows a lack of good faith.

Being honest: The subjective duty of good faith

Subjective good faith requires "honesty in fact." This makes sense, because if you're being dishonest, you're probably not acting in good faith. Proving that a person is in fact dishonest, however, may be difficult. To do so, you need evidence that proves the person had ulterior motives for her actions.

Assume, for example, that a buyer orders widgets to be delivered by noon on the 28th. The widgets arrive a half-hour late, and the buyer rejects them. Unless stated otherwise by the parties or the circumstances, the time of delivery is merely an immaterial breach, and the buyer should be able to recover damages in the unlikely event that the slight delay resulted in damages (see Chapter 14 for info on material and immaterial breaches). But according to the "perfect tender rule" of UCC § 2-601, a buyer may reject goods if the tender fails *in any respect* to conform to the contract. Here, although the tender did not conform, the buyer must still act in good faith. Did it honestly reject the widgets because they were delivered a half-hour late, or did the buyer have some other motive, such as a decline in the market price so it could obtain cheaper widgets elsewhere? To prove that the rejection was in bad faith, the seller would have to prove the buyer's motive, which isn't easy.

Furthermore, proving a breach of good faith probably isn't worth the trouble, because such a breach is just an ordinary breach of contract — nothing terrible happens to the person who failed to act in good faith. Courts don't generally award punitive damages for breach of contract. If the seller proves that the buyer failed to act in good faith, the seller gets the same damages for breach of contract as if the buyer had acted in good faith.

Some courts may award punitive damages in cases in which an insurance company acts in bad faith, knowing it should pay a claim but disputing that claim.

Being reasonable: The objective duty of good faith

Objective good faith is the duty to observe reasonable commercial standards of fair dealing. This concept is consistent with Code jurisprudence, which seems to think people in a particular business adhere to certain identifiable standards. If that's the case, then testimony from someone in that business could be proof of those standards.

In the case of a buyer who rejects widgets because they're delivered half an hour late, the buyer may have had a good reason to reject the goods. If he didn't, the seller could use another person in the widget business as a witness and ask, "Is it reasonable for a person in this business to reject a shipment of widgets just because they're delivered a half-hour late?" If the answer to that question is no, then the seller has gone a long way toward establishing that the buyer didn't act in good faith.

Good faith requires that a person be both honest and observe reasonable standards. The case of *Neumiller Farms, Inc. v. Cornett* provides a good example of how each of these standards can be proven. Cornett was a potato farmer who agreed to sell potatoes to Neumiller for $4.25 per hundredweight. The contract required potatoes that "chipt to buyer satisfaction"; in other words, these potatoes had to be suitable to make potato chips. After Neumiller rejected Cornett's potatoes, Cornett had them tested by an expert from the county Cooperative Extension Service, who reported that the potatoes were suitable. Furthermore, Neumiller bought potatoes from another grower for $2.00; but when Cornett tendered the same potatoes for the contract price of $4.25, Neumiller rejected them. These facts show that Neumiller wasn't acting in good faith according to the *objective standard,* because a reasonable person would've found the potatoes satisfactory.

Cornett also proved that when he tried to tender potatoes under the contract, the buyer told him, "I'm not going to accept any more of your potatoes. . . . I can buy potatoes all day for $2.00." This fact shows that Neumiller wasn't acting in good faith according to the *subjective standard,* because he was being dishonest — his real motive in rejecting the potatoes was the price he would have to pay for them, not their quality.

Using freedom of contract to refine the definition of good faith

Not surprisingly, you don't have freedom of contract to get out of the obligation of good faith. The UCC states this limitation on freedom of contract in § 1-302(b). As enacted in North Carolina, it provides in part:

> The obligations of good faith, diligence, reasonableness, and care prescribed by [the Uniform Commercial Code] may not be disclaimed by agreement. The parties, by agreement, may determine the standards by which the performance of those obligations is to be measured if those standards are not manifestly unreasonable.

The first sentence of this provision states that, in addition to good faith, you can't disclaim the duties of "diligence, reasonableness, and care." Notice, however, that the second sentence says that you may define them if you use standards that are not "manifestly unreasonable." For example, your contract can't say, "Buyer does not have to be reasonable in deciding whether to accept the goods after inspection." But it can say, "Buyer is acting reasonably in deciding whether to accept goods after inspection if more than 5 percent of the goods do not meet Industry Standard 5.0."

Working with and around the Default Rules

Whether you're drafting contracts, preparing a contract defense, or trying to prove the enforceability of certain terms omitted from the contract, you need to be able to identify any default rule that applies and understand how the parties can substitute their own rules.

This section tells you where to look for and how to identify the default rules and explains how the parties to an agreement can use freedom of contract to override the default terms and make strategic changes to shift the risk to the other party.

Recognizing default rules when you see them

To determine the default rule for a certain issue, consult the usual sources: federal and state statutes, including the UCC in a contract involving the sale of goods, and the common law, which you can find in general terms in the Restatement of Contracts. The hard part is determining whether the rule is a default rule or an immutable rule, because the rules don't come with flags attached telling you which is which.

In the UCC, look for the words "unless otherwise agreed" or some other indication that the parties are free to override the rule. This phrase tells you that unless the parties include a term that addresses this particular issue, then the Code supplies a default rule. However, the Code also says in § 1-302(c) that "The presence in certain provisions of the UCC of the phrase 'unless otherwise agreed' . . . does not imply that the effect of other provisions may not be varied by agreement." In other words, if the Code says that you can otherwise agree, then you can, but if it doesn't say that, then you still might be able to otherwise agree!

Using freedom of contract to change the rules and shift the risk

Freedom of contract (see Chapter 4) gives everyone of legal age and ability the freedom to bargain fairly for contracts allowable by law. Within certain limits, this freedom extends to setting terms in the contract that override the default rules.

For example, by default, the UCC in § 2-314(1) states that a merchant seller gives the buyer a warranty of merchantability — a promise that the goods will do what they're supposed to do. As a buyer, then, you don't have to bargain to get a promise from the seller that when you bring that new refrigerator home, it'll work. Contract law already supplied that promise. However, merchants are free to sell products without that warranty as long as they override the default rule by adding clear and conspicuous language to the contract. (For more about warranties, see "Protecting Buyers through Warranties," later in this chapter.)

When negotiating contracts, look for opportunities to use freedom of contract to shift the risk to the other party. If you're representing the seller, for example, you may want to shift the risk of loss of goods to the buyer. If you're representing the buyer who carries the risk that the price of goods will fall after the contract is signed, you may want to shift that risk to the seller. That's all part of negotiating.

A seller in Salem, North Carolina, agrees to sell goods to a buyer in Boston, Massachusetts. The default rule that governs the place of delivery of the goods is supplied by UCC § 2-308(a). As codified in North Carolina, it provides:

> Unless otherwise agreed . . . the place for delivery of goods is the seller's place of business.

This is bad news for the buyer — all the seller has to do is have the goods ready at his place of business for the buyer to pick up. The buyer wants to change that. Note that the statute contains the words "unless otherwise agreed," which is a signal that this is a default rule the parties are free to change. Knowing the default rule and taking advantage of that freedom of contract provision, the buyer may suggest a provision something like this:

> The seller shall deliver the goods to the buyer at buyer's address in Boston at seller's sole expense.

The seller may not agree to that and may suggest a compromise:

> The seller shall deliver the goods to UPS for shipment to the buyer at the buyer's expense.

The next section provides a closer look at how risk-shifting plays out in the law of warranty.

Protecting Buyers through Warranties

Sometimes contracts contain detailed terms regarding the quality of the performance the buyer has contracted to receive. But more often, the contract is silent on this question, so the law must supply a term to specify the quality the buyer is entitled to. In contracts for services, such as construction contracts, the court usually reads in that the contractor must provide something like "workmanlike performance." This standard is similar to the tort standard of performance: You're entitled to the quality you can reasonably expect from a person in a similar business in your community. With the purchase of a new home from a builder, in most jurisdictions you get an *implied warranty of habitability* — a promise that the home is fit to live in.

Under Article 2 of the UCC, the quality terms for the sale of goods are spelled out by using warranties, including the following:

- ✔ Express warranty
- ✔ Warranty of title and against infringement
- ✔ Warranty of merchantability
- ✔ Warranty of fitness for a particular purpose

This section describes each of these warranties and how the courts are likely to read them into a contract.

Making express warranties

As defined in UCC § 2-313, an *express warranty* is "an affirmation of fact or promise made by the seller to the buyer which relates to the goods and becomes part of the basis of the bargain." The two key phrases here are "affirmation of fact or promise" and "basis of the bargain."

An *affirmation of fact or promise* is a statement that can be proven in fact or something the seller promised. If a car dealer sells you a 2003 Ford Windstar, then the express warranty is that Ford made the car and it's a Windstar 2003 model. Contract law is more accustomed to warranties that don't just affirm facts but make a promise, such as, "If anything goes wrong with this car during the next 12 months or 10,000 miles, whichever comes first, we'll repair or replace the defective part." Statements that are puffing or opinion like "This car will run like a dream" or "You won't find a better deal anywhere in town" probably don't cut it.

Not everyone agrees what *basis of the bargain* means when the Code says that the warranty must become a part of the basis of the bargain. Here are two interpretations:

✔ One understanding is that the buyer relied on the warranty as part of the deal. Under this theory, if the buyer knew he was getting something different from what the seller expressly promised, then the buyer didn't get the warranty. For example, assume that you looked at the vehicle the seller was selling as a 2003 Ford Windstar, and you knew it was a 2002 model. The seller could claim that you didn't get that warranty because you didn't rely on the statement when you made the purchase.

✔ Another understanding is that whether the warranty is part of the basis of the bargain is a matter of timing. Under this theory, specifying that the warranty must be part of the basis of the bargain eliminates statements that didn't make it into the final contract based on the parol evidence rule (which I discuss in Chapter 9). For example, if just before I sell you my used refrigerator, I tell you, "I promise it will work for 30 days," that's an express warranty. But if we then sign a writing that contains the final and complete statement of our agreement, the parol evidence rule will probably say that that promise isn't part of our agreement. Some argue that the warranty is not part of the basis of the bargain if it comes later, like when you buy a TV and later open up the box and find a warranty inside.

With the sale of goods, look for any affirmation of fact or promise, and you'll find an express warranty. That's why you see all that fine print in ads on TV — the seller is trying to tell you that it's not making any affirmations of fact or promises!

Looking for an implied warranty of title or warranty against infringement

When someone transfers ownership of goods, such as a car or an electronics gadget, the transfer typically carries some implied warranties:

✔ An implied warranty that the seller owns the item

✔ An implied warranty against infringement of intellectual property rights in it

You don't see these warranties in the contract — the law supplies them by default.

The *implied warranty of title,* under § 2-312(1) of the Code, gives the buyer of goods a claim for damages for breach of contract if the seller doesn't in fact own the goods or have the right to transfer them. Furthermore, this warranty covers liens and encumbrances that cloud the title. For example, if a lender has a lien against property, that lender may have the right to take the property even from someone who bought it without knowing about the lien. However, the implied warranty of good title would give the ill-informed buyer a claim against the seller for breach of that warranty.

The *implied warranty of infringement,* under § 2-312(2) of the Code, applies to intellectual property, including software, inventions, literary and artistic works, and designs used in commerce. Unless otherwise specified in the contract, the seller warrants that the goods are delivered free of the intellectual property infringement claims of third parties. This warranty is becoming increasingly important as more "smart goods" that contain computer chips enter the market.

Suppose Developer A sells the architecture for a new cellular device to Xphones, Xphones sells the device to your local electronics store, which sells it to you. At each point in the distribution chain, the seller warrants the product against infringement to the buyer. If Developer B, who actually invented the architecture, wins an infringement claim against Developer A that results in your cellular device not working, each buyer has a claim for breach of warranty against the party higher in the distribution chain: You have a claim against your local electronics store, which has a claim against Xphones, which has a claim against Developer A, who's ultimately the responsible party.

Checking for an implied warranty of merchantability

When merchants who deal with a certain kind of product sell products of that kind, they give buyers the implied warranty of merchantability. You don't see the implied warranty in a contract, because the law supplies it by default. Although UCC § 2-314 provides a number of definitions of *merchantability,* the definition the courts most commonly apply is that the goods "are fit for the ordinary purposes for which such goods are used." In other words, the thing does what it's supposed to do.

The implied warranty of merchantability applies only to merchants who sell a particular kind of good. If a car dealer sells you a car, he's giving you an implied warranty that the car is fit for the ordinary purposes for which cars are used. On the other hand, if I, a law professor, sell you a car, you don't get that warranty, because I don't deal in cars.

You may wonder whether this implied warranty of merchantability applies to used-car dealers. The answer is yes and no:

✔ **Yes, because used-car dealers are merchants who deal in cars.** However, they're promising you only that the car is fit for the ordinary purposes of this particular kind of car. If you buy a car with 100,000 miles on it, they're warranting only that it's as fit as a car with 100,000 miles on it. If the transmission fails, you'd have to prove that the ordinary transmission should last longer than that.

✔ **No, because the implied warranty is merely a default rule.** If the used-car dealer slaps a sticker on the car that clearly communicates to buyers that this car is offered "AS IS," then that term overrides the implied warranty. (See the later section "Shifting the Risk by Disclaiming or Limiting Warranties" for more about warranty disclaimers.)

Seeking out an implied warranty of fitness for a particular purpose

Although the implied warranty of merchantability (see the preceding section) warrants that goods are fit for their ordinary purpose, it doesn't warrant that those goods are fit for any special purpose. To fill this gap, UCC § 2-315 provides an *implied warranty of fitness for a particular purpose.* Any seller, not just a merchant, can give this warranty, but it applies only under the following conditions:

✔ The buyer informs the seller about the special purpose the goods are to be used for.

✔ The seller selects goods that are supposedly suitable for the buyer's stated purpose.

For example, if you enter a sporting goods store and say, "I need footwear to climb Mt. Everest," and the clerk hands you a pair of hiking boots, then the merchant is promising more than footwear fit for the ordinary purpose of outdoor wear. He's promising that the boots are fit for the particular purpose you specified — climbing Mt. Everest.

Shifting the Risk by Disclaiming or Limiting Warranties

The general rule of warranties is this:

> *What the bold print giveth, the fine print taketh away.*

Well, that's a bit of an exaggeration, because the UCC requires more than fine print, but you get the idea. Implied warranties are merely default rules. Freedom of contract allows the parties to contract around the default rules, which sellers usually do by doing all of the following:

✔ Disclaiming the implied warranties

✔ Presenting an express warranty (as I explain earlier in "Making express warranties")

✔ Limiting the remedy for breach

Whether you're drafting a disclaimer or evaluating a contract to determine whether it has disclaimers and limitations that are likely to stick, you need to know what the Code says about it and how the courts are likely to form their decisions. This section provides the guidance you need.

Making warranty disclaimers specific and conspicuous

When a contract includes a disclaimer, the UCC wants to make sure that the buyer knows about it, so sellers and their attorneys must do the following:

✔ **Use specific language to disclaim the implied warranty of good title:** The disclaimer must use specific language that addresses the warranty of title, such as "Seller gives no warranty that he has good title to the goods sold." General language, such as "There are no warranties express or implied," doesn't cut it.

✔ **Use specific language to disclaim the implied warranty of merchantability:** According to UCC § 2-316(2), the disclaimer must be specific and include the word *merchantability,* as in "NO WARRANTIES, INCLUDING THE IMPLIED WARRANTY OF MERCHANTABILITY, ARE INCLUDED."

The Code provides sellers with an exception — UCC § 2-316(3) allows sellers to use expressions like "AS IS" to disclaim the implied warranties of merchantability and fitness for a particular purpose, because "AS IS" generally communicates to buyers that they're not getting a warranty.

✔ **Make the disclaimer conspicuous to the buyer:** According to UCC § 2-316(2), the disclaimer must be conspicuous, meaning presented in a way that a reasonable person is expected to notice it. This is why you often see big print in contracts stating something like the following:

THERE ARE NO WARRANTIES INCLUDING BUT NOT LIMITED TO THE IMPLIED WARRANTY OF MERCHANTABILITY.

This particular language would probably qualify under the Code. It disclaims the implied warranty of merchantability because it uses the word *merchantability,* is conspicuous, and disclaims all other warranties, including the implied warranty of fitness for a particular purpose, which must be conspicuous but doesn't require any particular words.

Sellers rarely disclaim all warranties, because if they did, they'd probably drive away many prospective customers. Instead, they typically disclaim all implied warranties (to clear the slate), offer an express warranty with a limited scope, and limit the remedy for breach. These three strategies reduce the seller's exposure to risk while still offering buyers some assurance that the seller is willing to stand behind the product.

Limiting the remedy for breach

Sellers often give an express warranty but limit the remedy for breach of that warranty. They may do so by

- ✔ **Limiting the amount the buyer can recover for direct damage (loss of the product itself):** Sometimes sellers limit the amount that buyers can recover for breach of warranty to the purchase price of the product, repair costs, or the cost of parts (excluding labor).

- ✔ **Limiting the consequential damages (losses resulting from the loss of the product):** Frequently, although sellers may agree to pay to fix defects in the goods themselves, they disclaim liability for consequential damages, such as ruining your vacation because your car broke down. (See Chapter 17 for info on consequential damages.)

- ✔ **Limiting the duration of the promise to provide a remedy:** Sellers often limit the duration of the time during which they'll repair defects, such as one year from the purchase.

The UCC allows these limitations with the exception that sellers can't disclaim liability for personal injury caused by consumer goods. Section 2-719 provides buyers with additional recourse. As enacted in North Carolina at 25-2-719(2), this section states that "where circumstances cause an exclusive or limited remedy to fail of its essential purpose, remedy may be had as provided in this act."

This section of the Code is sometimes used when the seller provides an express warranty to "repair or replace" defective products. If, after the seller has made a number of attempts at repairing the product, the buyer still doesn't have a working product, then the remedy hasn't accomplished its essential purpose, which is to give the buyer a working product. In that case, other remedies that the Code allows may become available, such as revocation of acceptance — giving back the goods and getting the money back. This same relief is offered for defective cars covered by warranty under the lemon laws enacted in most jurisdictions.

Drafting a disclaimer of warranty

No disclaimer of warranty is suitable for every seller's needs, but when drafting a disclaimer, most sellers include the following:

- ✔ A disclaimer of the implied warranties
- ✔ An express warranty
- ✔ A time period during which they'll honor the express warranty
- ✔ A disclaimer of consequential damages or some other limitation of remedy
- ✔ The possible remedies, such as replacing or repairing the product or offering credit
- ✔ Who determines what the remedy is (You probably want to give your client, the seller, the sole right to choose the remedy.)

In the following example, the first paragraph states the express warranty, the second presents the disclaimer of all implied warranties, and the third provides a disclaimer of consequential damages:

> If within one year from the date of sale, any product sold under this purchase order, or any part thereof, shall prove to be defective in material or workmanship upon examination by the Manufacturer, the Manufacturer will supply an identical or substantially similar replacement part f.o.b. the Manufacturer's factory, or the Manufacturer, at its option, will repair or allow credit for such part.
>
> NO OTHER WARRANTY, EITHER EXPRESS OR IMPLIED AND INCLUDING A WARRANTY OF MERCHANTABILITY AND FITNESS FOR A PARTICULAR PURPOSE, HAS BEEN OR WILL BE MADE BY OR ON BEHALF OF THE MANUFACTURER OR THE SELLER OR BY OPERATION OF LAW WITH RESPECT TO THE EQUIPMENT AND ACCESSORIES OR THEIR INSTALLATION, USE, OPERATION, REPLACEMENT OR REPAIR.
>
> NEITHER THE MANUFACTURER NOR THE SELLER SHALL BE LIABLE BY VIRTUE OF THIS WARRANTY, OR OTHERWISE, FOR ANY SPECIAL OR CONSEQUENTIAL LOSS OR DAMAGE RESULTING FROM THE USE OR LOSS OF THE USE OF EQUIPMENT AND ACCESSORIES.

Note that in this particular disclaimer, the Manufacturer (the seller) has the right to determine whether the product is, in fact, defective and has the choice of supplying a substantially similar replacement part, repairing the part, or providing credit.

Holiday hassles: A case study in disclaimers of warranty

A typical example of how the courts deal with warranty terms is *Murray v. Holiday Rambler, Inc.* The Murrays bought a Holiday Rambler motor home that came with an express "repair or replace" warranty, a disclaimer of implied warranties, and an exclusion of consequential damages. The Murrays immediately had numerous problems with different systems. They kept bringing the motor home in for repair, and the defendant always fixed it, but the problems kept recurring. On one vacation trip, they had to abandon the vehicle and return home by car.

The court found that the contract contained an effective disclaimer of implied warranties and an express "repair or replace" warranty. However, even though Holiday Rambler had always lived up to this promise, the court found that the remedy failed to serve its essential purpose: providing the Murrays with a decent motor home. Therefore, all remedies became available. The Murrays were allowed to return the motor home and get their money back.

Holiday Rambler had also disclaimed liability for consequential damages, such as damages for loss of use of the vehicle during their vacation. Courts are split on the issue of whether the disclaimer of consequential damages falls when the limited remedy falls, but this court found it did — in other words, the Murrays qualified to receive consequential damages. However, they were able to prove only $500 in consequential damages because they had poor records. They also didn't receive attorney's fees, because the default rule is that each side pays its own fees, so they were out what they had to pay their lawyer.

The Murrays might've been better off making their claim under a lemon law. For one thing, most lemon laws provide for a speedier resolution through nonbinding arbitration and for attorney's fees if the consumer is successful in court. On the other hand, in many jurisdictions, lemon laws don't apply to large vehicles like mobile homes.

Recognizing the statutory regulation of disclaimers

Contract law doesn't allow sellers to disclaim everything. Federal and state statutes directly regulate certain transactions (see Chapter 5), requiring sellers to put certain terms in the contract or forbidding them from including certain terms. For example, many states regulate contracts with dance studios and gyms. Other consumer protection legislation is directed toward particular aspects of the transaction, such as the financing or warranties. The Magnuson-Moss Warranty Act, for example, provides remedies for breach of certain warranties.

As you draft a disclaimer or evaluate disclaimers in existing contracts, be aware of any statutes that may govern transactions of the type addressed in the contract.

In warranty cases, you may be better off making a claim under a state lemon law rather than under warranty law. Most states have enacted lemon laws that expressly apply the rule of UCC § 2-719(2) to automobiles under warranty. Lemon laws provide protection when a limited remedy doesn't serve its intended purpose. If a dealer is unable to fix a major problem after a number of attempts or a number of days in the shop, then the manufacturer must buy back the car.

An example of a statutory regulation in federal law is the FTC Used Car Regulation Rule, which is designed to ensure that buyers of used cars understand the warranty terms of the transaction. The used-car dealer must put a sticker on the side window of the car that clearly informs the consumer either that they're buying the car "AS IS — NO WARRANTY." Or if the buyer is getting a warranty, the sticker must state exactly what those warranty terms are.

If a buyer purchases a used car from someone who's not a dealer, the buyer receives no implied warranty of merchantability. If the buyer wants a warranty, he must use his freedom of contract to bargain for an express warranty from the seller.

The Magnuson-Moss Warranty Act: A good idea . . . in theory, anyway

The federal Magnuson-Moss Warranty Act was an interesting innovation. Congress wanted to improve the warranties that buyers were getting, but it didn't want to interfere with freedom of contract. So instead of regulating the terms of warranties, it required that sellers clearly inform buyers what warranty terms they were getting. If the warranty provided a certain level of quality, sellers could label it a "Full Warranty," but if it didn't, they had to describe it as a "Limited Warranty."

The theory was that if consumers knew what they were getting, they would shop for the best warranty, encouraging manufacturers to compete in offering the best warranty. Voilà! Warranties would be improved! Furthermore, the act encourages attorneys to bring breach of warranty claims by providing that an attorney bringing a successful claim under it can recover attorney's fees.

In spite of these goals, I'm not sure that the act has worked because you don't see many Full Warranties, and few attorneys are bringing claims under the act. Nevertheless, it's an interesting experiment in using disclosure rather than regulation to influence the market.

Chapter 11

Interpreting Contracts

. . . .

. . . .

Contracts consist of words. What the parties meant by the words and phrases they used in stating their agreement is often open to interpretation, which can be somewhat subjective and unreliable. To make contract interpretation more objective, consistent, and predictable, contract law has established certain techniques and guidelines.

As an attorney, you must be able to interpret contracts to figure out what they mean and to write a contract in a way that makes its meaning clear to others. Furthermore, you need to be familiar with the techniques used in contract law to interpret contracts so you're better equipped to anticipate how judges and juries are likely to rule. This chapter provides the requisite guidance.

Grasping the Basics of Ambiguity

Ambiguity arises when a word or phrase has two or more conflicting meanings. Ambiguity in a contract may lead one party to claim that the language means one thing while the other party says that it means something else. One party usually claims that under its interpretation, the other party is in breach, and the other argues that under its interpretation, it's not in breach.

For example, a buyer orders "oranges and grapefruit from Florida." The seller sends grapefruit from Florida but oranges from elsewhere. The buyer claims that the seller is in breach. Here, whether "from Florida" modifies only "grapefruit" or both "oranges and grapefruit" is ambiguous.

In resolving such disputes, the goal of contract interpretation is to carry out what the parties intended. On this point, everyone agrees. But that's about all they agree on. Courts disagree on *how* to determine whether language is ambiguous and then, if they find it ambiguous, on *how* to resolve the ambiguity.

Don't confuse ambiguity, which is almost always a bad thing, with vagueness, which may be desirable. *Vague* means uncertain in meaning; however, with vagueness, the intended meaning revolves around a narrow range of meanings rather than the conflicting meanings that often arise with ambiguity. Vague words like *reasonable, satisfactory, usual,* and *promptly* are the lawyer's stock in trade, serving as tools to give one or both parties some breathing room. Here's an example:

> ✔ **Ambiguous wording:** "Notice of defects must be given within 10 days."
>
> ✔ **Explicit wording:** "Buyer must give notice of defects within 10 days after receipt of the goods."
>
> ✔ **Vague wording:** "Buyer must give notice of defects promptly after receipt of the goods."

The first example is ambiguous because it's not clear who has to give notice — the buyer or the seller. Furthermore, the statement doesn't say when the 10 days starts running. The explicit wording makes these terms clear. The vague wording uses "promptly" rather than "within 10 days." The disadvantage of this language is that it's hard to tell whether a party has complied. The advantage is flexibility, because what is "prompt" may depend on the facts and circumstances or trade usage. Prompt notice in the case of delivery of an ice sculpture, for example, probably differs from prompt notice in the case of delivery of a jet airplane.

To avoid the morass of ambiguity, use clear, unambiguous language when drafting contracts.

Is ambiguity ever a good thing?

Although I think detecting and avoiding ambiguity is the best practice, some authorities see "calculated ambiguity" as sometimes necessary to hold a deal together. Situations may arise when parties are deadlocked and would prefer an agreement with possible future uncertainty rather than no agreement at all.

For example, the parties to a labor agreement may provide for a "cost of living adjustment."

Employees may think that "cost of living adjustment" means only that wages increase if the cost of living rises, and management may interpret it to mean that they can reduce wages if the cost of living drops. If this issue becomes a sticking point during negotiation, the parties may agree to address the ambiguity in the future rather than suffer the consequences of having no agreement.

Doing the Interpretation Two-Step

When facing the task of deciding the meaning of allegedly ambiguous language, courts divide the task into two parts:

1. **Decide whether certain language is ambiguous.**

   Whether the language is ambiguous is a question for a court to resolve as a matter of law. The challenge is in deciding which evidence to admit to help make this determination.

2. **Declare or determine the meaning:**

   - If the court finds that the language isn't ambiguous, the court may declare the meaning.

   - If the court finds that the language is ambiguous, the court must decide which evidence is admissible to determine the meaning and then seek ways to use that evidence to find the meaning. If determining the meaning involves deciding fact questions, then a jury may decide the meaning.

To resolve questions of ambiguity, the courts often admit extrinsic (parol) evidence, but the parol evidence *rule* doesn't come into play here (see Chapter 9 for details on the parol evidence rule). The court isn't deciding which terms are in the contract — that's been resolved — but rather what the words mean. In other words, a court first uses the parol evidence rule to find the terms of the contract and then uses the tools of interpretation to determine whether those terms are ambiguous and, if they are, what they mean.

Nevertheless, policy questions regarding which evidence to admit in making ambiguity determinations are very similar to those that arise as a result of the parol evidence rule. The hardest question for a court to resolve when applying the parol evidence rule is whether the parties intended the agreement to be found just in the writing or in the writing plus other understandings. Just as authorities are divided on where to look to answer that question, they're divided over which evidence courts should consider in determining whether certain language is ambiguous.

The process of deciding whether the language is ambiguous and the process of deciding what it means overlap to a great extent. The court often uses the same evidence and techniques to determine whether the language is ambiguous as it does in determining the meaning and intent of that language.

Understanding How Courts Decide What's Ambiguous

To decide whether certain language in a contract is ambiguous and to determine its meaning, courts may consult a number of resources, the most obvious of which is the contract itself. Beyond that is a spectrum of resources, ranging from the most objective to the most subjective, that may include the following (see Figure 11-1):

✔ The language of the contract

✔ Rules of interpretation

✔ Course of performance, course of dealing, and trade usage

✔ Objective sources, such as dictionaries

✔ Contextual understandings of the parties

✔ Testimony of the parties and their attorneys

This section addresses each of these resources in turn.

Figure 11-1:
The spectrum of evidence for determining ambiguity begins with the contract.

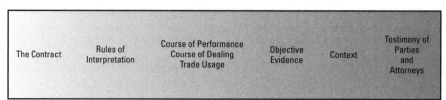

| The Contract | Rules of Interpretation | Course of Performance Course of Dealing Trade Usage | Objective Evidence | Context | Testimony of Parties and Attorneys |

Applying the rules of interpretation

Certain rules govern the reading and interpretation of contracts. These rules provide the courts, attorneys, and parties some guidance in determining whether certain language is actually ambiguous and, if it is, how to determine its intended meaning. This section describes these rules and explains how to apply them.

Applying the plain-meaning rule: Looking at the contract itself

According to the *plain-meaning rule,* the court should look only at the contract itself to determine whether the language is ambiguous. In other words, if a judge reads the contract language and concludes that its meaning is clear, the judge won't consider other evidence about what the contract means or the parties intended it to mean.

This rule, which is the most widely held view, has the advantage of efficiency: Courts only have to look at the contract and don't have to consider other evidence. Critics challenge this rule by arguing that words mean something only in context. This criticism has some validity, but the plain-meaning rule doesn't ignore looking at the context in a legal sense.

For example, if a contract provides for a "floor" and a "ceiling," the court would certainly look at the context to determine the type of contract — a construction contract or a financing arrangement. But the court would look at that context only to determine what's reasonably meant in that context and not what the parties may have actually meant.

Using tools of interpretation

Historically, courts use a number of devices to interpret the meaning of certain words and phrases without looking beyond the "four corners" of the contract. Collectively, you can refer to these as the *rules of interpretation*. Here is one listing of the rules of interpretation taken from Laurence P. Simpson, *Contracts* (West, 1965):

> The three primary rules of interpretation are:
>
> 1. Words are to be given their plain and normal meaning, except:
>
>> (a) Usage may vary the normal meaning of words.
>>
>> (b) Technical words are to be given their technical meaning.
>>
>> (c) Where possible, words will be given the meaning which best effectuates the intention of the parties.
>
> 2. Every part of a contract is to be interpreted, if possible, so as to carry out its general purpose.
>
> 3. The circumstances under which the contract was made may always be shown.
>
> If after applying the primary rules the meaning of the contract is yet not clear, there are secondary rules tending to the same end — to ascertain and effectuate the intention of the parties. They are:
>
> 1. Obvious mistakes of writing, grammar or punctuation will be corrected.
>
> 2. The meaning of general words or terms will be restricted by more specific descriptions of the subject matter or terms of performance.
>
> 3. A contract susceptible of two meanings will be given the meaning which will render it valid.
>
> 4. Between repugnant clauses, a possible interpretation which removes the conflict will be adopted.

5. A contract will, if possible, be interpreted so as to render it reasonable rather than unreasonable.

6. Words will generally be construed most strongly against the party using them.

7. In case of doubt, the interpretation given by the parties is the best evidence of their intention.

8. Where conflict between printed and written words, the writing governs.

Think of these rules as the application of common sense. For example, if a contract provides for a seal to be placed on it, you could look to Rule 5 for guidance: "A contract will, if possible, be interpreted so as to render it reasonable rather than unreasonable." Reasonable is determining the word "seal" in the given context to mean a stamp. Unreasonable would be to define "seal" in this context as a sea mammal.

Making sense of some Latin expressions

Many rules of interpretation originated in Roman law and go by their Latin names. Here are the two most important:

- ✔ **Expressio unius est exclusio alterius ("the expression of one thing excludes another"):** According to *expressio unius est exclusio alterius,* if the contract lists several items but excludes another, then the parties probably intended the excluded item to be excluded.

- ✔ **Ejusdem generis ("things of the same kind"):** According to *ejusdem generis,* wording like "including but not limited to," which is commonly used to avoid the pitfalls of *expressio unius est exclusio alterius,* applies only to things of the same kind.

For example, the parties include in their contract a *force majeure* clause that lists the events that excuse the seller's nonperformance (read more about *force majeure* in Chapter 13). They write:

Seller's performance is excused in the event seller is unable to perform because of fire, flood, earthquake, or hurricane.

This term is ambiguous because the intention seems to be to excuse the seller's performance in the event of a major catastrophe, but not all major catastrophes are listed. Suppose a tornado hits the seller's plant, and he claims that the intention of this clause was to excuse him. The buyer would say, "Sorry, I don't see *tornado* on that list of excusing events. According to *expressio unius est exclusio alterius,* the fact that fire, flood, earthquake, and hurricane are listed and tornado isn't indicates intent to exclude tornado damage." The buyer would probably win the argument.

Having learned his lesson, the seller redrafts his *force majeure* clause by using the handy expression "including but not limited to":

> Seller's performance is excused in the event seller is unable to perform for any reason, including but not limited to fire, flood, earthquake, or hurricane.

Now the seller can't perform because his workers went on strike. The buyer can't claim *expressio unius,* but she can now claim *ejusdem generis.* That is, when the seller listed "fire, flood, earthquake, or hurricane," he meant things that are of the same kind as natural disasters, and a strike is not that kind of thing. The buyer would probably win that one, too, so the seller may try again with something like this:

> Seller's performance is excused in the event seller is unable to perform because of fire, flood, earthquake, or hurricane, or other excusing event whether of the type enumerated or not.

This wording affords the seller additional protection.

Construing against the drafter: Contra proferentem

One of the rules of interpretation that many courts are fond of is *contra proferentem,* which I jokingly translate as "stick it to the insurance company" but which actually means "against the one who offered it" — that is, against the side that drafted the contract. This is a very handy weapon to use against big businesses like banks and insurance companies that draft *contracts of adhesion* (boilerplate contracts that readers often merely skim and sign without much thought).

The trouble with this rule is that it doesn't really attempt to determine from the language what the parties intended. Instead, it takes a shortcut to resolve the dispute. Some courts are quick to use *contra proferentem* right off the bat, and others use it as a last resort when all other attempts at interpretation fail.

Examining the baggage the parties bring to the contract

Going beyond the contract language itself, courts often look to the past experience of the parties, which may not appear in the contract — the parties are so accustomed to the practice that they assume it's part of the contract. This past experience may include terms they intended to be part of the contract and meanings they've assigned to certain words and phrases. If not expressed in the contract, these terms and meanings may come from

- ✔ Course of performance
- ✔ Course of dealing
- ✔ Usage of trade

This section explains how each of these factors may contribute to revealing and clearing up ambiguities.

According to Official Comment 1 to UCC § 2-202, evidence of past experience should be admitted to show that language is ambiguous regardless of whether the court first finds that the language is ambiguous.

Looking for a course of performance

Course of performance is a pattern of performance, under a single contract, that one party establishes and the other accepts or at least doesn't object to within a reasonable amount of time. The course of performance sets the standard of performance between the parties under that contract.

For example, a business contracts with a trash pickup service to have the business's trash hauled away for six months. For the first six weeks, the service picks up the trash once a week. The business then complains that the trash should be picked up more often. With no express term in the contract addressing the frequency of trash pickup, a court is likely to look at the course of performance. Because the trash pickup service picked up the trash once a week for six weeks without the business complaining about it, the parties established a course of performance that becomes part of the contract. The decision would probably favor the trash pickup service because the course of performance established the meaning of the language.

The number of performances required to establish a course of performance has never been established, but I can confidently tell you that it's more than one. Put yourself in the shoes of the trash pickup service in this example. After performing once a week for some time without objection by the business, the trash pickup service reasonably concluded that the term had been established.

Checking for a course of dealing

Course of dealing is a pattern established through performance of a series of previous contracts between the same parties. When interpreting contract language, courts may look at the parties' transaction history to determine meaning.

For example, suppose a contract between a buyer and a seller states that the buyer is to pay within 30 days of delivery. In performing previous contracts with this seller that contained the same term, the buyer has always taken a 5 percent discount when it pays within 10 days of delivery. When the buyer does this with the next purchase, the seller can't complain that this term is not part of the agreement, because the course of dealing established a pattern that has led the buyer to believe that this term is part of it. If the seller wants to put an end to the practice, he can say in this contract "no discount for early payment" or "evidence of course of dealing is not admissible to supply terms or meaning to this contract."

Seeking usage of trade

Trade usage refers to language that has a special meaning in a certain industry or to customs that prevail in that industry. If parties engage in a dispute over what a term or phrase means and the word or phrase has a specific meaning that industry insiders all know, then courts often look to trade usage to determine meaning.

For the most part, you must be in a trade in order to be bound by trade usage. In the notorious "chicken" case, *Frigaliment Importing Co. v. B.N.S. International Sales Corp.*, an experienced buyer purchased chicken from a novice seller and received stewing chickens rather than the broilers he was expecting. The buyer claimed that in the trade, "chicken" meant broilers, not stewing chicken. The seller said it couldn't be expected to know that because it was new to the trade. The court said that even if you're new to a trade, you're bound by trade usages if either (1) you actually knew it or (2) it's such common knowledge that it would be imputed to you. (In the end, the buyer was unable to prove either of these points.)

This reasoning shows that contract law often looks for objective, not subjective, understanding. That is, if a reasonable person in that same position would've known something, then a party in that position is assumed to know it, regardless of whether the party actually knew it. In legal circles, you say that the knowledge is *imputed* to him.

Suppose you're renovating your basement and you buy a bunch of two-by-fours from the lumber store. You then claim breach of contract because the two-by-fours measured only 1.5 inches by 3.5 inches (the standard dimensions of a two-by-four). After squelching a chuckle, the lumber store rep claims that trade usage of the term *two-by-four* describes wood with the standard dimensions of 1.5 x 3.5 inches, not 2 x 4 inches. You could claim that you're not in the trade, but that wouldn't matter, because just about everybody who's hammered a nail knows that. The knowledge is imputed to you, and you lose.

Don't be afraid to ask a lot of dumb questions to get to know your client's business. Parties in the trade frequently neglect to put trade usages expressly in their contracts because they're so steeped in the norms of that business that they don't even think about it. This can make the task of reading a client's contracts difficult if you don't know which special meanings they have or practices they follow that they haven't stated in the contract.

Resolving conflicts through the hierarchy of meaning

When evidence of course of performance, course of dealing, and trade usage conflict, resolve the conflicts by following the *hierarchy of meaning* that establishes which one governs over the others. The hierarchy, as found in UCC § 1-303, is as follows:

Trade usage driving you crazy?

If dealing with trade usage drives you crazy, seeing a therapist might not be a good idea. Suppose she tells you she charges $100 an hour. You see her for four 45-minute sessions, and she sends you a bill for $400. When you complain that you've seen her for only a total of three hours, she explains, "Oh, no. The 'therapeutic hour' is 45 minutes."

---

1. **Express term**

   Obviously, an express term should and does trump evidence from any and all of the other sources, because this is the rule that the parties say they want to govern their agreement. For example, in the chicken case (see the preceding section), if the contract had included the definition "In this contract, 'chicken' means broilers," then how the parties define "chicken" from course of performance, course of dealing, or trade usage wouldn't matter. The one exception occurs when course of performance leads to a waiver, as I explain in the next section.

2. **Course of performance**

   Lacking an express term, the pattern of behavior that the parties establish in performing the terms of the contract carries the most weight in establishing its meaning.

3. **Course of dealing**

   Evidence from previous transactions between the two parties carries less weight than course of performance but more weight than trade usage in determining the meaning.

4. **Trade usage**

   When all else fails, the industry standard determines the meaning.

Following are examples that demonstrate how a court might apply the hierarchy of meaning to resolve disputes.

The present contract contains no express term defining the word "chicken," but under previous contracts, the seller always supplied this buyer with broilers. Under the present contract, which calls for multiple shipments, the seller supplies stewers. After four shipments of stewers, the buyer wakes up and says, "Hey, our course of dealing called for broilers. That's what you should be sending us." Unfortunately, it's too late for the buyer to complain. Although the course of dealing initially established that "chicken" meant broilers, the buyer acquiesced in a course of performance by accepting repeated performances without objecting. In the hierarchy, course of performance trumps course of dealing, so the seller wins.

Assume now that the seller has always supplied broilers under previous contracts. Under the present contract, the seller supplies stewers and the buyer immediately protests. "But," the seller argues, "the trade usage calls for stewers, so we're just doing what's the normal trade practice." Unfortunately for the seller, course of dealing trumps trade usage, so by establishing through course of dealing that "chicken" means broilers, the seller loses this one. (The seller would've been right if it had followed the trade practice initially, but it didn't.)

Determining when a waiver exists

In certain cases, course of performance may result in a waiver of an express term, meaning course of performance then trumps the express term (perhaps only temporarily). Such cases arise when one party lulls the other into thinking that the express term won't be enforced. The party doing the lulling passively waives its right to enforce the express term but can undo the waiver by giving notice that it expects the other party to honor the express term in the future.

Assume, for example, that a car buyer promises the seller to make 24 payments on the first of the month. The contract expressly states that if the buyer doesn't do so, the seller has the right to declare the full amount due and repossess the car. For six months in a row, the buyer pays on the fifth or sixth day of the month. When the buyer doesn't pay on the first day of the seventh month, the seller declares the full amount due and repossesses the car. Here, the express term called for payment on the first, but the course of performance led the buyer to believe that making payments a few days late is acceptable. This waiver moves course of performance above express term in the hierarchy, so the seller had no right to repossess the car.

However, the displacement could be temporary. The seller could inform the buyer that it won't tolerate any more late payments. The seller is no longer leading the buyer to believe that the late performance is acceptable, so the buyer is once again bound by that express term.

Bringing in objective meaning from outside the contract

After looking at the contract itself and evidence of course of performance, course of dealing, and trade usage, many courts look at objective meanings from outside the contract to decide whether language is ambiguous. Objective meaning comes in two types, depending on the definition of *objective.* Objective meaning may be

- ✔ **Meanings used by reasonable people, as opposed to whatever meaning a party conjures up:** This is the usual meaning of *objective.* For example, a dictionary definition and a trade usage are meanings by reasonable people.

- ✔ **Meanings that the parties to the contract have manifested in some way, as opposed to being found only in their heads:** The discussions the parties had prior to signing the contract and earlier drafts of their agreements are examples of sources of this kind of objective meaning.

An extreme example of the second meaning of *objective* would be a secret code that the parties had worked out. For example, suppose a stock trader works in a cubicle where he's afraid his fellow workers can hear his telephone conversations. He and his broker agree to use coded language in which "buy" means to sell and "sell" means to buy. He calls and tells his broker to "sell 100 shares of XYZ." The broker proceeds to sell 100 shares of XYZ. Under the meaning of "sell" used by reasonable people, this isn't breach of contract.

However, under the meaning the parties agreed to, it is breach. Can the trader introduce evidence that the parties had agreed on this meaning? Not surprisingly, courts are divided on this question.

Considering subjective evidence: Context and testimony

In determining whether language is ambiguous, some courts go to the far end of the spectrum to look not only at the contract itself and objective evidence but also at all evidence in and around the contract in context. This differs from the plain-meaning approach because the plain-meaning approach considers only what *reasonable people* would have intended, whereas the context approach looks at what the *actual parties* would have intended.

At the subjective end of the spectrum of meaning are meanings that the parties had in mind or the meanings their lawyers had in mind when they drafted the contract — evidence gathered from testimony of the parties and their attorneys. Most courts, however, reject this subjective evidence, because making it up after the fact is far too easy.

Deciding What Something Means

After reviewing the evidence to determine whether certain language is ambiguous, the court may determine that the language isn't ambiguous and simply declare its meaning based on what the evidence indicates. If the court instead decides that the language is ambiguous, it moves on to the second step: deciding which evidence to admit to resolve the ambiguity. Admissible evidence usually consists of evidence heard during the first step (determining whether the language is ambiguous) and may include additional evidence from a larger part of the spectrum (refer to Figure 11-1).

If a court applying the plain-meaning rule determines that the language is ambiguous, it may resolve the ambiguity by using the rules of interpretation, including *contra proferentem* (against the offeror). However, it may also consider other objective evidence.

For example, a contract for the sale of a house states that the sale price is "$130,000 (one hundred twenty thousand dollars)." On its face, this is an obvious ambiguity — a conflict between the numbers and the words. Resolving this one against the party who happened to draft the contract would seem arbitrary. A court could resolve it by using the rule of interpretation that words govern over numbers on the theory that when you take time to write something out, that more likely expresses your intent. However, those techniques don't really get at what these parties intended. It would seem more reasonable to look to other evidence like preliminary agreements and earlier drafts of the contract to determine the price the parties intended.

Usually, courts are able to use these devices to resolve a problem of interpretation. They either determine what the parties intended or what reasonable parties would've intended, and the parties have to live with that. In either event, the contract lives on. In some cases, however, courts are unable to determine the intended meaning and must declare that the parties have a misunderstanding, as I explain next.

Dealing with Misunderstanding

When courts are unable to resolve a conflict between two meanings, the parties have a *misunderstanding* — a problem of interpretation that can render a contract void. Some folks like to define "misunderstanding" as a failure of the parties to achieve a "meeting of the minds," but that's not accurate. The problem is that the language manifested in the contract has two meanings and that the court is unable to determine which meaning the parties intended or which meaning reasonable parties would've intended.

The classic example is the infamous case of *Raffles v. Wichelhaus,* which involved the good ships *Peerless.* The parties entered into a contract to buy and sell cotton to arrive in London "*ex Peerless,*" meaning delivered on the ship *Peerless.* Apparently, however, two ships named *Peerless* were scheduled for London, one to arrive in October and the other to arrive in December. Because of fluctuating market prices, the time of delivery was crucial.

Of course, the parties wouldn't admit that they were thinking about the same ship *Peerless.* The buyer said he had in mind the October *Peerless,* and the seller, the December *Peerless.* Contract formation depends more on what reasonable people would have in mind (objective intent) than what the parties actually had in mind (subjective intent), as I explain in Chapter 2. Therefore, you need to ask two questions:

- ✔ Would a reasonable person in the shoes of the buyer have known the seller intended the December *Peerless?*
- ✔ Would a reasonable person in the shoes of the seller have known the buyer intended the October *Peerless?*

If the answer to *either* of these questions is yes, then the parties have a contract for arrival on the *Peerless* that one party actually had in mind and the other party should've had in mind. If the answer to *both* questions is yes or no, then you have to throw up your hands because you're unable to determine whether the parties had a contract for arrival on the October *Peerless* or for arrival on the December *Peerless.* In that event, no contract is formed.

Including outside evidence: What is *chicken?*

The famous case of *Frigaliment Importing Co. v. B.N.S. International Sales Corp.* is a trial court opinion that shows how a court goes about resolving ambiguities in contracts. Under a contract calling for the shipment of chicken, the seller shipped stewing chicken. The buyer cried foul, claiming that "chicken" meant broilers.

Judge Friendly wasted little time making the initial determination that the language was ambiguous — "chicken" may mean stewers or broilers or both. So which meaning did the parties intend? More important, what would a reasonable party have meant?

The judge considered a wide spectrum of evidence — evidence from the contract and from government regulations referenced in the contract along with prices in the contract that may have indicated what a reasonable party would've expected at that price. Other evidence came from what the parties told each other during negotiation, the documents they exchanged, and the course of performance, because the chicken arrived in more than one shipment.

Most of the argument revolved around trade usage — what members of the trade thought they were getting when they bought and sold chicken.

Considering the contradictory evidence, Judge Friendly concluded that the plaintiff buyer had not satisfied the burden of proving that its meaning, broilers only, was more reasonable. A few years later, he had second thoughts and realized that he could've decided this as a misunderstanding case. If the contract used the word "chicken" and the parties ascribed different meanings to it, and if neither party was able to show that its meaning was more reasonable, then the judge could've concluded that the parties didn't form a contract.

Fortunately, as a practical matter, few interpretation cases end up this way. Either the term is immaterial, or the application of the many tools of interpretation reveals that one interpretation is more reasonable than the other.

Part IV
Performing the Contract or Breaching It

The 5th Wave   By Rich Tennant

©RICHTENNANT

"The defendant is required to answer the question.
At the time the contract was executed, did you
or did you not link pinkies with the plaintiff?"

In this part . . .

*F*orming a contract is pretty easy. Performing it is more difficult, which is why contract disputes often arise over one party's failure to keep his promise.

The chapters in this part address nonperformance issues: how contract law determines whether a party's nonperformance constitutes breach. Here you find out whether changes made to a contract after formation are enforceable, whether the occurrence of unforeseen events or the nonoccurrence of certain conditions excuses performance, and how one party may breach a contract even before performance is due.

Chapter 12

Evaluating Whether Contract Modifications Are Enforceable

In This Chapter

▶ Evaluating the enforceability of modifications made during performance

▶ Knowing when *no oral modification clauses* carry weight

▶ Recognizing when a party can make modifications unilaterally

▶ Using accord and satisfaction to determine when a partial payment discharges a debt

Contracts usually call for future performance, and because no one can predict the future, parties may modify their contracts to accommodate unforeseen circumstances. Unfortunately, when parties modify a contract, they often don't take the steps necessary to make the modifications clearly enforceable. As a result, after agreeing to a modification, one party may claim breach during performance while the other party claims it's not in breach because the original contract was modified. Or after one party has performed, the parties may enter into an accord in which they agree that the other doesn't have to pay as much as they originally agreed to. The courts must then determine whether the modification or the accord is enforceable.

When the parties modify the contract makes a big difference:

✔ **Before completing performance:** An *executory contract* is a contract that neither party has fully performed. When parties modify an executory contract, the courts analyze the contract according to the law of modification.

✔ **After one party has fully performed:** When the modification occurs after one party has fully performed, you're dealing with a *contract fully executed by one party.* The courts analyze the contract according to the law of accord and satisfaction. (*Accord* is an agreement to discharge a debt by the payment of less money. *Satisfaction* is performance of that accord.)

This chapter explores some of the ways parties modify contracts before and after a party has fully performed. You discover how courts respond to these modifications in each case so that you're better equipped to advise your clients and represent them when such modifications become the basis of a dispute.

Considering Modifications Made during Performance

To determine whether a contract modification made during performance is enforceable, you must examine several factors, including whether consideration was required, whether the modification falls within the statute of frauds, and whether the original contract has a *no oral modification* (NOM) clause or a clause that gives a party the right to make modifications unilaterally. This section explains how to evaluate these factors to determine whether a modification made during performance is enforceable.

Determining whether consideration is required

In theory, a contract modification is a new contract, requiring offer, acceptance, and consideration (see Chapters 2 and 3). Contract modifications, however, don't always require consideration. To determine whether a modification is enforceable, the courts first consider whether the contract falls within UCC Article 2 (contracts for the sale of goods):

✔ **Within the UCC:** The courts must follow the Code rule enacted by the legislature, § 2-209(1), and according to that rule, no consideration is necessary for a modification.

✔ **Not within the UCC:** If you have a common-law case, some courts follow the old rule that if consideration is absent, then the modification is not enforceable. Other courts follow the Restatement, which says in § 59 that the modification is enforceable as long as it's "fair and equitable."

For example, a business rents a store in a shopping mall for two years at $1,000 per month, as reflected in a written lease. Shortly after the store opens, the economy slides into recession and the store isn't doing so well. The business asks the mall whether it will agree to reduce the rent to $800 a month.

The mall agrees, and the parties shake hands on it. After the business has paid $800 a month for six months, the mall claims that the business owes $1,200 — the balance of the unpaid rent for six months. The business claims it modified the contract and the mall agreed, but the mall says, "Ha-ha! You don't remember your contract law. Consideration is required to make a promise enforceable. We promised you a reduction in rent of $200 a month, but you didn't promise us anything in return. Therefore, our promise isn't enforceable."

The mall is technically right as a matter of general contract law, but given the fact that the parties agreed to a modification in good faith, letting the mall back out of its agreement to accept $200 less per month seems unjust. Contract law has struggled to find a theory to enforce modifications like this that the parties enter into in good faith. Here are some of the ways contract law has gotten around the problem:

- ✔ **A party can provide something new or different as consideration.** The business could avoid the consideration problem by bargaining to give something in return for the reduced rent. For example, the business could say, "We'll give you rent of $800 and a peppercorn rather than $1,000." If the mall agreed, they'd have a bargained-for consideration. Is a peppercorn worth $200? If the parties say it is, the answer is yes — why should contract law disturb their agreement?

- ✔ **The parties can tear up the old agreement (a process called *mutual rescission*) and enter into a new one.** This solution works because mutual rescission gives each party consideration (something of value): the release of their obligations under the contract. In effect, this process involves making three different contracts:

  - **The original contract:** The business rents the store for $1,000 per month.

  - **The mutual rescission:** The mall gives up rights against the business, and the business gives up rights against the mall.

  - **The new contract:** The business rents the store for $800 per month.

  The problem with this approach is that parties rarely take these three steps, so a court that finds they did often uses a *legal fiction,* pretending something happened in order to achieve a desirable outcome.

- ✔ **Contract law can change the rules so that the modification is enforceable even without consideration.** Contract law has taken this approach but has done so differently in the common law and the UCC, as the next two subsections explain.

Dispensing with consideration: The UCC approach

The UCC has taken a straightforward approach to the problem of requiring consideration for a contract modification: It says that no consideration is necessary in such situations. Section 2-209(1) provides, "An agreement modifying a contract within this Article needs no consideration to be binding."

Statutes have this advantage — the legislature can make a sweeping change to the law. Of course, because this provision appears in Article 2, it applies only to the sale of goods. If a seller of widgets agreed to reduce its contract price from $1,000 to $800, this provision would make the modification enforceable. But it wouldn't help a business that agreed to a $200 rent reduction in leasing a store from the mall.

Just because the UCC does away with consideration in a modification doesn't mean all modifications become enforceable. Other formation defenses (see Chapters 5 and 6) still apply. For example, if the widget buyer threatened the seller with bodily harm if the seller didn't agree to a price reduction, that modification wouldn't be enforceable because the seller entered into it under duress.

A more subtle Code limitation on the enforceability of modifications is the doctrine of good faith and fair dealing (see Chapter 10). This doctrine is part of every contract, regardless of whether the parties expressly include it in their agreement. Just because the Code says that a modification doesn't require consideration, not every modification lacking consideration is enforceable. The doctrine of good faith can be used to prevent enforcement of a modification that may otherwise be enforceable.

In *Roth Steel Products v. Sharon Steel Corp,* the plaintiff had agreed to purchase various kinds of steel at various times from the defendant. At the time they made the contract, the market for steel favored the buyer. But when the market later changed and steel became harder to obtain, the seller sought to modify the price. The buyer initially agreed to the modification but then sought to avoid it.

The Sixth Circuit Court of Appeals, applying the Ohio UCC, acknowledged that lack of consideration was not an argument that the buyer could use to avoid the contract because § 2-209(1) specifically provides that a modification does not need consideration to be binding. However, the court pointed out that, as indicated in Official Comment 1 to § 2-209(1), "modifications made thereunder must meet the test of good faith imposed by this Act."

Good faith requires both the "observance of reasonable commercial standards of fair dealing in the trade" and "honesty in fact," as I explain in Chapter 10. The court found that the first prong had been satisfied because the seller was experiencing a loss on the contract, and a reasonable seller in that situation would request a modification. However, the seller did not satisfy the second prong because it wasn't honest in requesting the modification. Instead of explaining that it believed the contract entitled it to pass on higher prices (an argument it came up with only during the litigation), the seller had threatened the buyer, saying that it would not ship any steel to the buyer if it did not agree to the price increase. That behavior is coercive and inconsistent with good faith.

The case makes clear that even though the UCC has done away with the requirement of consideration for a modification, that doesn't mean that all modifications without consideration are enforceable. The courts can use the doctrine of good faith to police behavior such as coercion, even if that behavior does not rise to the level of duress, which was the principal way to avoid a modification under the common law.

Although a party must perform a contract in good faith, no requirement stipulates that a party must agree to a modification. If one party requests a change, the other party is free to say no.

Enforcing reasonable modifications: The common-law approach

In common law, courts set precedents, which lower courts in the jurisdiction must follow, but which have only persuasive authority in other jurisdictions. If enough courts follow the same rule, then it becomes the general rule, and it may become the black-letter rule of the Restatement.

Over time, a number of courts in common-law cases began to find contract modifications enforceable even with consideration missing. The Restatement states the rule this way in § 89(a):

§ 89. Modification of Executory Contract

A promise modifying a duty under a contract not fully performed on either side is binding

> (a) if the modification is fair and equitable in view of circumstances not anticipated by the parties when the contract was made

If a court were to apply this rule to the rent-reduction scenario involving the mall (see the earlier section "Determining whether consideration is required"), the court would probably find that the modification was enforceable. The circumstances changed because of the economic recession, and the parties freely agreed to the modification.

The Restatement is not the law, and courts are free to ignore it. Rules in the Restatement are merely what the drafters found to be the rules. Usually the drafters state the rules that a majority of jurisdictions follow, but sometimes they state a rule they prefer even if it isn't followed in the majority of cases. In a common-law case, the court may follow the rule in the Restatement or ignore it and stick to the old rule — in this case, refusing to enforce the modification when consideration is absent. In a Code case, however, courts must follow the UCC rule enacted by the legislature, and according to that rule, no consideration is necessary for such modifications. (See Chapter 1 for details on the UCC, the Restatement, and common law.)

Written requirements: Seeing whether the modification is within the statute of frauds

Even if a modification passes the consideration test, the agreement is still subject to the other formation defenses, including the statute of frauds (see Chapter 8) — the collective name for statutes that require written evidence of a contract. If the agreement is within the statute of frauds, then oral modifications don't count.

In the example presented earlier in this chapter, the parties orally agree to reduce the rent on a two-year lease from $1,000 to $800. Because this agreement is related to real estate and real estate leases for more than one year are within the statute of frauds in most jurisdictions, the modification is not enforceable, even if it passes the consideration test. To be enforceable, the agreement would need to be in writing.

In the UCC, this rule appears in § 2-209(3), which provides that

> (3) The requirements of the statute of frauds section of this Article (Section 2-201) must be satisfied if the contract as modified is within its provisions.

The UCC statute of frauds, § 2-201(1), requires contracts for the sale of goods for $500 or more to be evidenced by a writing. The rule of § 2-209(3) clearly applies if the parties made an oral agreement to sell four widgets for $400 (not within the statute of frauds) and then orally modify it to a sale for $600 (within the statute of frauds) — the modified agreement would have to be evidenced by a writing to be enforceable. The rule is less clear if the parties had a written agreement to sell the four widgets for $1,000 and then orally agreed to drop the price to $800. The contract as modified is within the statute of frauds. Written evidence of the modified agreement exists; however, it doesn't include the new price term. You could argue that the writing doesn't have to contain all the terms, as I discuss in Chapter 8.

Courts are divided on whether oral modifications to written agreements like this are enforceable. One thing they do generally agree on, however, is that if the *quantity* is modified, that modification has to be evidenced by a writing. For example, if the parties orally modify the agreement from four to five widgets for $1,000, most authorities would find that the writing does not evidence this agreement.

Dealing with "no oral modification" clauses

One of the most common terms found in the boilerplate of contracts is the *no oral modification clause* (NOM). It functions as the parties' own private statute of frauds providing that oral modifications don't count. The UCC expressly permits parties to create an NOM. Section 2-209(2) provides in part that "A signed agreement which excludes modification or rescission except by a signed writing cannot be otherwise modified or rescinded." This clause has a positive channeling effect, encouraging the parties to get their modifications in writing. The problem is that nine times out of ten, they don't realize that the provision is there, or they ignore it, and they make an oral modification anyway.

Most courts find that an oral modification made in the face of a NOM is enforceable, especially when it induces reliance. (I cover reliance in Chapter 4.) Contract law authority Arthur Corbin says that the written contract the parties make today can't change what they agree to tomorrow. In other words, today they agree that all modifications must be in writing. Tomorrow, by making an oral modification, the parties imply an agreement to change their original rule and allow oral modifications. Courts frequently invoke the doctrine of waiver to get around the NOM. (A *waiver* is a knowing relinquishment of a legal right.)

For example, a bank has a written agreement with a borrower for a car loan. The contract says that the customer agrees to make payments on the first of the month, and if she doesn't, the bank can accelerate the debt (make the entire amount due) and repossess the car. The customer calls the bank and says, "I'm having a temporary cash-flow problem. Would it be okay if I pay next month on the tenth rather than the first?" The bank employee says, "No problem." However, the bank employee neglects to tell the department that deals with defaults, and when the payment doesn't arrive on the first, the bank repossesses the car.

Outraged, the customer says, "You agreed that I could have until the tenth to pay." The bank says, "Ha-ha! No consideration! We gave you another ten days to pay, but what did you do for us?" The customer says, probably rightly, "This is a case where the modification may be enforceable without consideration under the rule found in Restatement § 89." The bank says, "That may be true, but the contract that you freely agreed to has a NOM clause stating that oral agreements don't count."

Rarely would a court let the bank get away with that argument. Most courts say that the bank had the right to insist on the NOM, but it waived that right when it agreed to the oral modification, which led the customer to believe that nothing terrible would happen if she paid ten days late. Her reliance on the oral agreement makes it enforceable.

The UCC recognizes the waiver doctrine, providing in § 2-209(4) that both an agreement in violation of the NOM clause and an agreement in violation of the statute of frauds are subject to waiver: "(4) Although an attempt at modification or rescission does not satisfy the requirements of subsection (2) or (3) it can operate as a waiver."

Agreeing to future, unilateral modifications

A cutting-edge question in contract law is whether the parties can agree that one party has the right to make unilateral (one-sided) modifications during the performance of the contract. In a number of cases, banks have done this to raise credit card interest rates in response to market changes.

A contract would be illusory if one party in effect said to the other, "You're free to make whatever terms you want, and I will agree to them." Such a provision would undermine the idea that contracts represent the agreement of two parties. On the other hand, allowing unilateral modifications based on future events makes sense in cases in which the parties can't possibly predict a change in circumstances.

A rule that provides a good balance would permit the agreed-upon unilateral modifications when they're based on some objective standard. Under that approach, a party that had reserved the right to make unilateral modifications would be allowed to change a term like a price or interest rate to meet a market standard but prohibited from changing terms unrelated to market fluctuations.

For example, in a long-term written agreement, a seller sets the price of goods at $1,000 each, says nothing about dispute resolution, and reserves the right to change the terms of the agreement. A few months later, the seller informs the buyer that because of an increase in the price of its raw materials, starting next month, the price of the goods will be $1,050 each and all disputes will go to arbitration. Are these modifications enforceable? Although not all courts will agree, I think the best answer is yes and no. Assuming that the price increase reflects a change in the market, the modified price increase is enforceable. However, the new language concerning how arbitrations are to be handled is not enforceable, because it's not tied to some future, objective change in circumstances.

Making Changes after One Party Fully Performed: Accord and Satisfaction

After one party has fully performed, the other party owes the contract price for that performance. The party who performed is a creditor, and the party who hasn't performed is a debtor. In this case, only the debtor has something to bargain with (the unpaid debt), so allowing modification without consideration doesn't make sense. Either the debtor must pay up, or the parties may cut a deal through accord and satisfaction.

An *accord* is a contract in which a creditor agrees to accept less than the full amount of the debt in order to discharge the debt *(satisfaction).* Because an accord is a contract, all the elements of a contract I discuss in Part I, including offer, acceptance, and consideration, must be present without any of the defenses I discuss in Part II, including fraud, duress, and mistake.

For example, a painter has agreed to paint a house for $10,000. When the painter finishes the job, the painter is now a creditor, and the owner owes a debt of $10,000. The contract has been fully performed by one party — the painter — and the contract price is now due. If the debtor now offers to pay less, any agreement that results falls under the law of accord and satisfaction rather than modification.

Determining whether the parties formed an accord: Offer and acceptance

Like any contract, an accord requires offer and acceptance, but what constitutes offer and acceptance in this case can get fuzzy. For example, if the debtor owes the creditor $10,000 and sends the creditor a check for $8,000, a reasonable person in the shoes of the creditor would think this was just a *payment on account* (a partial payment made with the intention of paying the rest later) and that the remaining $2,000 is still owed.

If the debtor intends the creditor to discharge the debt by accepting this partial payment, the debtor must make that clear in the offer. This issue often arises with a *conditional check,* in which the debtor writes the offer to discharge the debt in fine print on the check. Although courts are divided on the issue of whether the fine print notice on the check is enough to constitute an offer, a wise debtor makes the offer clear in a separate communication to avoid any dispute.

If the debtor makes a clear offer, the creditor has two choices:

- ✔ Accept the offer, thus discharging the debt upon acceptance of the partial payment (the satisfaction).
- ✔ Reject the offer, in which case the debt remains.

What the debtor can't do is accept the payment (the offer) and claim the right to recover the rest of the debt. The acceptance must match the offer. The offeree can't change the offer and then accept the changed offer. This choice may be tough for a creditor, because a creditor may live to regret not accepting that offer of partial payment.

Finding consideration: Doing something additional or different

Assuming that the agreement to enter an accord passes the offer and acceptance test, it must then pass the consideration test without breaking the pre-existing duty rule. (The *pre-existing duty rule* states that a party's promise to do what it's already bound to do doesn't constitute consideration; see Chapter 3 for details.) To get around the pre-existing duty rule, the debtor must agree to do something additional to or different from what he promised in the original agreement.

For example, assume that a debtor owes a creditor $10,000 on June 1. If the debtor offers to pay $8,000 on June 1 to settle the debt, this isn't consideration because the debtor is merely promising to pay part of what he was obligated to pay on the same date specified in the original contract. If, instead, the debtor offers to pay $8,000 on May 31 to satisfy the debt and the creditor accepts, that's consideration. The creditor got something he wasn't legally entitled to: early payment. Is paying one day early worth $2,000? The law doesn't inquire into the adequacy of consideration. If the creditor bargained for payment a day early, then consideration is satisfied.

Finding consideration in unliquidated debts and debt-dispute settlements

You can often find consideration in either liquidation of an unliquidated debt or in settlement of a dispute between the parties, including a tort claim, as I explain in this section.

Liquidation of an unliquidated debt

A debt is *liquidated* if the parties or a court fixes the amount of the debt. It is *unliquidated* if the parties have entered into a contract without specifying the amount to be paid. Similarly, a tort claim is unliquidated because how much the debtor will have to pay is unclear. If the debt is unliquidated, a dispute as to the amount owed may arise. Consideration in resolving that dispute exists because each side is getting something.

If a painter offers to paint the owner's home for $10,000 and the owner accepts, they've liquidated the debt. On the other hand, if the painter offers to paint the owner's home for some unspecified amount and the owner accepts, the debt is unliquidated. The contract is still valid, but the parties or a court must supply the contract price (see Chapter 10 for details on supplying terms). Suppose the painter has finished painting and says, "That'll be $10,000." The owner says, "I don't think it's worth that much. I'm only willing to pay you $6,000." If the painter refuses, the parties can ask a court to fill in the gap with an amount. Or they can fix the amount themselves. The painter may say, "I'll take $8,000," and if the owner agrees, then they have an accord — they've liquidated the amount at $8,000. Both parties bargained to get something because if the court had liquidated the debt, the amount could've been more or less than $8,000.

Settlement of a dispute between the parties

A debt is *disputed* if — even though the amount was agreed to originally — one party raises a good-faith defense to payment. If the parties then settle the dispute, consideration exists, because each party got something out of the settlement.

For example, an homeowner and a painter agree that the painter will paint the owner's house for $10,000. After the painter finishes painting the house, the owner says, "You did a terrible job painting. I don't think you've lived up to the implied standard of workmanlike performance I read about in Chapter 10 of *Contract Law For Dummies*. But I'm willing to pay you $6,000." The painter is perfectly free to reject the offer, sue the owner for $10,000, let the owner assert the defense as a breach of contract claim, and let the court determine the amount due. Or the painter can say, "I'll take $8,000," and if the owner agrees, then they've reached an accord by settling the dispute for $8,000. Both parties bargained to get something, because if a court had resolved the dispute, the amount could've more or less than $8,000.

Settlement of a tort claim

Accord and satisfaction is a quick and dirty dispute-resolution mechanism that also arises when an injured party makes a tort claim against the party who allegedly caused the injury. The injured party is a creditor, and the party who caused the injury is a debtor. The tort claim is clearly unliquidated and disputed, so consideration exists if the parties negotiate a *release* (an agreement to settle the claim), as I explain in Chapter 7.

Figuring out what happens when the accord has been satisfied . . . or not

After the parties form an accord, it hovers like a fairy, awaiting performance (satisfaction). If the debtor pays according to the terms of the accord, he performs the accord and satisfies the underlying debt. If the debtor fails to perform, he's breached the accord, and the creditor may sue either on the accord or on the underlying debt (the greater amount).

If you're representing the creditor and the underlying debt is unliquidated or disputed, consider suing on the accord (the lesser amount), because that amount has been established. If you sue on the underlying debt, the court may say you're entitled to an amount that's even less than the amount agreed to in the accord.

For example, suppose the parties entered into an accord to settle a disputed $10,000 debt for $8,000. If the debtor fails to perform (satisfy) the accord, then the creditor can sue on the underlying debt of $10,000. But the debtor can raise the dispute as a defense to that debt, and the creditor may end up recovering less than $8,000. If the creditor sues on the accord of $8,000, however, the debtor has agreed that that's a liquidated and undisputed amount. The debtor can't raise a defense to payment, so the creditor should get judgment for $8,000.

Distinguishing accord and satisfaction from substituted contract

When a debtor breaches an accord, the creditor may sue on the accord or on the underlying obligation. This rule has one exception that seldom arises. Sometimes the debtor claims that the creditor agreed to discharge the debt in return for the debtor's *promise* to pay a lesser amount, not for the debtor's *payment* of the lesser amount. Such an agreement is called a *substituted contract* because the new agreement presumably replaces the original contract. Whether the parties entered into an accord or a substituted contract is a matter of interpretation, as I discuss in Chapter 11. The more reasonable interpretation usually favors the creditor. To create a substituted contract, the parties must be very clear that that was their intention.

For example, a debtor says to a creditor, "I dispute owing you the $10,000 you claim. I promise to pay you $8,000 in return for your agreement to discharge the debt." The creditor agrees. The debtor then fails to pay the $8,000, and the creditor sues for $10,000. The debtor defends this claim by arguing that the consideration for resolving the dispute was the debtor's *promise* to pay the $8,000, not the *payment* of $8,000. Whether this falls under substituted contract or accord and satisfaction is a matter of interpretation:

- ✔ **Substituted contract:** If the creditor said in effect, "I'll accept your *promise* in exchange for my discharge of the debt," then you're looking at a substituted contract, and the creditor discharged the debtor from the underlying debt as soon as he stated that promise.

- ✔ **Accord and satisfaction:** If the creditor said in effect, "I'll accept your *payment* of $8,000 in exchange for my discharge of the debt," then the parties have an accord, and the underlying debt is discharged only when the debtor pays the $8,000.

Because a reasonable creditor is likely to discharge an underlying debt only upon payment of the new amount, courts lean toward interpreting agreements like these to be accords unless evidence clearly shows that the parties intended to form a substituted contract.

One way to slash an electric bill: *Con Edison v. Arroll*

In *Consolidated Edison v. Arroll*, Arroll was a customer of Con Edison, which supplies electricity to New Yorkers. Arroll thought his bill was too high, so he sent Con Edison a check in partial payment along with an accompanying letter that explained the dispute and informed Con Edison that if they cashed the check, the debt was settled. Con Edison cashed the check and sued for the balance due.

Arroll raised the affirmative defense of accord and satisfaction. Con Edison claimed that Arroll didn't prove that his bill was in error. The court agreed, but it found that Arroll had raised the dispute in good faith. Even if a claim isn't a valid claim, it's consideration if raised in good faith.

Con Edison then claimed that as a practical matter, it has to process thousands of checks and can't be bothered to sort out the ones that are sent to resolve a dispute. Too bad, said the court. The same rules apply to you as to everyone else. You were on notice that if you accepted this check to resolve a disputed debt, the debt would be satisfied.

Before you start sending checks in partial payments to all your creditors, realize that the debt is settled only if they accept a check that you sent in good faith to settle an unliquidated or disputed debt.

Applying the rule of UCC § 3-311 to settlements by check

The discussion of the UCC in this book is mostly confined to Article 1, Definitions and General Provisions, and Article 2, Sale of Goods. Article 3 governs negotiable instruments such as checks and includes a rule that governs an accord and satisfaction entered into by check. This provision will probably become less important as fewer and fewer transactions use checks, but it makes for a good review of the rules. The statute provides the following in part, as enacted in North Carolina at 25-3-311:

> § 25-3-311. Accord and satisfaction by use of instrument.
>
> (a) If a person against whom a claim is asserted proves that (i) that person in good faith tendered an instrument to the claimant as full satisfaction of the claim, (ii) the amount of the claim was unliquidated or subject to a bona fide dispute, and (iii) the claimant obtained payment of the instrument, the following subsections apply.

(b) Unless subsection (c) applies, the claim is discharged if the person against whom the claim is asserted proves that the instrument or an accompanying written communication contained a conspicuous statement to the effect that the instrument was tendered as full satisfaction of the claim.

(c) Subject to subsection (d), a claim is not discharged under subsection (b) if either of the following applies:

> (1) The claimant, if an organization, proves that (i) within a reasonable time before the tender, the claimant sent a conspicuous statement to the person against whom the claim is asserted that communications concerning disputed debts, including an instrument tendered as full satisfaction of a debt, are to be sent to a designated person, office, or place, and (ii) the instrument or accompanying communication was not received by that designated person, office, or place.

> (2) The claimant, whether or not an organization, proves that within 90 days after payment of the instrument, the claimant tendered repayment of the amount of the instrument to the person against whom the claim is asserted. This paragraph does not apply if the claimant is an organization that sent a statement complying with paragraph (1)(i).

(d) A claim is discharged if the person against whom the claim is asserted proves that within a reasonable time before collection of the instrument was initiated, the claimant, or an agent of the claimant having direct responsibility with respect to the disputed obligation, knew that the instrument was tendered in full satisfaction of the claim.

Subsections (a) and (b) lay out the common-law rules of offer, acceptance, and consideration. Subsection (c) provides two rules that give the creditor an escape from an accord it entered under subsections (a) and (b). And subsection (d) states a situation in which a party would not be allowed the escape under (c).

- ✔ Under subsection (a), this provision applies only when (1) the debtor sends a check, (2) the claim was unliquidated or subject to a good-faith dispute, and (3) the creditor accepted the offer by cashing the check.

- ✔ Under subsection (b), the accord is satisfied only if the debtor, on the check or in an accompanying communication, informs the creditor that the check was offered in full satisfaction of the debt.

✔ Subsection (c) gives the creditor two escape routes. First, the creditor may have informed the debtor that offers to enter into accords must be sent to a particular office. If the creditor did so and the debtor didn't comply, then the accord doesn't discharge the debt. Second, if the creditor doesn't have such an office, it can return the debtor's payment within 90 days of cashing the check to avoid the discharge of the debt.

✔ Subsection (d) removes the subsection (c) escape routes if the creditor knew that it was entering into an accord before receiving the check. In this case, the partial payment discharges the debt.

Doing away with consideration by statute or case law

Many authorities would like to see accord and satisfaction used even when consideration for the settlement is missing. For example, if I owe you $10,000, you may have perfectly good reasons to willingly discharge that debt in return for my payment of $8,000 even if I offered no consideration for the reduced amount. You may just want to cut your losses and be done with me, especially if you think that collecting from me would be difficult. Therefore, many jurisdictions, by statute or by case law, have established a mechanism for discharging even a liquidated and undisputed debt. In such a case, carefully follow the procedure established in your jurisdiction in order to effectively discharge the debt.

Chapter 13

Deciding Whether Unforeseen Events Excuse Performance

. . . .

In This Chapter

▶ Recognizing when unforeseen events excuse a seller's performance

▶ Excusing a buyer whose purpose was frustrated

▶ Anticipating the possible outcomes of excused performance

▶ Allocating risk with freedom of contract

. . . .

A party's failure to perform isn't breach if their nonperformance is excused. If performance is subject to an express condition that doesn't occur, then nonperformance is excused and doesn't constitute breach (see Chapter 14 for details). But even if a contract omits such a conditional clause, an unforeseen event that makes performance impossible or very difficult may excuse nonperformance if a court reads that condition into the contract.

This chapter explains how courts decide whether certain events excuse performance, how the courts are likely to resolve issues that result from excused performance, and how to draft clauses to allow and disallow excused performance.

Deciding Whether a Nonperforming Party Is in Breach

Centuries ago, performance-excusing events had to be enumerated in the contract: If an event wasn't in the contract, its occurrence didn't excuse nonperformance. Now the rule has flip-flopped, so contract law assumes that an unforeseen event excuses nonperformance unless the contract assigns the risk that the event will occur to one of the parties.

For example, most courts would agree that if a tornado wipes out the manufacturing plant of a seller who had promised widgets from that factory, the manufacturer would be excused from performance. The manufacturer may not be excused, however, if the contract stipulates something like "Manufacturer bears the risk if it is unable to perform because of tornado damage to its manufacturing facilities."

When an unforeseen event occurs and the risk is not allocated in the contract, a seller may claim that the event has made performance *impracticable* (impossible or unrealistic). To analyze a claim of impracticability, determine whether the following four conditions are met:

- ✔ The event occurred after the contract was made.
- ✔ Performance became impracticable because of the event.
- ✔ The nonoccurrence of the event was a basic assumption of the parties when they entered the contract.
- ✔ The party seeking to be discharged didn't carry the risk of the event's occurrence.

This section examines each of these factors in turn.

Did the event occur after contract formation?

First determine whether the unexpected event occurred before or after the parties formed the contract. If the unknown, adverse condition already existed at the time the parties made the contract, then the adversely affected party may have a choice. That party could claim that the parties acted on a *mistaken* belief that may *avoid the contract* (provide a defense to contract formation). (See Part II for more about the mistake defense.) Alternatively, that party could claim that the unexpected event discovered during performance discharges him because of existing impracticability.

The main difference between these claims is conceptual. If a court finds mistake, then the contract is voidable. If the court finds that performance was impracticable because of a fact that existed at the time of contract formation but which the adversely affected party had no reason to know about, then the parties have a contract, but the adversely affected party's duty to perform that contract never arose.

If the event occurred after the parties made the contract, then you're dealing only with contract performance rather than formation, and *supervening impracticability* comes into play.

Suppose a manufacturer agrees with the government to develop a superwidget that has capabilities not shared by existing widgets. The manufacturer is unable to achieve the technological breakthrough required to perform and claims relief from the contract. The manufacturer could claim relief either through mistake or impracticability:

- ✔ **Mistake defense:** The manufacturer claims that both parties shared a belief that was not in accord with the facts (that the breakthrough could be achieved), and this basic assumption on which the contract was made had a material effect on the exchange of performances. The case would come down to whether the adversely affected party, the contractor, bore the risk of that mistake.

- ✔ **Existing impracticability:** The contractor claims that his performance is impracticable because of a fact he had no reason to know (the breakthrough could be achieved only at tremendous expense) and the nonexistence of which was a basic assumption on which the contract was made. The case would come down to whether, under the circumstances, the contractor bore the risk of such facts.

The mistake defense may be easier to prove if the manufacturer can convince the court that the parties shared a mistaken belief about the facts and not just a mistaken prediction about the future. One problem with the impracticability alternative is that courts may not excuse nonperformance merely because performance turned out to be more expensive than anticipated. Obviously, the best solution would've been to address the possibility in the contract.

Did performance become impracticable?

The UCC uses the term *impracticability* to mean performance that's not necessarily impossible but considerably more difficult than anticipated. When the event occurs after the parties form a contract, the party claims that performance is considerably more difficult because of *supervening impracticability*. In these cases, the person adversely affected always admits contract formation but claims that his duty is discharged due to the occurrence of a certain event.

Determining how hard performance has to be to constitute impracticability is somewhat subjective. If performance is destined to drive a company into bankruptcy, that's probably enough to constitute impracticability. If a company's performance merely means it won't earn a profit from the exchange, that's probably insufficient reason to excuse its performance.

A problem courts often face arises when a party claims that it should be excused because an event dramatically increased the cost of its inputs. For example, if I promised you cotton goods from my factory at a certain price and a flood prevents my factory from operating, clearly I'm excused from nonperformance. But what if a flood in cotton-growing regions drives up the price of cotton? I'm still able to perform but at a dramatically higher price because it cost me more to buy the cotton I needed.

Official Comment 4 to UCC § 2-615, which deals with Excuse by Failure of Presupposed Conditions, provides an answer that involves considerable waffling:

> 4. Increased cost alone does not excuse performance unless the rise in cost is due to some unforeseen contingency which alters the essential nature of the performance. Neither is a rise or a collapse in the market in itself a justification, for that is exactly the type of business risk which business contracts made at fixed prices are intended to cover. But a severe shortage of raw materials or of supplies due to a contingency such as war, embargo, local crop failure, unforeseen shutdown of major sources of supply or the like, which either causes a marked increase in cost or altogether prevents the seller from securing supplies necessary to his performance, is within the contemplation of this section.

One way contract law limits the application of the doctrine is by asking not whether this party, in its financial situation, is able to perform, but whether any objective, reasonable party would be able to perform. If another party was able to perform under the same conditions, then performance wouldn't be excused.

For example, because a downturn in cattle prices prevents a feedlot from being able to get credit, the feedlot is unable to continue feeding cattle under the contract and claims that it's excused. Contract law would say that although this party was unable to perform, another party in its place would've been able to perform, and the feedlot's nonperformance is unexcused. On the other hand, if the feedlot was unable to perform because of a government quarantine, then it would be excused because any party in that situation would've been unable to perform.

Was nonoccurrence of the event a basic assumption?

When figuring out whether nonperformance is excused, the most difficult determination is whether nonoccurrence of an event is a basic assumption of the contract. Put yourself in the shoes of the parties at the time they formed the contract. They didn't address this situation in the contract, so contract law has to supply it for them. Ask whether the parties, when making the agreement, were likely to have thought that the event wouldn't occur. If the answer is yes, then nonoccurrence of the event was a basic assumption.

The kinds of events that qualify as basic assumptions and often excuse nonperformance are the sudden natural disasters that people often refer to as *acts of God* — flood, hurricane, tornado, earthquake, and so on. A government action such as an embargo or quarantine is also an excusing event.

In some cases, courts use the *foreseeability* test to determine whether nonoccurrence of an event was a basic assumption. Under this test, if the occurrence of an event isn't predictable, then the nonoccurrence of that event is a basic assumption of the contract. However, this isn't a very good test, because you can easily demonstrate that just about any event was predictable.

For example, I say, "Let's put it in the contract that I'm excused if a meteorite destroys my factory," and you say, "That'll never happen!" So we omit that clause from the contract and sign it. Five minutes later — Bam! — a meteorite hits my factory. The event was clearly predictable, because I said it might happen. Technically speaking, it was foreseeable, but any reasonable person probably wouldn't consider that a foreseeable event.

Because contract law is essentially trying to determine whether the law should imply that a certain event excuses nonperformance, contracts expert Allan Farnsworth suggests looking at the parties' situation when they entered the contract and asking whether this was a risk that reasonably would be assumed. To solve the meteorite problem under this test, ask whether reasonable parties at the time they entered the contract would've expected performance if a meteorite later hit the seller's factory. If the answer is no, then the nonoccurrence of that event was a basic assumption. Similarly, every farmer knows a drought is possible, but reasonable parties would intend that if a drought wipes out a farmer's crop, that farmer's nonperformance is excused.

Did the party seeking to be discharged carry the risk?

A frequent theme of contract law is the interplay of two rules:

- ✔ **What's reasonable:** This often supplies the default rule.

- ✔ **What the parties agree to:** The parties often have the freedom of contract to change the default rule.

The interplay of these two concepts is evident in the area of impracticability. Contract law can determine whether excusing a party's nonperformance because of a certain unanticipated event is reasonable. Freedom of contract enables the parties to override that default rule. For example, a party generally bears the risk of rising or falling markets. In other words, circumstances hold the party to bear the risk. However, parties may use language in the contract to protect themselves from certain risks (for details, see the later section "Using Freedom of Contract to Allocate Risk").

In a number of cases, a farmer has promised, say, 50,000 pounds of tomatoes to a buyer. An unanticipated event wipes out the farmer's crop, but the farmer isn't excused. Why not? Because the farmer promised 50,000 pounds of tomatoes and not 50,000 pounds of tomatoes *from his farm*. Under this interpretation, the farmer is still liable for performance and will be in breach if he doesn't obtain the tomatoes elsewhere. He should've put in the contract that the tomatoes were to come from his farm. Similarly, if a seller relies on a certain source of supply and that source of supply becomes unavailable, whether the seller is excused depends on whether his getting the goods from that source was a basic assumption of the contract. To make it clear, he should put language to that effect in the contract.

Determining Whether a Buyer's Purpose Was Frustrated

A seller may claim impracticability if he can satisfy all the elements: That is, after contract formation, an unforeseen event made the seller's performance impossible or unrealistic, nonoccurrence of the event was a basic assumption of the contract, and the seller didn't carry the risk of that event. A buyer's obligation, however, is usually to pay money. Lack of money is not an excuse for nonperformance, because that's a subjective factor. A buyer may, however, be able to claim excuse because of frustration of purpose.

The elements of *frustration* are the same as the elements of impracticability, except that the party seeking to be discharged from the contractual obligations must prove that a certain event *frustrated the principal purpose of the contract.* In the case of frustration, the party is able to perform, but the performance no longer holds any value for him.

For example, in 1919, a tenant leases space from a landlord, intending to use the space as a drinking establishment. Immediately afterward, the government enacts Prohibition, banning the sale of alcohol. An event has occurred, and its nonoccurrence was a basic assumption of the contract. The principal purpose of the contract has been frustrated because of the event, which clearly had a material effect on the transaction. The duty of the tenant would be discharged unless he bore the risk under the language of the contract or under the circumstances. The case would likely turn on whether a reasonable party under the same circumstances would've known that Prohibition was likely.

Frustration comes in handy to get a buyer off the hook when certain events undermine the buyer's ability to reap the expected benefits of the exchange. Claiming impracticability is rarely an option, because buyers can't claim that their nonperformance is excused by something like a natural disaster. After all, the buyer's main obligation is to pay money — an act that's easy to perform even when serious events occur. In addition, subsequent events often place the buyer at a disadvantage in the contract, and contract law doesn't want to provide the buyer with an easy exit just because she made a bad deal.

For a buyer, frustration is a better claim than impracticability, but the buyer has to come up with a better claim than saying, "My principal purpose was to make money, and because I am no longer going to make money under this contract, the purpose of it has been frustrated."

Many modern cases arise because of changing government regulations. For example, if a particular crop is limited, such as through a quota of fish that can be caught, then a person may buy a share of that quota. If the quota is then lifted, the person's purpose in obtaining that right has been frustrated by an event. As a result, his performance is excused.

The case of *Krell v. Henry* stands out as a clear case of frustration. The setting was London in 1902, and Queen Victoria's reign had finally ended with her death. Like Prince Charles today, Prince Edward had been sitting around forever singing "Oh I Just Can't Wait to be King," and finally he was going to have his chance. A magnificent coronation parade was planned through London, and the route just happened to pass by Krell's house, which afforded a great view of the procession. He advertised that his house was available for rental on June 26 and 27, the days of the coronation parade. Henry saw the sign and struck a deal to rent it on those days for £75.

Then disaster struck. Edward was stricken with appendicitis and the parade was canceled. Henry expected to be released from the contract, but Krell refused. He said in effect, "The house did not burn down. Nothing is stopping you from renting it on June 26 and 27. Have a nice time!" Henry's response, of course, was that although the contract could be performed, its principal purpose had been frustrated, so performance no longer held any value to him. The court agreed, and the modern view of frustration was born.

Figuring Out What Happens When a Party's Performance Is Excused

When impracticability or frustration excuses a party's performance, the party is not in breach, so no damages are payable. But when a party suffers a loss as a result of the nonperformance, that party may ask a court to make some financial allocation. The law's views on this have changed over time.

For example, in *Krell v. Henry* (refer to the preceding section), Henry had already made a down payment when his performance was excused, and he didn't get it back. This was standard practice established by other coronation cases. The English courts decided in these cases to leave the parties where they would've been under the contract at the moment the event occurred — if the renter had made a down payment before the event occurred, he wouldn't get it back, and if he was scheduled to make a payment before the event occurred, he'd have to pay it.

This result seems arbitrary, and its only advantage is that the rule is easy to apply. Modern contract law has other, more-logical and messier approaches, as I explain in this section.

Using our old friends reliance and restitution

Restatement § 272 says that courts may use principles of restitution and reliance to allocate the resulting losses when performance is excused. This solution is fairer than leaving the parties where they are, but it's fuzzy.

For example, in *Krell v. Henry,* a modern American court would undoubtedly award Henry restitution of his down payment and wouldn't require further scheduled payments to be made. This solution makes a great deal of sense because the coronation parade will be rescheduled and Krell will have another opportunity to rent out the house. He'd be unjustly enriched if he were able to collect two rentals.

Courts have awarded reliance to a party who reasonably prepared for performance before the event occurred, as when a contractor has spent money for plans to work on a building and the builder's performance is excused because of impracticability when the building burns down. Allocating the loss between the parties seems fair.

Don't call such an allocation of losses *damages*. Damages are payments for breach of contract. When a party's performance is excused, the party hasn't breached.

Allocating the loss when a performance is partially excused

When a party's performance is excused but he still has some production available to supply under two or more contracts, contract law needs a rule for allocating the available supply among buyers. UCC § 2-615(b) provides the rule, stating that "he may so allocate in any manner which is fair and reasonable."

For example, a farmer was expecting to produce 200,000 pounds of cotton on his farm and agreed to sell 100,000 pounds from his farm to each of two buyers. An unanticipated event limited his cotton harvest to 80,000 pounds. The event excused his performance, so he's not in breach, but under UCC § 2-615(b), he's obligated to allocate his cotton crop in a fair and reasonable manner. This doesn't necessarily mean that he has to offer 40,000 pounds to each buyer. One buyer may be a more established customer or have greater need.

Because a natural disaster often drives up the prices of goods by making them scarcer, the farmer may be able to get contracts to sell the cotton at prices higher than his original customers were bound to pay. Because the farmer must act in good faith, however, he probably should not favor those prospective customers over his regular customers.

On the other hand, the buyers are under no obligation to accept less than they bargained for. Under the mechanism of UCC § 2-616, the seller must notify the buyer of the allocation. If the buyer affirmatively agrees, then the contract is modified to the allocated quantity. But if the buyer wants, she may terminate the contract, and if she doesn't respond to the seller's notice, her silence will be interpreted as terminating the contract.

A peculiar ruling: *ALCOA v. Essex*

In the case of *ALCOA v. Essex*, ALCOA promised to covert ore into aluminum from 1967 to 1983. Knowing that conditions would change over the years during this long-term contract, ALCOA consulted an expert, the noted economist Alan Greenspan, to develop a formula for how much it should charge each year. The resulting formula provided that the price ALCOA charged would increase each year by the percentage the Wholesale Price Index (WPI) rose each year. That worked fine until 1973, when the OPEC oil embargo drove up the price of oil, which is a key factor in the price of electricity, which is a major input in aluminum production. When the cost of electricity rose faster than the WPI, ALCOA was stuck with a formula for the price of its services that didn't cover its expenses. ALCOA calculated that it would lose $75 million over the remaining term of the contract. It sought to have its duty to perform the contract excused under mistake, frustration, or impracticability.

ALCOA won in the trial court on all three grounds. The court found that the parties shared a mistaken belief at the time they entered the contract that the formula would accurately predict the cost of production, and this turned out not to be true. Therefore, the contract was voidable by ALCOA. (I don't agree with that analysis, because I would've found that ALCOA had asked for the formula and therefore assumed the risk of its not working out.)

The court also found impracticability and frustration. This situation is one of those cases where a party was able to perform but claimed it suffered hardship because of the additional cost of its inputs. The court was persuaded that although increased cost doesn't generally excuse performance, this was a dramatic increase. The *ALCOA* case is one of only a few cases where a seller was excused because of the increased cost of its inputs.

Similarly, ALCOA claimed that its principal purpose in entering the contract was to make money and that this purpose was frustrated by the unanticipated event. The court agreed, even though loss of money has generally been held not to excuse nonperformance. (Again, I don't agree with that analysis, because I would've found that ALCOA had assumed the risk of higher costs.)

Furthermore, having held that the parties had no contract because of mistake and that nonperformance was excused because of impracticability and frustration, the court then decided that the remedy was to continue the contract with a revised price formula that was more favorable to ALCOA. Although parties frequently negotiate such solutions for themselves, rarely does a court come up with a remedy that's so at odds with traditional contract law.

A trial court decided ALCOA v. Essex, and the parties settled before an appellate court could reach its decision, so this case probably has little precedential value, but it is interesting as an outlier case that's inconsistent with most of the law in this area.

Using Freedom of Contract to Allocate Risk

Instead of letting a court decide after the fact whether a particular event excuses nonperformance, parties can use their freedom of contract to add a clause to the contract that enumerates the events that excuse nonperformance. Such a provision is often called a *force majeure* ("greater force") clause. Although parties often incorporate an off-the-rack force majeure clause in the boilerplate provisions of their contract, you're better off drafting a provision that addresses the particular needs of the parties, as I explain next.

Drafting a "force majeure" clause to identify events excusing nonperformance

A force majeure clause usually identifies the events that excuse nonperformance. One approach is to just state the default rule:

> Seller's performance is discharged if seller is unable to perform in whole or substantial part because of events beyond its control.

Unfortunately, such a clause offers no more protection than if the clause were omitted. To draft a solid force majeure clause, include the following elements:

- ✔ **A list enumerating the most common events that excuse performance:** This list may include natural disasters, such as fire, flood, hurricane, and tornado.

- ✔ **Language stating that the events listed "include but are not limited to" those most common events:** If you merely enumerate the events, you leave the seller vulnerable to the rule of *expressio unius est exclusio alterius* ("expression of one excludes the other"), as I discuss in Chapter 11. The fact that the parties listed other events but omitted "meteorite" indicates that they didn't intend a meteorite strike to be an excusing event. By adding "include but not limited to," you cover other types of natural disasters, including meteorite strikes.

- ✔ **Language stating "whether the event is of the same class as the enumerated events or not":** Including all natural disasters is better, but it doesn't protect the seller if his workers go on strike. If such an event occurred, the buyer could invoke another rule: *ejusdem generis,* which means that the excusing events are "of the same kind" as the enumerated items, and a strike is not the same as a natural disaster. Adding language that includes excusing events that are not in the same class as the enumerated events protects against this rule.

- ✔ **A price escalator to protect against changes in input costs:** A price escalator allows the seller to pass on the higher costs of its inputs to the buyer.

Here's an example of a solid force majeure clause that incorporates the first three elements:

> Seller's performance is discharged if seller is unable to perform in whole or substantial part because of events beyond its control, including but not limited to fire, flood, hurricane, or tornado, whether the event is of the same class as the enumerated events or not.

And here's a portion of a price-escalator clause that allows the parties to adjust the terms if hardship results from the initial terms — for example, if the price of an input increases:

> If a new situation beyond the reasonable control of either party arises during the term of this agreement, and if that situation results in a severe hardship to one party without an advantage to the other party, then the parties shall promptly consult to seek a mutually acceptable agreement that deals with the situation.

No excuses: Drafting a "hell or high water" clause

In theory, the parties could draft around the default rule and put in the contract a clause stating that performance is not excused even if unanticipated events arise. In the Texas oil business, these are known as *hell or high water clauses* because, as the expression goes, you have to perform come hell or high water. If an athlete or entertainer has a lot of bargaining power, she can get a term in the contract that provides that in addition to her nonperformance being excused if she is unable to perform (for example, because of an injury), she still gets paid in the event of that injury.

Chapter 14

Checking for Conditional Language

. . . .

In This Chapter

▶ Grasping the basics of conditions

▶ Recognizing express and implied conditions

▶ Deciding who performs first and why it matters

▶ Gauging substantial performance

▶ Getting out of a condition

. . . .

Almost all contracts contain at least one condition — an implied condition that goes something like this: "If you don't perform, I don't have to perform, either." Parties are free to add express conditions to their contracts as well, such as "If payment in full is not received within 30 days of the billing date, finance charges may begin to accrue at the maximum rate allowable by law."

Parties generally use conditions to encourage performance by the other party or to protect themselves when their ability to perform hinges on unpredictable future events, such as qualifying for a mortgage loan to purchase a home. Parties may also try to use conditions to excuse their performance by saying that their performance was conditional on the occurrence of a certain event that never happened.

This chapter brings you up to speed on what conditions are (and aren't). It then explains how to use conditions to give your client more leverage in getting the other party to perform a contract and how to use conditions to give your client an escape hatch from the contract.

Defining Condition in Legal Terms

The Restatement defines *condition* as "an event, not certain to occur, which must occur, unless its non-occurrence is excused, before performance under a contract becomes due." This definition is pretty clear, but sometimes people confuse conditions with promises. To further muddy the waters, conditions may be *express* or *implied.* This section helps clarify these important distinctions.

When people refer to the "Terms and Conditions" that govern a contract, they're usually referring to only the terms of the contract. Saying the "Terms" that govern the contract is more precise because terms may be promises or conditions.

Telling the difference between a promise and a condition

A term in a contract may be a promise, a condition, or both:

- ✔ **Condition:** An event that must occur but isn't certain to occur before some performance is due

- ✔ **Promise:** A commitment to do or refrain from doing something

- ✔ **Both (sometimes called a *promissory condition*):** A commitment to do something that's also an event that must occur before the other party's performance is due

Suppose I agree to sell my Ted Williams autographed baseball to you for $400 if the Red Sox win this year's World Series, and you agree to pay 30 days after I give you the ball. This example contains all three types of terms:

- ✔ **Condition:** One condition is the Red Sox's winning the World Series. Neither party has promised to make this happen. It's an event that has to occur, but isn't certain to occur, before our performances are due.

- ✔ **Promise:** You promise to pay me $400. You have a commitment to do this. However, your payment isn't an event that has to occur before my performance is due, because I'll already have performed.

- ✔ **Both:** My promise to give you the baseball is a promissory condition. It's a promise because I have a commitment to do it, and it's a condition because it's an event that has to occur before your performance of paying me the $400 is due.

These distinctions have practical implications. Breach of promise gives the non-breaching party only the right to seek damages, whereas breach of a promissory condition excuses the non-breaching party's performance (because it's conditional) *and* gives her the right to sue for damages (due to the breach).

Suppose I agree to sell you the baseball and you agree to pay me $400 for it (no 30 days to pay, no winning the World Series condition). If I refuse to deliver the baseball, you can refuse to pay me (not perform), buy one elsewhere for more money, and sue me for the extra money it cost you. Likewise, if you refuse to pay me the $400, I can refuse to give you the baseball (not perform), sell the baseball to someone else for less, and sue you for the difference.

Making your client's performance conditional can be powerful leverage to secure performance from the other party. If your client extends credit, she gives up that leverage.

Notice that if I agree that you can pay me $400 in 30 days in exchange for the baseball instead of paying on delivery, I give up one of these rights: If you don't pay, I can still sue you, but I can't refuse to give you the baseball (not perform), because I've already performed. By extending credit, I didn't make my performance conditional on your performance.

You may encounter vocabulary describing the promises as *dependent* or *independent.* Here's the difference:

  ✔ A *dependent promise* is conditional on the occurrence of some event, usually the performance of another promise.

  ✔ An *independent promise* is unconditional — no event that has to occur before the promise must be performed.

For example, in a separation agreement, a husband promises to pay $100 per week child support, and the wife promises to give him weekend visitation with the kids. One week, he doesn't pay. The wife retaliates by saying he can't have visitation with the kids. She's treating the promises as *dependent* and claiming that because he didn't perform his promise, she doesn't have to perform hers. But as a matter of policy, courts say that these promises are *independent* — she has to perform even though he hasn't performed. Note that she still has a remedy — she can recover damages for breach of contract.

Determining whether a condition is express or implied

Conditions are either express or implied:

- **Express conditions:** Express conditions are those that the parties include in their contract by stating that some performance is conditional upon the occurrence of one or more events. An express condition is easy to detect. Look for words like *if* or *it is a condition precedent that.* For more about express conditions, see the next section.

- **Implied conditions:** Implied conditions are found by a court. Under the rule of *constructive conditions of exchange,* courts generally find that each party's performance is impliedly conditional on the other party's performance. To discover how courts find implied conditions, skip ahead to "Determining Whether Courts Will Find an Implied Condition."

For example, assume that I say, "I'll sell you my Ted Williams baseball for $400 if the Red Sox win the World Series this year," and you agree to the deal. Our contract has both types of conditions:

- The express condition is that I'll sell you the ball only if the Red Sox win the World Series. This condition is directly stated in our contract.

- The implied condition is each of our performances. I'm obligated to perform if you perform, and you're obligated to perform if I perform. These conditions aren't stated in the contract; they're implied.

Tapping the Power of Express Conditions

Express conditions are valuable in protecting a party from unforeseen circumstances that may prevent her performance. Homebuyers often use express conditions when presenting a purchase offer to a seller; they may make the offer on the condition that they're able to sell their own house by a certain date or that they're able to secure a mortgage loan. If the specified event doesn't happen, the buyer doesn't have to perform and isn't in breach for nonperformance.

If a party has some control over the occurrence of the conditional event, he has a good-faith duty to see that it occurs and not to prevent its occurrence.

For example, a homebuyer can't agree to a purchase conditional upon securing a mortgage loan and then do nothing to secure that loan — the courts won't allow it. The buyer may say, "How can I be in breach? My offer was conditional upon securing the loan, and that didn't happen." But because the occurrence of the condition was within the buyers' control, a court will read in an implied promise based on the obligation of good faith, as I discuss in Chapter 10. If the buyer had put a good faith effort into securing a mortgage loan and failed to accomplish that task, then the court would probably excuse the buyer's performance.

Determining Whether Courts Will Find an Implied Condition

If the parties haven't made performances expressly conditional, then a court has to determine whether the contract contains implied conditions. The biggie here is that each party's obligation to perform is impliedly conditional on the other party's performance.

To understand how and why this rule came into being, suppose I agree to sell you the baseball and you agree to pay me $400 for it. Before I give you the baseball, you say to me, "Ha-ha! I'm not going to give you the $400." I say, "Then I'm not going to give you the baseball." You say, "I don't see that in the contract. The contract says that you promised me the baseball. It doesn't contain an express condition saying that if I don't pay you the $400, then you don't have to give me the baseball."

You would've been right until about 1775, but fortunately after that the law changed to recognize the implied conditions that are called *constructive conditions of exchange*. Under this sensible rule, if one party refuses to perform, then the other party is excused from performance. I win the argument because the condition is implied as a matter of practicality. And because our promises are conditions as well, then if one party doesn't perform, the other party has two remedies:

- ✔ Refuse to perform because an implied condition to the other party's performance didn't occur.
- ✔ Recover damages for breach of promise.

Sorting Out Conditions Precedent, Concurrent, and Subsequent

The Restatement doesn't differentiate between classes of conditions, but the rules of Civil Procedure and some commentators muck things up by categorizing conditions into three types:

- ✔ **Condition precedent:** A condition precedent is an event that must occur before some promise has to be performed. For example, I agree that I will sell you my baseball if the Red Sox win the World Series. This event must occur before the promise has to be performed.

- ✔ **Condition concurrent:** A condition concurrent is an event that must occur at the same time as a promise has to be performed, such as when I promise to sell you the baseball and you promise to pay me $400 for it. Each party's performance is conditional on the other party's performance, and the performances must occur at the same time.

- ✔ **Condition subsequent:** A condition subsequent is an event that discharges a duty to perform a promise. Conditions subsequent arise when a person has a duty but an event that *discharges* that duty (excuses the person from performing it) occurs. Conditions subsequent arise most frequently in insurance contracts. Suppose an insurer has the duty to pay for losses you suffer in a fire. The duty to pay arises in the event of a fire, but the policy may also say that the insurer's duty is discharged if the insured doesn't give notice of the loss within 30 days from the date of the loss. If the event (failure to give notice within 30 days) occurs, it extinguishes the insurer's duty. That event is a condition subsequent.

The distinction between conditions precedent and conditions subsequent makes some difference in civil procedure, because a plaintiff has the burden of proving a condition precedent, whereas the defendant has the burden of proving a condition subsequent. For purposes of contract law, however, these distinctions aren't important. In the insurance example, whether the contract stipulates a condition precedent ("It is a condition precedent to the insurer's duty to pay that the insured give notice within 30 days of the loss") or a condition subsequent ("The insurer's duty to pay terminates if the insured does not give notice of the loss within 30 days"), the provision has the same effect — the insured will not be able to recover if he doesn't give notice within 30 days of the loss. For this reason, contract law simply calls both a *condition*.

When pleading conditions in the documents supplied to a court, both parties are obligated to state the conditions they think did or didn't occur, but the obligation is different depending on whether you're a plaintiff or a defendant. Rule 9(c) of the Federal Rules of Civil Procedure states the following:

> (c) Conditions Precedent.
>
> In pleading conditions precedent, it suffices to allege generally that all conditions precedent have occurred or been performed. But when denying that a condition precedent has occurred or been performed, a party must do so with particularity.

According to this rule, which most states use as well, the plaintiff must generally plead that all conditions have been satisfied, whereas the defendant must point out the specific conditions that haven't been satisfied and thus excuse its performance. This rule makes practical sense, because the plaintiff needs to know which conditions the other party is claiming excuse its performance.

Suppose we've agreed that I'll sell you my Ted Williams baseball for $400 if the Red Sox win the World Series. If I sue you for breach, I have to put in my pleading that "all conditions have been satisfied," because the events that conditioned your performance had to occur before your performance was due. On the other hand, you have to inform me what your defense is going to be by alleging with particularity which conditions you're claiming did not occur — either "The Red Sox didn't win the World Series" or "Burnham didn't offer to give me the baseball" or both.

Avoid using the phrase "breach of condition." If a condition is an *event,* then it can't be breached — it either occurs or it doesn't. Instead, say that a condition has been *satisfied* or *not satisfied.* If the person had a duty to bring about the event that had to occur before performance was due, then say, even though it's a mouthful, that there's "breach of the promise to bring about the condition" when that's the case.

Deciding Who Must Go First

Conditions create a lot of leverage, giving a party two ways to convince the nonperforming party to perform: (1) threaten to withhold performance and (2) threaten to sue for damages. However, the non-breaching party loses its leverage if it has already performed, so the party who performs first is at a disadvantage. This section explains how courts decide who has to perform first.

Checking out the default order of performance

By default, contract law says that both parties must perform at the same time, which gives each party leverage to ensure that the other party performs. Ideally, when I sell you the baseball, I hand it to you as you hand me the $400.

Exceptions arise when circumstances prevent the parties from exchanging performances at the same time or when parties contract around the default rule. The main circumstance that prevents the performances from being due at the same time is that one performance, such as a service, may take time to perform, whereas the performance of payment can be done instantly. In these cases, the rule is that the performance that takes time must go first. This is bad news for parties providing services, because they must perform before they're paid; however, they can work around this rule, as I explain next.

Making agreements about the order of performance

The party who performs first is at a distinct disadvantage, so if your client happens to be the party who has to go first, look for some way to reduce the risk. Because contractors have to build the building (the performance that takes time) before they get paid (the performance that can be done instantly), contractors traditionally find ways to contract around this rule. Contractors may have the benefit of statutory lien laws that give them a claim to the property they constructed to recover payment. In addition, contractors often require "progress payments" — payments tied to certain milestones. Similarly, because lawyers have to perform first, they often require clients to pay a *retainer* — an upfront payment so the lawyers don't have to worry about getting paid after performing a service.

Extending credit increases the creditors' exposure to risk, because they give up the right to make their performance conditional upon payment. For example, suppose I agree to sell you the baseball for $400 payable in 30 days. I have to give you the baseball now. If in 30 days, you don't pay me, my only remedy is to sue for breach of promise to recover the $400 you owe me, but I don't get the ball back. By extending credit, I relinquish my right to make my performance conditional on your performance.

When your client extends credit for the sale of goods, be sure that the contract contains language stating that your client has the right to repossess the goods if the other party fails to perform. If you omit that language, your client has no claim to the goods, only to the payment. The main remedy for breach of contract is the non-breaching party's right to the *expectancy* — what they would've had if the contract had been performed (see Chapter 16 for details). When I sell my baseball for $400 with 30 days to pay and you don't pay, I can claim only the $400, not the baseball. However, I can contract around this through the *law of secured transactions,* which allows the creditor to provide that if the other party doesn't perform, the creditor can repossess the property.

Determining Whether a Party Has Substantially Performed

According to the rule of constructive conditions of exchange, if one party doesn't perform at all, then the other party's entire performance is excused. That's easy. What's tough is determining whether performance of one party *in part* excuses the other party's performance. This is one of the toughest questions in contract law, and it's one your clients will frequently ask. Contract law says that if a party commits a *material breach,* then the other party's performance is excused. But if the breach is *immaterial,* then the other party must still perform.

For example, your client calls and says, "My contractor was supposed to build my swimming pool to a depth of 9 feet, but he built it only 8½ feet deep. I don't have to pay him, right?" Your client may not realize it, but he's claiming benefit of the rule of conditions — he thinks that because the other party didn't perform as specified in the contract, then he doesn't have to perform, either. But if that were the rule, then people wouldn't have to pay if they got anything less than perfect performance. The law doesn't want that to happen because it would result in a lot of people getting a lot of stuff without having to pay for it.

To prevent a party from refusing to perform because of a minor breach by the other party, contract law created the rule of *substantial performance.* This rule says essentially that if a breach is *immaterial,* then the party has substantially performed, and we'll pretend that performance was sufficient to satisfy the implied condition that one party has to perform before the other party's performance is due.

If you explained this to your client, he'd probably get impatient and ask, "So do I have to pay him for the swimming pool or not?" Your client, of course, doesn't want to wait for an appellate court to tell him whether the contractor has substantially performed — he wants to know now, from you. This section explains various ways to make this determination.

Considering how the type of breach affects the outcome

Whether a breach is material or immaterial matters because it determines how a dispute is resolved:

- ✔ **Immaterial breach:** An immaterial breach entitles the non-breaching party to recover damages but doesn't excuse that party's performance. For example, if a court found that the contractor had substantially performed the contract to build the swimming pool (committed an immaterial breach), then the owner would have to pay for the pool but could recover damages for the breach.

- ✔ **Material breach:** A material breach means that the breaching party didn't substantially perform. Not only can the other party recover damages, but their own performance is also excused. For example, if a court found that the contractor had not substantially performed, then the owner wouldn't have to pay for the pool under the contract. If that sounds like a harsh outcome for the contractor, contract law agrees with you and has some ways to reduce the harsh effects of conditions. To find out more about these methods, keep reading.

Running tests to find substantial performance

If I could predict when a court was going to find substantial performance, I'd be a millionaire. Contract law has no reliable test, because each situation is so different, but this section explains a few tests you can run to make an educated guess.

The mathematical test

Courts often start their discussions of substantial performance by saying that no mathematical formula is available. Technically, that's true, but dismissing the math option entirely is baloney. A mathematical test is often a good place to start. To perform the mathematical test, look at the amount of performance as a percentage. If the performance is close to 100 percent, it probably constitutes substantial performance. If a contractor completes 90 percent of the work, that's probably substantial, whereas 40 percent is not.

However, the math test isn't very useful in gauging quality and other subjective factors. If a telescope lens has to be ground to precision and the manufacturer claims, "I only missed by a thousandth of an inch!," that's not close enough if it prevents the telescope from working. Likewise, if an asphalt roof is supposed to be a certain uniform color but it comes out multicolored and streaky, calculating what part of the contract was performed is difficult.

The Cardozo test: Purpose served

In the famous case of *Jacob & Youngs v. Kent,* Judge Cardozo said to look at "the purpose to be served, the desire to be gratified, the excuse for deviation from the letter, the cruelty of enforced adherence." That's an elegant mouthful, but it makes sense. The "purpose served" looks at whether what the party received serves the essential purpose of what was promised.

For example, if you're an ordinary swimmer, whether your pool is 9 feet deep or 8½ feet deep would probably make little difference in the functioning of the pool — its "purpose to be served." In addition, "the cruelty of enforced adherence" — saying that the owners don't have to pay for it — would give the homeowners a windfall at the contractor's expense. As a result, a court would likely find substantial performance.

In the case of the streaky asphalt roof, even though the roof serves its purpose of keeping rain out of the house, the homeowner's "desire to be gratified," which probably meant getting a roof that was aesthetically pleasing, was not met. As a result, a court would likely find no substantial performance.

If what the party received serves the essential purpose of what was promised but isn't quite what was promised, the party not in breach is entitled to damages to make it right.

The Restatement test

Restatement § 141 looks at a number of factors, similar to the Cardozo test, and it is similarly difficult to apply. These factors include the following:

- The extent to which the injured party is deprived of the promised benefit
- The extent to which the injured party can be adequately compensated by damages
- The extent to which the breaching party will suffer a *forfeiture* (an out-of-pocket loss)
- The likelihood that the breaching party will cure his failure
- The extent to which the breaching party failed to act in good faith

The Get Smart test

On the popular '60s TV show *Get Smart,* Agent 86 often explained that he only "missed it by *that* much," holding up his thumb and forefinger to show just how close he was. Maybe if a party misses only by *that* much, the breach should be regarded as immaterial. I admit that this isn't a very helpful legal test, but it's hard to come up with a test!

Deciding whether a breach with respect to time is material

Parties often breach by failing to perform on time. The general rule is that stating a time for performance creates only a promise to perform at that time and doesn't create an express condition. The Restatement defines *condition* as an event that's "not certain to occur," and the passage of time *is* certain to occur. If we agree that I'll sell you a baseball for $400 on November 1, then the arrival of November 1 is not a condition to my performance; a promise to perform at a certain time is only a promise. If I deliver late, you can recover damages for my late delivery, but you still have to perform.

The parties are free to make performance on time an express condition. To do so, spell out the condition in the contract; for example, "If the baseball is not delivered by November 1, then the buyer does not have to accept it."

Don't use the stock phrase "Time is of the essence" to indicate that time is material, because many courts see this as a shopworn phrase that has lost its legal significance. Spell out the condition.

A court may determine that the circumstances make performance on time an implied condition. If I promised to tender the baseball on November 1 and still haven't delivered it a couple of months later, that's probably a material breach. Furthermore, circumstances may make even a short delay in performance material.

If you own a bar, I promise ten kegs of green beer on March 16, and I deliver it on the 18th, you can treat my nonperformance as though delivery on the 16th were a condition. The circumstances made the delivery date material, because a reasonable person in my shoes should've known that because March 17 is St. Patrick's Day, timely delivery was important in this case.

Solving the problem by drafting express conditions

There's no such thing as substantial performance of an express condition. Express conditions require strict performance, because a condition is an event — it's either satisfied or not. The Red Sox will either win the World Series or they won't — missing it by *that much* is irrelevant.

Because there's no such thing as substantial performance of an express condition, one way around the problem of having a person get away with substantial performance is to put an express condition in the contract. If having a pool with a depth of 9 feet is important to you, then put in the contract, "If the pool is not nine (9) feet deep, then the owner does not have to pay for it."

The courts have ways of getting around even express conditions, as I explain in the later section "Excusing Conditions," but they can't use substantial performance to do so.

Looking at Conditions in the UCC

The rules in UCC Article 2 are in practice very similar to the common-law rules. The UCC contains an express rule of constructive conditions of exchange. The default rule is that the performances are due simultaneously, so the obligation to pay is conditioned on tender of the goods, and the tender of the goods is conditioned on payment. Of course, frequently the buyer and the seller are at some distance from each other, and unless the seller arranges for delivery to be C.O.D. (Cash on Delivery), someone is going to have to go first — usually the buyer. As a result, the buyer takes on more risk.

As in common law, parties are free to contract around these rules and customs or use third-party payment services, such as PayPal, to reduce risk. Parties may also limit their exposure to risk by using an escrow service, which is common in international business transactions. With an *escrow service,* a third party such as a bank holds the buyer's funds and releases them to the seller only after the seller has performed.

Although the rules in UCC Article 2 are similar to common-law rules that apply to conditions, note the two important exceptions I explain next.

Rule § 2-601: Making a "perfect tender"

UCC Article 2 doesn't appear to have the rule of substantial performance, so if the seller fails in any respect to fully perform, the buyer seems to be excused from performance and pretty much call the shots. Section 2-601, as codified in North Carolina at 25-2-601, provides:

> Buyer's rights on improper delivery.
>
> Subject to the provisions of this Article on breach in installment contracts (G.S. 25-2-612) and unless otherwise agreed under the sections on contractual limitations of remedy (G.S. 25-2-718 and 25-2-719), if the goods or the tender of delivery fail in any respect to conform to the contract, the buyer may
>
> > (a) reject the whole; or
> >
> > (b) accept the whole; or
> >
> > (c) accept any commercial unit or units and reject the rest.

This rule is known as the *perfect tender rule* because it appears to say that the slightest defect in goods or delivery (even a few minutes late) excuses the buyer's performance. If read that way, sellers couldn't claim substantial performance, because only perfect tender would create a condition to the buyer's obligation to accept and pay for the goods.

Fortunately, few courts have enforced the rule as written. They avoid abuse by using principles such as good faith (being honest and reasonable, as I explain in Chapter 10). For example, if a buyer receives goods a day late but suffers no loss because of the delay and rejects them only because the contract price is higher than the market price, courts are likely to find that the rejection was not in good faith — the buyer didn't reject them because they were late.

Because of the many exceptions found by courts, you're probably safe to read the perfect tender rule as requiring the buyer to accept the goods — but allowing him to recover damages — in the event of the seller's substantial performance.

Rule § 2-612: Dealing with installment contracts

The UCC rule on installment contracts is useful for understanding how the Code expects parties to behave. The default rule under the Code is that the seller must deliver the goods in a single shipment. But the parties are free to contract around that rule by agreeing to an installment contract. According to UCC § 2-612(1), an *installment contract* is "one which requires or authorizes the delivery of goods in separate lots to be separately accepted."

A problem may arise when the parties agree to an installment contract and the seller materially breaches with respect to one of those installments. Depending on the situation, a buyer may become so annoyed with the seller that she not only rejects the installment but also cancels the rest of the contract, saying that she didn't want the other installments.

Not so fast, says the Code. Although the buyer can clearly reject an installment under § 2-601 when the seller materially breaches its obligations with respect to that installment, the buyer can't necessarily cancel the rest of the contract. The buyer must first determine whether the breach with respect to one installment "substantially impairs the value of the whole contract," in the words of § 2-612(3). If the seller is in breach with respect to one installment, the Code wants the parties to try to work it out rather than end their relationship immediately.

But how can the buyer determine whether the seller will perform in the future after a breach in delivering one installment? One technique the buyer can use is to demand assurances from the seller, as I discuss in Chapter 15. A party who received a nonconforming delivery may reasonably feel insecure about subsequent deliveries. If the concerned party makes a demand for adequate assurances and doesn't get them, then she can regard the contract as canceled.

For example, if a seller of chicken has promised to deliver broilers (young chickens) in installments and the first installment is stewing chicken (older chickens), the buyer can't necessarily cancel the contract. But the buyer can reject that installment and deliver a letter to the seller demanding assurances that the seller will deliver broilers in the remaining installments. If the seller demonstrates an ability to deliver broilers, the contract is back on track. If the seller says in effect, "You'll get what you get," then the buyer can probably cancel the contract.

Excusing Conditions

Certain conditions, express or implied, may cause hardship. For example, if a contractor builds 80 percent of a house and a court finds that the contractor didn't perform substantially, then the owner doesn't have to pay for the house. Obviously, such a ruling would cause the builder extreme hardship and give the homeowner an unfair windfall. To avoid the "cruelty of enforced adherence" of certain conditions, express or implied, the courts have several methods to provide relief: interpretation, restitution, divisible contract, waiver, and excuse of condition. This section explains these methods so you know what to expect and can put them to use in representing your clients.

Finding promise: Interpreting your way out of a condition

If an express condition causes hardship, courts frequently declare that the language allegedly creating the condition is ambiguous and interpret it as a promise rather than a condition. That way, the non-breaching party must still perform and can claim only damages resulting from the breach.

For example, suppose a contractor contracts with an owner to do some work. The contractor then contracts with a subcontractor to do a portion of the work. The contract between the contractor and the subcontractor provides, "Contractor will pay subcontractor when owner pays contractor." That sounds reasonable, but what happens if the owner doesn't pay the contractor? The contractor may tell the subcontractor, "I don't have to pay you because your payment is conditional on my receiving payment, and that didn't happen." This would create a hardship for the subcontractor, who wouldn't get paid for his work.

A court is likely to find that "when" is not language of condition under which the subcontractor took the risk of not getting paid. Rather, it would interpret the agreement to mean that the contractor promised to pay the subcontractor for the work and also promised to pay him at a reasonable time.

To avoid problems of interpretation, use clear language when writing contracts.

> ✔ **To create a condition:** Use "if" or "on condition that" or "it is a condition precedent to A that B occur."

> ✔ **To create a promise:** Use "shall" or "has an obligation to" or "agrees to."

For example, an insurance company contract provides that "the owner must give notice within 30 days of the loss." The owner gives notice on the 32nd day, and the insurance company claims that the condition is not satisfied. A court could say that "must" means "shall" and the owner only breached a promise, so the insurance company still has to perform. To prevent this outcome, the lawyers for the insurance company could change the language to something like, "If the owner does not give notice within 30 days of the loss, then the insurance company's duty to pay for the loss is excused." It would be hard to argue that *that* language doesn't create an express condition.

Using restitution when a condition bars recovery

When one party is unjustly enriched at the expense of the other party, restitution requires that the unjustly enriched party *disgorge* (relinquish) the benefit, returning the enriched party to the position he was in before the benefit was conferred (see Chapter 4 for details). Restitution can be very useful when a failure to substantially perform results in nonpayment under the contract. Restitution enables the breaching party to recover for the partial performance.

For example, if a contractor conferred a substantial benefit on the owner, like building 80 percent of the project, then the contractor could claim payment for the benefit conferred in restitution. A century ago, many courts didn't favor restitution in this situation because the courts didn't recognize claims from parties who didn't have clean hands, such as dirty contract-breakers. Today, however, the prevailing view is that even the breaching party may recover restitution.

The remedy for restitution starts with the value of the benefit conferred, which contract law can measure in a number of ways. But remember that the remedy for breach of promise by the non-breaching party comes before restitution for the breaching party. In other words, a court deals first with the breach and then with restitution.

Here's an example of how restitution works:

1. A contractor builds 50 percent of a $200,000 house and quits.

2. The owner refuses to pay the contractor because the contractor didn't substantially perform.

3. The contractor claims $100,000 in restitution.

4. The owner has a claim for damages for breach, which comes before restitution. So you need to look at what the homeowner has to pay to get the house completed before you determine how much the contractor is entitled to in restitution:

   • If the owner has the house completed at a cost of $110,000, then the contractor can't recover more than $90,000 in restitution because the owner bargained to pay $200,000 total for the house:

   $200,000 − $110,000 = $90,000

   • If the owner is able to get the house completed at a cost of $90,000 (for a total of $190,000 rather than $200,000), then the restitution would be limited to no more than the portion of the contract that was completed, which is 50 percent of $200,000, or $100,000.

The restitution argument is unnecessary in Code contracts. Section 2-607 of the UCC states that "The buyer must pay at the contract rate for any goods accepted." So if a store orders 100 shirts at $20 each and the seller delivers only 80 shirts, the buyer is free to accept or reject the shirts or a portion of them, but it has to pay for any shirts it accepts under the contract at a price of $20 per shirt.

Finding a divisible contract

A *divisible contract* is one in which the parties agree that a part performance by one party is the "agreed equivalent" of some part performance by the other party. In sorting out performance disputes, a court may look at such a contract as a series of minicontracts, enforcing a contract claim for the part performed.

For example, suppose I was going away for 30 days and agreed to pay you $20 for each day you fed and walked my dog ($600 total). You did it for 20 days and then bailed, so I had to find someone else to do the job for the remaining time. You materially breached, so I could claim that I owe you nothing. But contract law would look at this as 30 contracts for $20 each and would likely find that you performed 20 of those contracts, so you'd have a claim for $400 under the contract. But remember that the expectancy of the non-breaching party comes before any claim by the breaching party. If I had to pay someone else $25 a day for the remaining 10 days, that would come to $250 + $400 = $650 or $50 more than the $600 I would've paid had you fully performed, so the maximum you could claim would be $600 − $250 = $350.

If parties have a contract that's broken up into parts, that doesn't necessarily mean that those parts are agreed equivalents.

For example, suppose that you mastered contracts through your study of *Contract Law For Dummies* and agreed to tutor a first-year student for the 14-week semester for $420. You provide tutoring for two weeks and then decide to do something else with your time. You materially breached, so the tutee, showing that she learned something about implied conditions, says she doesn't have to pay you anything. You claim that this is a divisible contract — essentially 14 contracts to provide tutoring for $30/week. You performed two of those mini-contracts, so she owes you $60. Your tutee, however, would have a good claim that a week of tutoring and payment of $30 were not necessarily agreed equivalents — some weeks, particularly toward the end of the semester, may be more demanding, and others, such as during a break, may be less demanding. She'd argue that the contract was *entire* rather than divisible. If she's successful in that argument, then you'd have to fall back on a claim for restitution.

Claiming waiver to excuse a condition

A *waiver* is a knowing relinquishment of a legal right. Waivers often arise when a party has a right to treat a nonperformance as triggering a condition but the party doesn't do so. The waiver may lead the nonperforming party to believe that nothing terrible will happen if she doesn't perform exactly as promised, and this justifiable belief may bar the other party from exercising his right in the future. Note that a waiver arises by the conduct of the parties, so it's not a contract modification, which I discuss in Chapter 12.

For example, a consumer takes out an auto loan and promises to pay the lender a certain amount of money on the first day of the month for the next 24 months. The contract contains an express condition stating that if the consumer doesn't pay on the first of the month, then the lender may *accelerate the loan* (call the entire amount due) and repossess the car if the consumer doesn't pay the entire balance due. The consumer makes the first five payments on the 5th of the month, and the lender does nothing. When the consumer makes the next payment on the 5th, the lender exercises its right to accelerate and repossess. A court will likely find that because the lender repeatedly failed to exercise the right, the borrower was lulled into thinking that the lender wouldn't exercise that right.

Because a waiver arises by conduct rather than agreement, a party may retract a waiver by giving the other party proper notice. The lender can send the consumer a "No More Mr. Nice Guy" letter clearly informing the consumer that if future payments are not made on the 1st, the lender will exercise its contractual rights. This letter would retract the waiver, and the consumer can no longer claim that she didn't know the importance of timely payment.

Throwing yourself on the mercy of the court to excuse a condition

When all else fails, a party who didn't satisfy a condition can ask the court to excuse the condition. Courts do this reluctantly and only when the party has suffered a *forfeiture* (an out-of-pocket loss), as the wishy-washy rule from Restatement § 229 explains:

> § 229. Excuse of a Condition to Avoid Forfeiture
>
> To the extent that the non-occurrence of a condition would cause disproportionate forfeiture, a court may excuse the non-occurrence of that condition unless its occurrence was a material part of the agreed exchange.

This section explains a couple of applications of this rule.

Insurance cases

Courts apply excuse of a condition to avoid forfeiture most frequently in insurance cases.

Consider an insurance company that put in a fire-insurance policy an express condition that if notice is not given in 30 days, it won't pay for the loss. Suppose a policy owner gave notice on the 32nd day. None of the other forms of relief for avoiding the harsh effect of conditions would apply, but the court may excuse this condition because the owner will suffer a forfeiture — he would've paid his premiums for nothing.

The Restatement qualifies this rule with the language "unless its occurrence was a material part of the agreed exchange." In other words, the court looks at how important the condition was to the party who imposed it.

For example, an insurance company may put in its contract that it won't pay for a business's fire loss "if the business does not install a sprinkler system." The business makes a claim for fire loss, and the insurance company refuses to pay because the business didn't install a sprinkler system. Here, it seems that the condition was material — very important for the insurance company because a sprinkler system probably would've reduced the fire damage and the cost to the insurance company. The insurance company could make the same argument if in the previous example, the owner gave notice not on the 32nd day but on the 332nd day. The condition is less likely to be excused because the insurance company is harmed if it can't investigate within a reasonable time from the loss.

Conditions can give you powerful leverage to get the other party to perform. If the insurance company had put in the contract that the business promised to install a sprinkler system, then in the event of loss, the insurance company would still have to pay but could recover damages for breach of promise. Instead, it put in the contract that installation of a sprinkler system is a condition to its payment. Which method do you think would best induce the business to perform?

Jacob & Youngs v. Kent

The case of *Jacob & Youngs v. Kent* demonstrates the difficulty the courts face in sorting out promises and conditions. Jacob & Youngs, Inc., was a contractor that agreed to build a mansion for Mr. Kent. The contract contained numerous specifications, one of which was that "all wrought-iron pipe must be well galvanized lap welded pipe of the grade known as 'standard pipe' of Reading manufacture." When the house was completed, Kent discovered that the pipe was made by the Cohoes company rather than by the Reading company.

Kent claimed that he wanted the house rebuilt with the correct pipe, and he also refused to make the final payment under the contract, which was about 5 percent of the price. His first claim sounds like a breach of promise — if Jacob & Youngs promised him a house with Reading pipe, that's what he should have, even if it meant demolishing most of the building to get it. His second claim sounds like a condition — because Jacob & Youngs failed to perform an express condition, he didn't have to pay for the house.

During the trial, Jacob & Youngs offered evidence that Cohoes pipe was just as good as Reading pipe, but the trial judge excluded this evidence, presumably because it was irrelevant. If Reading pipe was a condition, then it didn't matter that some other performance was just as good, because the condition wasn't satisfied.

On appeal, Judge Cardozo said that "considerations partly of justice and partly of presumable intention" should be used to determine whether a term is a promise or a condition. He didn't think that reasonable parties in this situation could seriously have meant that performance of every single specification was to be a condition. Therefore, Jacob & Youngs had only *promised* to use Reading pipe. This conclusion drove the dissent crazy, because it appeared that the parties had drafted the term as an express condition.

But even if it was a promise, the contractors might still have materially breached the promise, and material breach would operate as the nonoccurrence of a condition, excusing Kent's performance. But Cardozo found the equivalent pipe served the purpose and that Jacob & Youngs had acted innocently. This also drove the dissent crazy, because Jacob & Youngs could not possibly have installed that much pipe without knowing what they were doing.

Even if it was only an immaterial breach, Kent would still be entitled to damages and, as I explain in Chapter 18, courts generally award money damages rather than order the party in breach to fix the problem. Kent would've been very happy to recover the amount of money it would take to tear out the Reading pipe and put in new pipe in order to give him what he was promised. But Cardozo wasn't going to let him get away with that — everyone knows that Kent wouldn't really use the money for that purpose but would gain a windfall at the expense of the contractors. So Cardozo instead awarded him the difference in value between what he was promised — a house with Reading pipe — and what he got — a house with Cohoes pipe. Because they were equivalent pipe, that amount was zero.

Although Cardozo undoubtedly thought Kent was a chiseler trying to get away with something, the dissent was concerned that this opinion would open the floodgates for contracting parties to cut corners and get away with not giving owners what they promised. However you feel about that, parties have learned at least two practical lessons from this case:

✔ If you're a contractor, don't promise to use a particular brand name, and in case you forget, include in the contract that if any brand is named in the contract, it's only to establish a level of quality.

✔ If you really want something to be a condition, spell it out clearly. I have no doubt that if the contract had said in big letters, "If Jacob & Youngs doesn't use Reading pipe, then Kent doesn't have to make the final payment," the court would've enforced that understanding.

Chapter 15

Breaching the Contract by Anticipatory Repudiation

. . . .

In This Chapter

▶ Understanding the two types of anticipatory repudiation

▶ Knowing when a party can and can't revoke a repudiation

▶ Recognizing when a party has repudiated

▶ Discovering what happens when a party repudiates

. . . .

*R*epudiation arises when a party refuses or fails to perform the entire contract. *Anticipatory repudiation* occurs when a party refuses or implies a refusal to fully perform before the performance deadline, thus breaching the contract.

Granted, calling anticipatory repudiation a breach isn't exactly logical, because by definition, breach doesn't occur unless a party fails to perform by the agreed upon deadline. If I have an obligation to deliver 1,000 widgets to you on August 1, and then on July 1, I say to you, "I'm not going to deliver those widgets," I could claim that logically I can't be in breach, because on July 1, I can't possibly have failed to perform my obligation to deliver the widgets by August 1.

Nevertheless, for practical reasons, contract law calls this act a breach. Contract law recognizes that if we treat my refusal as a breach on July 1, we mitigate the negative consequences that would be likely to arise if you had to wait until August 1 to order replacement widgets.

However, you need to be careful in claiming breach. Because you can't take action unless I've breached, you must first determine whether I've actually repudiated in the eyes of the law. This chapter explains how to recognize when a party has repudiated, whether a party may revoke a repudiation, and what you can expect when one of your clients or a party your client has contracted with repudiates before the performance deadline.

Recognizing the Two Types of Anticipatory Repudiation

Anticipatory repudiation may be expressed or implied. In other words, one party may refuse to perform his obligation either by his words or his actions.

An *express repudiation* arises when one party verbally (in speech or writing) informs the other party that he clearly and unequivocally refuses to perform. My saying on July 1, "I'm not going to deliver those widgets that I promised to deliver on August 1" would probably cut it. But in order to discharge my duties (as I explain in Chapter 14), the repudiation must be material. If a party substantially performs at the time performance is due, it's not a material breach.

To determine whether the repudiation is material, ask yourself, "If the breach occurred at the time for performance, would it excuse the other party?" If the answer is yes, you're dealing with a material breach. The same rule applies to anticipatory repudiation. A breach prior to the performance deadline isn't an anticipatory repudiation unless it's a material breach.

If I say on July 1, "I absolutely, unequivocally am going to deliver only 995 of the 1,000 widgets I promised on August 1," this doesn't qualify as a repudiation, because it's not sufficient to excuse you from performing your obligation — it wouldn't rise to the level of material breach if that was the performance I gave you on August 1.

An *implied repudiation* arises when a party does something that puts the power to perform out of his control, even if he doesn't say anything. If I have a contract to sell my house to you on August 1, and on July 1, you find out I sold it to someone else, that's clearly a breach by anticipatory repudiation. I didn't expressly inform you of my intention, but selling my house to someone else implied repudiation. My actions speak even though I'm silent.

The case of *Taylor v. Johnston* nicely illustrates both implied and express anticipatory repudiation. Taylor, who owned two racehorses, both mares, contracted with Johnston, who owned the great stallion Fleet Nasrullah, for stud services in California. Johnston then sold the horse to new owners in Kentucky. This constitutes an implied repudiation, because Johnston relinquished his power to perform. Instead of accepting the repudiation, Taylor protested and persuaded Johnston to retract the repudiation by getting the new owners to perform the contract for him (see more on retraction in the section "Deciding whether the breaching party can retract the repudiation"). So now the contract was back on track.

In Kentucky, however, Taylor got a runaround. Whenever he made a reservation for the services of Fleet Nasrullah, the new owners canceled it at the last minute. After this happened numerous times, Taylor became convinced that he wasn't going to get the services before the breeding season ended, so he finally sought other stud services. When that didn't work out, he sued.

The court noticed that the contract called for services during the year 1966 and couldn't understand why Taylor had given up in June, when six more months remained in the year. But both parties explained to the court that in a contract for stud services in the thoroughbred-racehorse world, the word "year" means "the breeding season of the year." (This is a great example of how trade usage replaces ordinary meanings when the parties are in the trade, as I explain in Chapter 11.)

The California Supreme Court held that there was no express anticipatory repudiation because Johnston had not made "a clear, positive, unequivocal refusal to perform." Therefore, Taylor was the breaching party. This decision strikes me as outrageous, because I think a reasonable person in Taylor's shoes would've concluded that he wasn't going to get the services. But it does reinforce an important lesson: Be careful about canceling a contract until you're sure that the other party has repudiated, either expressly or impliedly.

De La (European) Tour: The rule on anticipatory repudiation is born

The rule on anticipatory repudiation was established in Anglo-American law by the landmark case of *Hochster v. De La Tour,* decided by the Queen's Bench of England in 1853. In April of 1852, De La Tour hired Hochster to accompany him on a trip around the European Continent for three months, beginning on June 1. When De La Tour told Hochster on May 11 that he didn't require his services, Hochster wasted no time and sued on May 22. De La Tour claimed that Hochster couldn't claim damages until after he had held himself ready to perform on June 1.

The court had some precedent that involved implied repudiations where the breaching party had put itself out of its power to perform, but the court didn't recognize a distinction between the cases. The court said, "It seems strange that the defendant, after renouncing the contract and absolutely declaring that he will never act under it, should be permitted to object that faith is given to his assertion."

The court seemed particularly impressed with the economics of the situation. It didn't make economic sense for Hochster to sit around, waiting to see if De La Tour was going to change his mind. It made more sense for Hochster to seek alternate employment during that time, because money earned from the alternate employment would reduce his damages, thus benefiting De La Tour.

Determining Whether a Party Has Repudiated

Recognizing anticipatory repudiation in the real world isn't always easy. People don't always state their intentions in a clear and unequivocal manner. They make statements like, "The market price of widgets is going up. I'm not sure I'm going to be able to deliver those widgets you ordered at the old price after all." Or they may not say anything but demonstrate through their actions an unwillingness or inability to perform; for example, a buyer may hear from other buyers that the seller has failed to deliver to them, causing concern that the seller may not perform as promised.

The problem is that remarks and rumors like these are not clear and unequivocal refusals to perform. If you treat these somewhat ambiguous signs as repudiation and refuse to perform, then you run the risk of becoming the repudiating party.

Situations such as these present a dilemma. Say you're a seller who has agreed to sell on credit, giving the buyer 30 days to pay after delivery. You hear that the buyer hasn't been paying other creditors. This makes you reluctant to deliver to the buyer, but because the buyer hasn't actually repudiated, if you refuse to deliver the goods as promised, you take the chance of becoming the repudiating party.

Contract law has come up with a cool solution to this dilemma, as this section explains.

Insecurity and assurances: Using UCC § 2-609 to identify repudiation

The UCC has come up with an elegant solution to the fuzziness that often accompanies repudiation. The solution goes something like this:

1. One party has reasonable grounds for insecurity.

2. The insecure party demands written assurance from the other party.

3. If the insecure party receives adequate assurance, then the contract is back on track. If the insecure party doesn't receive adequate assurance, then the party who demanded assurance may treat the contract as repudiated by the other party and cancel the contract.

This procedure provides a way to turn wishy-washy expressions into the same certainty a party has when they receive an express repudiation.

Here's the official word from the Code found in § 2-609, as enacted in North Carolina at § 25-2-609:

> § 25-2-609. Right to adequate assurance of performance.
>
> (1) A contract for sale imposes an obligation on each party that the other's expectation of receiving due performance will not be impaired. When reasonable grounds for insecurity arise with respect to the performance of either party the other may in writing demand adequate assurance of due performance and until he receives such assurance may if commercially reasonable suspend any performance for which he has not already received the agreed return.
>
> (2) Between merchants the reasonableness of grounds for insecurity and the adequacy of any assurance offered shall be determined according to commercial standards.
>
> (3) Acceptance of any improper delivery or payment does not prejudice the aggrieved party's right to demand adequate assurance of future performance.
>
> (4) After receipt of a justified demand failure to provide within a reasonable time not exceeding thirty days such assurance of due performance as is adequate under the circumstances of the particular case is a repudiation of the contract.

The following subsections explain what constitutes reasonable grounds for insecurity and how to go about demanding and getting reasonable assurances.

Finding reasonable grounds for insecurity

A party can demand assurances only if they have "reasonable grounds for insecurity." Note that either party can use this device — a buyer concerned about performance or a seller concerned about payment. In typical Code fashion, subsection (2) explains that "Between merchants the reasonableness of grounds for insecurity . . . shall be determined according to commercial standards." The Code assumes that merchants, as people in business, have determinable (objective) standards for what they consider reasonable. Examples of reasonable grounds for insecurity may include a case in which a buyer hasn't paid the seller for a previous order or the seller has reliable reports that this buyer has failed to pay other sellers.

Demanding and getting adequate assurances

Assuming that a party has reasonable grounds for insecurity, she has the right to demand *adequate* assurances. The definition of what's adequate, however, can be elusive. Use the following guidelines to determine what the court is likely to consider to be a reasonable demand for adequate assurances and what qualifies as adequate assurances:

- **Reasonable demand:** A reasonable demand for adequate assurances is typically a demand for an explanation of
  - The circumstances that gave rise to the insecurity
  - How the circumstances have changed
  - How the party plans on making good on its promise

  The insecure party can't use this situation as an excuse to completely rewrite the contract in its favor. A seller who extends credit, for example, has taken some risk, and to demand an assurance of payment on delivery would probably go too far.

- **Adequate assurances:** Adequate assurances given in response to the demand typically consist of an explanation of
  - The circumstances that gave rise to the insecurity
  - How the party has resolved or is in the process of resolving these issues and plans to honor the terms of the contract

  If a buyer hasn't paid, for example, reasonable assurances may consist of explaining how the situation arose and why the seller can now expect payment. A statement from the buyer's bank might be helpful.

If the insecure party has delivered a proper demand and the other party has given no assurances or has given inadequate assurances, then the party making the demand may treat the contract as repudiated and *cancel* the contract, declaring that the contract ended because of the other party's breach.

The case of *AMF Inc. v. McDonald's* is a good example of how UCC § 2-609 works. In late 1968 and early 1969, McDonald's (yes, that McDonald's) ordered 23 cash registers of a new design from AMF to be delivered by January 1970. In March 1969, executives from the two companies held a meeting at which McDonald's expressed concern that insufficient progress was being made on the development of the cash registers. In May, they met again, and AMF failed to alleviate the concerns that McDonald's had raised. Shortly thereafter, McDonald's canceled the contract.

AMF claimed that McDonald's was the breaching party, because they had canceled the contract in July of 1969, even though the delivery date was in January of 1970. McDonald's claimed they were justified in canceling the contract because of AMF's anticipatory repudiation in spite of the fact that AMF had never absolutely and unequivocally refused to perform.

Unable to prove an express repudiation, McDonald's claimed that they had satisfied the elements of § 2-609. The court found that McDonald's had reasonable grounds for insecurity because of AMF's production problems, that McDonald's had made a demand for assurances at the March meeting, and that AMF had failed to give them adequate assurances at the May meeting. This looked pretty good for McDonald's in establishing that AMF had repudiated the contract, but one element of the statute was not satisfied: McDonald's had not made its demand for assurances *in writing*, as required by the statute.

The judge in the case found this element satisfied under the language from § 1-103(a) that the Code "must be liberally construed and applied to promote its underlying purposes and policies." On the one hand, this doesn't make a lot of sense, because even under the most liberal construction, "in writing" doesn't mean "not in writing." On the other hand, the purpose of the writing requirement is probably to make clear to the other party that a serious demand has been made that has legal consequences if they don't respond. The two meetings in March and in May probably served that purpose. In other words, little doubt exists that McDonald's had informed AMF of their concerns and expected action to be taken, and that AMF knew about the seriousness of the matter.

Applying the rule to the common law

In most jurisdictions, the common law follows the Code rule that addresses repudiation. Some jurisdictions may have established the common-law equivalent of UCC § 2-609, found in Restatement § 251. Sometimes even if the Code isn't applicable to a situation because it doesn't involve the sale of goods, a court nevertheless *analogizes* to the Code. In other words, the court may say that the Code has a good rule that should be followed even in non-Code situations.

Suppose that during the spring, the dean of a law school hears that a professor who's under contract has been looking for jobs at other law schools. Concerned about having the position filled by the time the school year begins, the dean demands assurances from the professor. The professor responds, "The semester starts on August 25, dean. Peek into my office at that time. Either I'll be there or I won't."

This situation clearly involves personal services, so the Code doesn't apply, but the rule seems to make sense in this situation. The law school has information that raises reasonable grounds for insecurity about whether the professor will perform his contract for the next year. Finding out in the spring, when lining up a replacement would be easier and cheaper, seems to make more sense than waiting until August when the professor's absence is likely to be disruptive. If I were a judge in that jurisdiction, I would analogize to the Code to come up with a rule for this common-law case that's similar to the Code rule. Based on the rule, I would find that the professor failed to provide adequate assurances and hence repudiated his contract.

 The purpose of the demand for assurances is to find out whether a party's equivocal statements or actions constitute a repudiation. If the party has made an express or implied repudiation, demanding assurances is unnecessary.

Figuring Out What Happens after Repudiation

After a party repudiates, any of the following events may occur in response to that repudiation:

- ✓ The repudiating party retracts the repudiation.
- ✓ The injured party accepts the repudiation and seeks remedies for the breach.
- ✓ The injured party ignores the repudiation.

This section explains these three events and their consequences in detail.

Deciding whether the breaching party can retract the repudiation

When one party repudiates, the other party usually gets a little miffed. If I agree to sell my house to you and then inform you, after you just sold your house, that I have no intention of selling to you, you're likely to get more than a little irritated. You're probably *not* going to say, "Oh, okay, I guess I just need to find another house in a hurry." More likely, you'll yell, threaten legal action, and employ other tools of persuasion to convince me to change my mind and *retract* (take back) my repudiation.

Retracting a repudiation is a good thing because it puts the contract back on track, so contract law allows dirty, lowdown contract-breakers to retract their repudiations with two exceptions. A party can't retract a repudiation after the other party has done one of the following:

  ✔ Made clear that they accept the repudiation

  ✔ Relied on the repudiation

So if after I told you I wasn't going to deliver the widgets on August 1 as promised, you told me, "You're so unreliable. I'll never deal with you again," then I can't retract the repudiation later. Similarly, if the day after my repudiation I tell you that I've decided to perform after all, you're free to tell me, "Sorry, I already ordered replacement widgets from someone else." Your reliance on my repudiation keeps me from retracting even if I didn't know about it before I tried to retract.

Seeking remedies for the breach when the injured party accepts the repudiation

When a party breaches by anticipatory repudiation, the non-breaching party can bring suit for breach of contract right then; she doesn't need to wait until the performance deadline passes. The UCC in § 2-610 states that the "aggrieved party may (a) for a commercially reasonable time await performance by the repudiating party; or (b) resort to any remedy for breach."

Acting in "a commercially reasonable time"

In UCC § 2-610, the reference to "a commercially reasonable time" shows the Code's sense of reality. The non-breaching party doesn't usually immediately accept the repudiation but may try to work things out with the repudiating party. Thus, the reasonable time is a time in which the non-breaching party can look around for alternative ways of obtaining performance while trying to get the repudiating party to retract.

However, the non-breaching party runs a risk if she waits beyond that reasonable time to obtain a remedy. Often a seller repudiates because prices are rising and he could get more money for his goods from other buyers. If the aggrieved buyer waits too long before obtaining goods in the market, then if prices continue to rise, she may not be taking reasonable steps to mitigate the damages, which is an important principle of contract damages (see Chapter 16). The same thing can happen, of course, if a buyer repudiates because of a falling market.

In *Oloffson v. Coomer,* the plaintiff, a grain dealer, contracted on April 16 with Coomer, a farmer, to buy 20,000 bushels of corn on October 30 and another 20,000 bushels on December 15 at a price of about $1.12 per bushel. On June 3, when the price of corn was $1.16 per bushel, Coomer informed Oloffson that he wasn't going to plant corn and that Oloffson should obtain it elsewhere. Oloffson insisted that Coomer perform and kept badgering him for months, even though Coomer had clearly not planted corn. Finally, Oloffson purchased corn on the delivery dates at prices of $1.35 and $1.49 per bushel and sued Coomer for the difference between those prices and the contract price.

The court correctly held that Oloffson had waited way past "a commercially reasonable time" before he *covered* (found an alternative source for the corn). Because Coomer had clearly repudiated on June 3, Oloffson should've covered soon after that date. His damages were limited to the difference between the market price on that date and the contract price.

Canceling a contract and excusing performance

Because anticipatory repudiation requires a material breach, the non-breaching party may cancel the contract when the repudiation occurs. This is an exception to the rule of constructive conditions I explain in Chapter 14. Under that rule, a party must tender performance in order to satisfy the condition that had to occur before the other party's performance was due. But an anticipatory repudiation by one party excuses the other from tendering its performance.

For example, I had a client who was an author. In his files he found a contract he had made with a publisher a number of years earlier in which he promised to write a book for them. Under the rule of the order of performances (see Chapter 14), he would be obligated to perform first by writing and submitting the book, and then the publisher would publish it and pay him royalties. I wrote a letter to the publisher, enclosing a copy of the contract and informing them that he planned to submit the book. Without considering the consequences, they wrote back, declaring that he was performing too late and they no longer wanted the book! This was an express anticipatory repudiation, with two consequences: (1) it discharged my client's obligation to write the book, and (2) it allowed us to sue for damages immediately. All without having to write the book!

If the publisher had simply ignored my letter, my client would've had to write the book and submit it. But because the publisher repudiated, my client didn't have to write the manuscript. However, if we then sued the publisher for breach, they'd defend by claiming that their performance was excused because the author committed material breach first by not delivering the book in a timely manner.

In either scenario, we'd need to prove that the author didn't breach. The big difference is that due to the anticipatory repudiation, the author doesn't have to submit the manuscript.

Repudiating a contract that includes installment payments

The rule that a material breach allows the other party to cancel the contract has one important exception. It comes into play when a party repudiates after receiving everything he was supposed to get in exchange for his performance. The exception usually arises in the context of a loan. A borrower receives full performance when she gets the money from the lender. If the borrower agreed to pay back the lender in installments, her anticipatory repudiation doesn't permit the lender to sue at that time for the entire balance.

Suppose I lend you $10,000, and you promise to pay back $500 per month. Later, you tell me, "I'm not paying you this month and am never paying you back!" Even though this sounds like an express anticipatory repudiation, I can sue you for only the $500, because your duty at that time was to pay that one installment.

When writing a contract that includes installment payments on behalf of the party who will be receiving payments, consider adding an acceleration clause. An *acceleration clause* provides that if the borrower defaults on one payment, then the lender has the right to accelerate the entire amount, declaring it immediately due and payable.

Ignoring the repudiation: Not the best option

Ignoring a party's repudiation is the worst course of action for the non-repudiating party for two reasons:

- ✔ As long as the non-breaching party hasn't accepted or relied on the repudiation, the repudiating party can revoke the repudiation.
- ✔ Even if the repudiation eventually results in breach, the non-breaching party may be limited to the damages it could've recovered if it had acted promptly after the repudiation.

Part V

Exploring Remedies for Breach of Contract

The 5th Wave   By Rich Tennant

"Or, we could just agree to disagree."

In this part . . .

This part deals with remedies for breach of contract. The goal is to give the damaged party the *expectancy* — the financial equivalent of what the party reasonably expected to receive from the performance of the contract. Although that seems easy enough, the actual calculations sometimes become complex, and contract law places certain limitations on remedies according to the principles of causation, certainty, foreseeability, and mitigation.

The chapters in this part explain how the courts generally calculate damages in the common law and the UCC and then examine different remedies, including unwinding the contract through rescission, reforming the contract, and settling the dispute via alternative dispute resolution (ADR).

Chapter 16

Examining How Courts Handle Breach of Contract

*W*hen a party fails to *perform* (do what he promised to do), resulting in breach of contract, the courts strive to exact justice by awarding the non-breaching party a remedy. Courts are vigilant to ensure that the non-breaching party is compensated, but not overcompensated, for the breach. Therefore, courts don't award punitive damages for breach of contract, because punitive damages don't compensate for a loss. Courts compensate the non-breaching party in three ways:

✔ **Expectancy:** The principal remedy is to award the non-breaching party money damages that give him the financial equivalent of what he would have gotten had both parties performed — no more, no less. Courts rarely force the breaching party to perform (however, exceptions do exist in unusual circumstances, as I discuss in Chapter 18).

✔ **Reliance:** Reliance is compensating the non-breaching party for out-of-pocket expenses incurred in anticipation of having whatever the breaching party had promised.

✔ **Restitution:** Restitution involves requiring the breaching party to *disgorge* (return) the value of any benefit he received from the non-breaching party.

This chapter addresses these three basic common-law remedies for breach of contract and explains how the courts limit damages for breach. This information makes you better equipped to pursue what your client is entitled to or to limit what your client is required to pay when breach occurs. (In Chapter 17, I explain the equivalent of these remedies as established in UCC Article 2. And in Chapter 18, I present additional information about remedies, including *equitable remedies,* where the court orders a party to perform or not to do something, and the parties' ability to change the rules.)

Mastering the Rule of the Expectancy

According to the rule of the *expectancy* or *expectation damages,* compensation for breach should put the non-breaching party in as good a position as she would've been in if both parties had performed the contract. The rule of the expectancy isn't just about compensating a party for what she actually lost out of pocket. It's about compensating a party for the loss of the expected benefit from the exchange.

To use the rule of the expectancy to calculate damages, take the following steps:

1. **Describe what the non-breaching party would've had if both parties had performed the contract.**

2. **Describe where the non-breaching party stands now.**

3. **Figure out what it would take to bring the non-breaching party from where she is now to where she would've been had both parties performed.**

For example, suppose I promise to sell you my car for $10,000. If the car is actually worth $10,500 and I breach before you've paid me, here's how the rule of the expectancy would apply:

1. Had the contract been performed, you would've had a car worth $10,500 for the price of $10,000 — an addition of $500 to your net worth.

2. You still have your $10,000, but you don't have the $10,500 car.

3. You'd need $500 to put you from where you are now (having an asset worth $10,000) to where you would've been (having an asset worth $10,500).

If you choose, you could buy a car equivalent to the $10,500 car I promised to sell you, and you'd have to pay $10,500 to buy it. So if I give you $500, then you're exactly where you would've been had I performed — you have a comparable car and are out $10,000. The bottom line is this: Whether you replace the car or not, I'd owe you $500.

However, if the car were worth only $10,000, your expected gain from the exchange would be $0, and the court would award you nothing. Likewise, if the car were worth only $9,500, you would've had an expected *loss* of $500 from the exchange and wouldn't be eligible for damages. In fact, I did you a favor by breaching!

Contract law is interested in compensating the party who lost something because of the breach. It's not interested in punishing a party for breaching a contract.

The following subsections explain how the expectancy plays out in common scenarios, how courts account for additional expenses when calculating damages, and how economists view breach as a good thing.

Seeing the expectancy in context

You can develop a better understanding of the rule of the expectancy by seeing how it plays out in particular situations, such as construction and employment contracts. To give you a better sense of how the courts are likely to apply the rule in each situation, I provide examples for both in this section.

Checking out a construction contract

A builder agrees to build a house on an owner's lot for $200,000. The builder plans to spend $190,000 on labor and materials and to make a profit of $10,000. As soon as the parties sign the contract and before the builder has lifted a finger, the owner breaches and says she doesn't want the house built after all. The builder is entitled to damages of $10,000 for breach of contract because that's what he would've had if both parties had performed the contract. It doesn't matter that he hasn't actually spent any money — the expectancy is what he *would have had.* He would've had $200,000 from the owner, but he would've needed to spend $190,000 to get it, so the amount he expected to gain is $10,000.

Now assume that the builder has started work and has built almost half the house at a cost of $90,000. If the owner breaches at this point, a court would have to award the builder $100,000 to give him the expectancy — the amount required to bring him from where he stands now (out $90,000) to where he would've been if both parties had performed the contract (having a profit of $10,000). Of course, in real life, this example would be messier, because the builder would have to prove that he would've had a profit of $10,000 and that he actually spent $90,000. In law school, however, you have the luxury of assuming facts and then discussing the law as it applies to the given facts.

If the builder breaches, computing the damages is more difficult. At this point, the owner finds another builder to complete the job. Based on what the second builder charges, the courts make sure that the owner gets her house built at a cost of $200,000. If the initial builder breaches immediately after the parties enter into the contract and the second builder reasonably charges $210,000 to do the same work, the owner is eligible for $10,000 in damages. If she pays the second builder $210,000 and then recovers $10,000 from the first builder, she has exactly what she bargained for — a house for $200,000.

If the builder breaches midway through, after incurring expenses of $90,000, the analysis is similar. The owner generally finds another builder to complete the house, and contract law awards the owner any damages necessary to give her the expectancy — getting the house built at a cost of $200,000. A complication, however, is whether the builder can recover for the expenses incurred (the $90,000). This recovery would not be damages for breach of contract. I discuss the builder's remedies in the section "Deciding whether dirty contract-breakers should get restitution," later in this chapter.

Examining an employment contract

Assume an employer hires an employee to work for one year for $100,000. The employer immediately discharges the employee without cause (if there were *cause* for the discharge, the employee would be the one who breached the contract). The employee would've had $100,000 if both parties had performed the contract, so that's the amount the employee would presumably be entitled to as damages.

Notice that the breach leaves the employee free for a year. If the employee lands another job that earns him $75,000 during that year, the employee is awarded damages of $25,000 ($100,000 – $75,000). This amount of money brings the employee to where he would've been (receiving $100,000) had both parties performed the contract.

Contract law expects the employee to work during that year and not just sit around watching reruns of *Buffy the Vampire Slayer*. So contract law requires the employee to *mitigate* — to find other work that will reduce the damages the employer must pay. For more about mitigation, see "Asking whether the non-breaching party mitigated the loss," later in this chapter.

If the employee breaches the contract, the employer is entitled to its expectancy — an employee who would perform that job for a year for $100,000. So if the employer has to pay someone $110,000 to do the job, the employer is entitled to $10,000, because that's the amount it would take to put the employer in the position it would've been in had both parties performed the contract. Of course, if the employer finds someone willing to do the job for $100,000, it suffers no damages. Breach of contract claims aren't very common in such cases because losses don't often result from breaches.

In an employment contract, if the employment is "at will" (no specific term), then either party can terminate the agreement without breach. But if the employment is for a term, then a party who terminates the agreement without cause is in breach.

Accounting for expenses

When calculating the damages that a plaintiff may be eligible for, make sure that your client accounts for expenses, or *transaction costs,* which usually include the costs of bringing a claim. In many cases, however, the transaction costs exceed the damages, and the plaintiff may not be entitled to recover these costs. These facts often keep the plaintiff from filing a claim. Consider the following costs:

- ✔ **Out-of-pocket costs for finding suitable performance:** If the plaintiff can document reasonable costs associated with procuring whatever the breaching party promised but failed to deliver, you can add those costs to the damages for breach of contract. However, contract law doesn't like parties to claim amounts they can't document. In other words, a plaintiff can't expect the defendant to pay for her "time and trouble."

- ✔ **Costs established by civil procedure statutes:** Civil procedure statutes may entitle a party, typically the prevailing party, to recover costs, but they're usually only minor costs, such as the cost of serving a summons, filing an action, or conducting depositions. Eligible costs don't include the biggest expense of bringing a lawsuit: hiring an attorney.

Under the so-called American Rule, each side pays its own attorney's fees — win or lose — which may discourage a party from bringing a claim because she may not come out ahead even if she wins. The English Rule is even more discouraging: If you lose, you have to pay the winner's attorney's fees, along with your own. This rule would certainly discourage the little guy from taking on a giant corporation.

The American Rule has two exceptions:

- ✔ **Some statutes provide for attorney's fees.** Examples are state consumer protection acts and numerous federal consumer protection statutes. If you can bring the claim under such a statute instead of bringing a common law or UCC claim, you may be able to recover attorney's fees.

Sometimes statutes that provide for attorney's fees essentially enact the English Rule, providing that the "prevailing party" gets the attorney's fees. In other words, if you bring suit and the other side wins, your client may have to pay all attorney's fees.

✔ **Parties may contract around the American rule.** The parties may use their freedom of contract to contract around the default rule and include a provision that the loser must pay the winner's attorney's fees. Sometimes in a *contract of adhesion,* the more powerful party drafts the attorney's fee provision so it's a one-way street: If he wins, you pay, but if you win, he doesn't have to pay. By statute or case law, many states have decided that such a provision must be read as reciprocal. That is, if the contract says that only one party is entitled to attorney's fees, the court will read it as if it said that the prevailing party is entitled to the fees.

Justifying breach: The economist's notion of the efficient breach

Contract cases usually lend themselves to settlement rather than litigation because, in general, nothing terrible happens to the breaching party. In the typical scenario, the breaching party is usually no worse off by breaching than if she performed.

For example, suppose a contractor bids $10,000 to do a job and then discovers that the actual cost of doing the work is $12,000. If she completes the job, she'll be out $2,000. If she breaches the contract, another contractor may do the job for $12,000, meaning that the breaching party will be liable for only $2,000 in damages for breach of contract. In fact, the breach is likely to be less costly than performance because the first contractor knows that the other party faces transaction costs in bringing a claim and will probably settle for less than $2,000 to avoid those costs.

In many cases, breach may actually produce better economic results than performance! Economists describe this scenario as the *theory of efficient breach.* An *efficient,* or *Pareto-optimal,* breach is one that leaves at least one party better off and no party worse off than they were before the breach. This situation arises when a party breaches to take advantage of a better opportunity and uses some of the gains to pay damages to the non-breaching party.

Suppose, for instance, that an employee has agreed to work for an employer for $100,000. She's offered another job that pays $120,000, but she must break her contract to take it. She can figure that her initial employer will incur some out-of-pocket costs to find a replacement and that it may have to pay the replacement a bit more than her salary. Say these damages for breach come to $12,000. When she pays the employer these damages, the employer is no worse off; after recovering the damages, the employer has its expectancy — an employee for the year at a cost of $100,000. And the employee is better off with the new job, earning $108,000 ($120,000 – $12,000) rather than the $100,000 if she had stayed at the first job.

You may wonder why so many people perform their contracts if breach carries no penalty. The simple answer is this: Even though breach may not hurt them financially, they see breaching as a moral issue, not an economic one. In other words, they don't want to be dirty contract-breakers. In fact, contract-breaking can adversely affect an individual's or business's reputation. You wouldn't want to hire a contractor who's known to be unreliable. In the business world, however, customary business norms often trump both moral and legal norms. Contracts expert Stewart Macaulay discovered that people in the business world often follow their way of doing things rather than the dictates of contract law, even though it may drive their lawyers crazy. (You can read more about Macaulay and his contributions to contract law in Chapter 22.)

The case against punitive damages

Economists make a pretty good case against awarding punitive damages for breach, arguing that the fear of punitive damages would be bad for business and, therefore, the economy. For example, if an auto manufacturer ordered steel and then realized it didn't need it because of a decline in business, the threat of punitive damages may discourage the manufacturer from canceling the order, paying damages, and letting the steel go to where it could be used most efficiently.

The goal of punitive damages is to deter certain behavior, and contract-breaking is not necessarily behavior that should be deterred. Breaking a contract may be in a party's best economic interests, and contract law in theory provides that the breaching party compensates the other party for the breach. Of course, in practice, the breaching party rarely offers to pay all the damages, and the transaction costs involved in recovering damages typically leave the non-breaching party worse off after a breach. Still, a system based on allocation of resources through contract is more effective than alternatives such as systems that enforce all contracts or that allocate resources through central planning.

Recognizing How Contract Law Limits the Damages for Breach

REMEMBER

The plaintiff in a breach of contract case faces an uphill battle. Any damages the court awards are limited by the following considerations:

- **Causation:** The plaintiff must prove that the breach caused the loss.

- **Certainty:** The plaintiff must prove the damages to a reasonable certainty.

- **Foreseeability:** The plaintiff can recover only the losses that the defendant would reasonably have known, at the time the parties made the contract, would likely result from the breach.

- **Mitigation:** The plaintiff must make reasonable efforts to minimize the cost of the breach.

I discuss all these points in this section.

Concluding whether the breach caused the loss

The rule of *causation* requires a plaintiff to prove that breach caused the loss. Proving that the loss resulted from the breach is usually obvious and generally not an issue. Sometimes, however, causation gets tangled up with consequential damages and mitigation and can become an issue when the breach has multiple causes. (See the later sections "Limiting damages with the rule of foreseeability" and "Asking whether the non-breaching party mitigated the loss.")

For example, in the case of *Freund v. Washington Square Press,* the plaintiff was Freund, a college professor and author who sued his publisher because the publisher failed to publish his book as promised. In addition to suing for the expectancy, Freund also claimed that because his book wasn't published, he didn't get a promotion. But the court found that in spite of the breach and his failure to publish, he had been promoted without delay. Therefore, the breach didn't cause that loss.

In other cases, certain losses may be traced back to a plaintiff's failure to mitigate rather than to the breach itself. In a Montana case, a rancher claimed that defective bull semen caused the loss of his cattle crop. He then got carried away and claimed that the loss of that crop prevented him from getting another crop, and that crop would have had another crop, and so he lost an infinite number of cattle! The court pointed out that all the rancher had to do was get the cattle reinseminated to prevent any further loss.

To handle the problem of multiple causes, a court may determine whether the defendant's breach was a substantial contributing cause of the loss, even if it wasn't the only cause. For example, assume that a manufacturer was making boots for the army and lost the contract because several of its part suppliers breached their contracts. If the manufacturer sued only one of the suppliers, the supplier would claim that even if it had delivered its parts, the manufacturer still wouldn't have been able to deliver the boots to the army, because other suppliers failed in their contracts. Thus, it didn't cause the loss. The other suppliers could make the same claim, leaving the manufacturer with no damages from anyone. To handle this problem, the court would likely hold responsible any of the suppliers whose breach was a substantial contributing cause of the loss.

Determining whether the loss is established with certainty

In a case of breach of contract, the plaintiff must prove damages to a reasonable certainty. In other words, contract law doesn't award speculative damages.

In *Freund v. Washington Square Press* (introduced earlier in the section "Concluding whether the breach caused the loss"), the trial court awarded Freund $10,000, which an expert testified was the cost of getting the book published. But the appellate court found that an author's expectancy isn't the cost of getting the book published — that's the publisher's cost of performance. Instead, the author's expectancy is the royalties he would've had from sales of the book. But Freund was unable to prove to a reasonable certainty how many copies of a book that was never published would've sold. Because he could prove he was damaged but couldn't prove the amount of the damage, the court awarded him nominal damages of six cents!

The certainty problem can be difficult to overcome. An existing business, for example, can project losses based on its earnings over a similar period, but a new business can't. The rule, however, doesn't require absolute certainty — it requires only *reasonable* certainty. If Freund had published other books, or if a new business can show what comparable businesses would've earned, the evidence may have satisfied the requirement. So be sure that you can provide some hard evidence of losses.

Limiting damages with the rule of foreseeability

Damages come in two types: direct and consequential. *Direct damages* are losses that result from the promisee's not getting what was promised. Those losses always result from breach. *Consequential damages* are losses set in motion by the loss of what was promised, which could significantly exceed direct damages if they weren't limited. For example, a factory may order a $5 part. If the seller of the part breaches by not delivering it, the factory has to buy a replacement part, which may cost only a few dollars more. But while waiting for the part, it may have to close its assembly line, causing hundreds of thousands of dollars in damages, all for the want of a $5 part. Those are the consequential damages.

In 1854, an English court decided whether the party who contracted to sell that part would be liable for those resulting damages, and the rule is still around today, as I explain next. This section explains the *rule of foreseeability,* which determines whether a breaching party like the $5-part seller is liable for consequential damages, and it provides guidance on how to draft a provision that excludes or limits such damages.

Working with Hadley v. Baxendale: The rule of foreseeability

The 1854 English case of *Hadley v. Baxendale* continues to set the standard for determining whether a party can recover consequential damages. Hadley operated a steam-powered mill — a technological wonder of the early Industrial Age. A steam engine generated the power to turn a crankshaft, which turned a wheel that ground the grain. A crankshaft at Hadley's mill broke, so he arranged to have it taken to the manufacturer for repair or replacement. The carrier, Baxendale, agreed that if Hadley got the crankshaft to him by noon, the carrier would deliver it to the manufacturer the next day. The carrier breached its promise, and Hadley was without a crankshaft for a longer period than if Baxendale had performed as promised. Hadley sued Baxendale for the profit he would've made from the mill's operation if the crankshaft had been available at the time promised. The jury, apparently without any rule to guide them, found for Hadley. Baxendale appealed.

On appeal, the court described the two kinds of damages: direct damages, which always arise from the breach, and consequential damages, which the breaching party, when entering the contract, would know would likely result from the breach. But how would the breaching party know about the likely damages that might result from breach? Either because he had actual knowledge (the other party told him) or he had imputed knowledge (a reasonable person would have known it).

In the case of Hadley and Baxendale, the direct damages were the loss of the crankshaft for a time; the damages for that loss would probably be the rental cost of a crankshaft. The consequential damages were the lost profits that were set in motion by the delay. The court held that Hadley wasn't entitled to the consequential damages because a reasonable carrier wouldn't have known that Hadley was unable to operate the mill without a crankshaft (Hadley may have had a spare crankshaft lying around, or maybe other parts of the mill didn't work as well and Hadley didn't tell them otherwise).

The rule of _Hadley v. Baxendale_ has become known as the _rule of foreseeability,_ which states that the breaching party is liable only for the losses that a reasonable party in the shoes of the breaching party would have known, at the time of the contract, would likely result from the breach.

This rule is practical because it allows the parties to negotiate which damages the breaching party will be liable for. Assume that Hadley has learned his lesson. The next time he takes a broken crankshaft to a carrier, he tells the carrier, "My good man. This is my only crankshaft, and if you are late delivering it, I will hold you liable for all the losses that result from the late delivery." The carrier, now knowing of his potential liability, uses his freedom of contract to shift the risk back to Hadley. "Sorry, my good man," he says, "but I won't accept the shipment on that basis. I will accept it only if you sign this contract that clearly states, 'Shipper is not liable for consequential damages.'"

Protecting your client with a consequential damages provision

According to the rule of foreseeability (discussed in the preceding section), you're not liable if you don't know or have no reason to know about the consequential damages that may result from breach. However, if your client does know or has reason to know about potential consequential damages, consider drafting a disclaimer to contract around such damages. Provisions that disclaim consequential damages or limit them to a certain amount frequently arise in the terms of service and in warranties, as I discuss in Chapter 10.

Shipping services, for instance, state that they're liable only for the cost of shipping and not for any consequential damages. If customers want to cover those losses, they're free to purchase insurance.

A tire seller, for example, knows that if it sells a defective tire, it's responsible for the direct damages that result from the defect — the cost of repairing or replacing the tire. Without being told, the seller also knows that the defective tire may cause other damage, such as property damage or personal injury. So under the rule of foreseeability, the tire seller would be liable for those consequential damages. To protect itself against those losses, most tire sellers include a provision clearly stating that they're not liable for consequential damages.

Civil procedure: Pleading special damages

When preparing a pleading (a summons and complaint), be careful about how you state your claim for damages. You have to alert the defendant to your claim for consequential damages, which are called *special damages* in civil procedure. Rule 9(g) of the Federal Rules of Civil Procedure, adopted by most states, provides the following:

> (9)(g) Special Damages.
>
> If an item of special damage is claimed, it must be specifically stated.

Your pleading doesn't need to spell out the direct damages (called *general damages* in civil procedure) because those damages always result from breach, so the defendant ought to know she may be liable for them. But if the plaintiff intends to claim special damages, the pleadings have to put the defendant on notice of exactly what the plaintiff intends to prove, because as the rule of foreseeability points out, these damages don't always occur and may come in different shapes and sizes.

For example, in a Montana case, a musician took the seller of some sound equipment to court because he claimed the equipment didn't work. Fine, said the seller, we'll pay to repair the sound equipment. But the musician then explained that he was a professional musician and the equipment had failed at a concert, costing him thousands of dollars. The defendant said, "We didn't know that from your pleadings." Because these are special damages, the court had to throw out the claim for those losses. When pleading *special damages* on behalf of a plaintiff, be sure to spell out those damages in the pleading.

Although provisions excluding or limiting consequential damages are generally legal, one exception limits the seller's right to protect itself in that way. According to UCC § 2-719(3), the limitation of consequential damages for personal injury in the case of consumer goods is *prima facie* (on its face) unconscionable. In other words, the tire seller could disclaim liability for consequential damages for personal injury if it sold the tire to a truck driver but not if it sold the tire to a commuter.

Asking whether the non-breaching party mitigated the loss

Contract law doesn't like to give one party something at the expense of another party, so it expects plaintiffs to take reasonable steps to reduce the amount of the loss. According to the *rule of mitigation*, also known as the *rule of avoidable consequences,* the defendant isn't liable for any losses that the plaintiff reasonably could've avoided. To encourage parties to mitigate their losses, parties may recover as damages any reasonable expenses incurred for mitigating the losses.

If a factory must shut down its assembly line because a supplier didn't deliver a $5 part as promised and if the buyer can satisfy the rule of foreseeability (see the earlier section "Limiting damages with the rule of foreseeability"), the supplier may be responsible for consequential damages — the amount of money the factory lost due to the shutdown. But the buyer has a duty to try to mitigate the losses, perhaps by finding another part and getting the assembly line going again. The buyer may then recover damages that include the cost of procuring that other part. The plaintiff doesn't have to make heroic efforts, just reasonable efforts to reduce the loss.

A party has a duty to mitigate only if the breach freed the party to use that time to earn money. In other words, if the party could've earned the money anyway, it has no duty to mitigate. For example, when a builder agrees to build a house and is told immediately not to build it, the builder isn't mitigating when it takes another job during that time. It could've built both houses by subcontracting the work, so the breach didn't necessarily free the builder to do additional work.

When an employer wrongfully terminates an employee, he frees the employee to perform other work, so the employee has a duty to mitigate. If a comparable position opens and the employee takes it or the defendant can prove that the employee could've taken it but didn't, the employee can only recover damages equal to the total damages minus what he earned or would have earned by taking the new job. If the employee looked for a comparable job with comparable pay and couldn't find one or wasn't hired, the employee would be eligible to collect 100 percent of the damages. In addition, the employee could recover the cost of trying to find a job. Because mitigation benefits the employer, contract law awards as damages the cost of reasonable attempts to secure employment, even if those attempts are unsuccessful.

In the famous case of *Parker v. Twentieth Century-Fox Film Corp.,* Shirley MacLaine (Parker) was hired as the female lead in a movie called *Bloomer Girl.* The movie company then breached the contract by deciding not to make the movie. In mitigation of MacLaine's damages, the company offered her a role in another movie called *Big Country, Big Man,* to be filmed at the same time for the same compensation. When MacLaine refused to accept this offer, the company refused to pay her any damages because of her failure to mitigate.

The majority of the California Supreme Court found that the case turned on whether the employment offered in mitigation was "different or inferior" from the original employment, because historically an employee doesn't have to lower her status in order to mitigate. The court found that the two roles had substantial differences, including (1) she had the right to approve the director of one but not the other, (2) one was the lead in a song-and-dance production, and the other was the female lead in a western, and (3) one was filmed in Hollywood, and the other was filmed in Australia. A strong dissent pointed out that of course another job is always different, but different does not necessarily mean inferior. Furthermore, whether the distinctions really did make the second job inferior was a fact question that shouldn't be resolved by an appellate court.

Using Reliance and Restitution as Remedies

In addition to the expectancy damages, courts may use reliance and restitution as remedies to obtain financial justice for breach. Here's a rundown of each remedy:

- ✔ **Reliance:** Reliance arises when a party reasonably changes her position in response to another party's promise, as I explain in Chapter 4. Reliance damages consist of the amount of money required to put the party back to her original position by compensating her for out-of-pocket expenses.

- ✔ **Restitution:** Restitution arises when, after one party confers on another party a benefit that's not officious (forced on him) and not a gift, contract law requires that the recipient *disgorge* (return the value of) the benefit. The measure of restitution is the value of the benefit he received.

This section explains how courts are likely to apply reliance and restitution as remedies.

Seeking reliance damages for breach

In a contract case, the non-breaching party generally claims the expectancy (as I explain in the earlier section "Mastering the Rule of the Expectancy"). Parties may also seek reliance damages in addition to or rather than the expectancy damages.

To qualify for reliance damages *in addition* to the expectancy, a party must prove that she incurred a certain expense due to her reliance on the other party's performance. For a party to be eligible for reliance damages, the loss must be suffered because of the breach. If the losses would've been incurred regardless of the breach, they're not eligible.

For example, suppose you promise a pizza oven for my business, and I build a platform for it. You breach by failing to deliver the oven, and I have to buy a different oven. If the platform works for the new oven, I can't recover the cost of the platform in reliance, because I would've had that expense even if you had performed. If I can't use the platform for the new oven, however, I should be able to recover that expense, because I built the platform relying on your performance, the loss was caused by the breach, and I would not have incurred the cost of two platforms. I'm also entitled to the expectancy damages, which may include direct damages if I paid more for the replacement oven, and consequential damages if the lack of an oven resulted in a loss of revenue that you should've reasonably foreseen.

A party may also recover reliance damages when the party is unable to prove the expectancy. Think of this as a fallback position, because the expectancy damages are likely to be greater, and a court may limit the reliance damages if the party wasn't eligible for the expectancy damages.

In a famous case, a boxer canceled a prizefight after the promoter had spent money promoting it. Theoretically, the promoter was entitled to the expectancy damages — the profit he would've earned had the fighter honored the contract — but those damages were speculative (uncertain). However, the promoter was able to fall back on recovering the out-of-pocket expenses he had incurred in reliance on the fight being held, including ticket printing and advertising. However, if the fighter could demonstrate that the fight would have lost money (no expectancy damages), the court would likely not award reliance damages.

Granting restitution for breach

If one party confers a benefit on another without intending it as a gift or forcing it on the other party, the party conferring the benefit may have a claim for restitution (see Chapter 4 for details). In addition, when one party performs fully or partially before the other party breaches the contract, the party who conferred the benefit can then claim restitution from the breaching party.

The clearest example of restitution is return of a down payment. Assume that I promise to sell my house to you for $200,000, and you give me a $10,000 down payment. I then breach by refusing to sell the house to you. You may be entitled to the expectancy damages if the house was worth more than $200,000. But regardless of whether you recover the expectancy damages, I would clearly be forced in restitution to disgorge the benefit you conferred on me when you gave me the $10,000 down payment.

A party who can't establish any expectancy damages, perhaps because it's a losing contract or because the amount of the expectancy is speculative, sometimes claims restitution instead. By *losing contract,* I mean that if both parties performed, the non-breaching party would have had a loss rather than a gain.

Suppose a contractor agrees to build a home for $200,000, thinking that he will incur $180,000 in costs and earn a $20,000 profit. After the builder has completed 90 percent of the house at a cost of $190,000, the owner breaches. (Note that the *owner* breaches, not the contractor.) Clearly, if the contractor had finished the house, it would've cost him more than $200,000 (probably more like $211,000) and he would've been paid $200,000. Therefore, the contractor would've had no claim for the expectancy because if both parties had completed the contract, he would've had a loss rather than a gain. Instead, he can seek restitution for the value of the benefit he conferred on the owner.

Calculating the benefit conferred is one of the more interesting challenges of contract law. In the case of the contractor, the portion of the house he built is probably worth a minimum of its cost — but the contractor may claim it's worth $209,000 because if he had put $190,000 into it, he could've sold the incomplete structure for $209,000 when his 10 percent profit was added. The owner would probably claim that $209,000 is absurd, because it's more than the contract price, but the contractor can say he's not claiming under the contract, where recovery is measured by the contract price, but in restitution, where recovery is measured by the reasonable value of the benefit conferred.

Unfortunately, contract law has no clear solution to this problem. The solutions range from $180,000 (90 percent of the contract price for a 90 percent completed house) to $209,000 (what the price would've been if the parties had contracted for that unfinished dwelling) to whatever a third-party appraiser would say it was worth.

Deciding whether dirty contract-breakers should get restitution

When a party performs only partially and then breaches, the courts must determine whether the dirty contract-breaker is entitled to any recovery. Recall that the courts aren't interested in penalizing either party; the goal is financial justice. How a court deals with situations like this depends on many factors, initially including whether the contract-breaker substantially performs. Here's what happens in each instance:

- ✔ **The contract breaker substantially performs:** A party who substantially performs and then breaches can recover on the contract (see Chapter 14 for details). She would recover whatever was promised her in the contract minus the damages due the other party.

  Assume that a contractor completes 90 percent of the work on a $200,000 house and then quits, and the owner has the house finished by another contractor at a cost of $30,000. If the court finds that the first contractor substantially performed, he can recover the contract price of $200,000 minus the damages of $30,000, which is $170,000. The owner in this case has the expectancy of a house at a cost of $200,000, which she gets by paying the initial contractor $170,000 and the second contractor $30,000.

  You may be wondering what happens if the cost of completion is lower, say $15,000. Does the contractor still recover the contract price minus the cost of completion ($200,000 – $15,000 = $185,000)? Most courts would limit the contractor's recovery to the pro rata part of the contract that the contractor completed. If she did 90 percent of the work on a $200,000 house, she should get no more than 90 percent of the contract price: $200,000 × 0.90 = $180,000. Notice that this solution lets the non-breaching party, not the contract-breaker, keep the benefit of the lower cost of completion.

- ✔ **The contract breaker doesn't substantially perform:** If the court finds that the breaching party didn't substantially perform, that party can't sue on the contract. As I explain in Chapter 14, the breaching party is entitled to nothing under the contract because she didn't bring about the event that had to occur before she could get paid. So this party must fall back on a claim in restitution.

  Most (but not all) courts allow a breaching party to recover restitution, but the measure of restitution varies widely. Some courts handle scenarios like this as if the breaching party had substantially performed; the courts start with the contract price and subtract the amount required to put the non-breaching party where he would've been had he received what he was promised. Other courts start with the value of the benefit conferred to the non-breaching party but cap the restitution to give the non-breaching party the expectancy.

Computing the value of the benefit conferred

In the old days, dirty contract-breakers didn't get restitution, which doesn't seem fair, because under this rule, the more the party performs before breach, the more he loses. If a contractor knew he wasn't going to get anything if he didn't finish, he'd be more inclined to breach early rather than try to complete the project.

The modern rule gives restitution to the breaching party, but contract law is still left with the problem of how to measure that restitution. Some courts award the contract price minus the cost of completion, which is a bit odd, because restitution is supposed to be based on the value of the benefit conferred.

A better approach would be to start by trying to measure the value of the benefit conferred, while keeping in mind that the expectancy of the non-breaching party comes first. Assume that a contractor does 50 percent of the work on a $200,000 house and then quits, and the owner hires a second contractor to finish the house at a cost of $110,000. If you start with the contract price, restitution based on the value conferred is 50 percent of the contract price: $200,000 × 0.50 = $100,000. Because the owner hired the second contractor to complete the project for $110,000, however, the first contractor can't recover in restitution more than $90,000.

If you start with the value of the benefit conferred on the owner, the contractor is going to claim that the value is $110,000, because a reasonable contractor would've charged that much for that job. However, the fact that a party racked up a lot of time doing work doesn't mean it's worth that much. A good tip to use in a situation like this is to measure the value of the benefit conferred from the point of view of the non-breaching party. That is, ask how much the work is worth to the owner. The answer will be a maximum of $90,000, but it may well be less if the work was poor quality. As Arthur Corbin said in another context, you need the wisdom of Solomon to compute the value of the benefit conferred in a restitution claim.

Chapter 17

Exploring Remedies in Article 2 of the UCC

. . . .

In This Chapter

▶ Comparing UCC to common-law remedies

▶ Awarding remedies to buyers when sellers breach

▶ Handing out remedies to sellers when buyers breach

. . . .

*I*n transactions that involve the sale of goods, contract law turns to Article 2 of the Uniform Commercial Code (UCC) for guidance in awarding damages for breach of contract. The UCC approach differs somewhat from the common-law approach I describe in Chapter 16, but the desired result is pretty much the same: to give the non-breaching party what it would've had if both parties had performed.

This chapter compares the UCC and common-law approach to remedies and explains how the courts use the UCC formulas and the principles behind them to calculate remedies for both buyers and sellers.

Comparing Common-Law and UCC Remedies

The goal of common-law remedies for breach is to give both parties the *expectancy,* or what they would've received had both parties performed (see Chapter 16). UCC remedies have the same goal, but the statutes use a more for-mulaic approach, using actual formulas in some cases to calculate remedies.

But don't let the formulas lull you into thinking that the UCC makes calculating remedies an exact science. According to UCC § 1-305, the remedies "should be liberally administered." In other words, the courts are instructed not to be rigid in following the formulaic approach but instead to act in the spirit of the more liberal common-law rules. Furthermore, when applying the UCC formulas, consider some common-law rules, including causation, foreseeability, certainty, and mitigation, that may not be expressly stated in the statutes.

UCC remedies are more similar to their common-law cousins than they are different. This section highlights the key difference and similarity between the two.

Recognizing the key difference

The key difference between the common-law and UCC approach to arriving at remedies for breach is this: Goods can usually be bought and sold in a market, and even if no actual sale occurs, a market price can be determined. In this respect, a contract to buy 100,000 widgets differs from a construction contract or an employment contract, because the non-breaching party in contract or employment agreements won't find a handy market with established prices.

Many goods are *fungible* (interchangeable). As defined in UCC § 1-201(b)(18), *fungible* means that "any unit, by nature of usage or trade, is the equivalent of any other like unit." So if I promise to sell you 100,000 bushels of winter wheat, this commodity could come from any supplier of winter wheat. Furthermore, we can readily find a market price in a place where winter wheat is regularly traded.

Of course, although a market to buy and sell the goods usually exists, Article 2 of the Code applies to all sales of goods, even when no market for the goods exists. When no market exists, the buyer may seek *specific performance,* which means a demand that the seller provide the goods (see "Seeking specific performance: Getting the promised goods," later in this chapter).

Understanding just how similar they really are

If a contract involves the sale of goods, you can look to UCC Article 2 for the rules that govern remedies. For the most part, the UCC is another way to express common-law rules. So if you understand the common-law rules that govern remedies, you already have a good grasp of the UCC rules.

According to the Code, remedies must be "liberally administered" to serve the general purposes of remedies. As enacted in North Carolina at 25-1-305(a), § 1-305(a) states the following:

> § 25-1-305. Remedies to be liberally administered.
>
> (a) The remedies provided by this Chapter shall be liberally administered to the end that the aggrieved party may be put in as good a position as if the other party had fully performed, but neither consequential or special damages nor penal damages may be had except as specifically provided in this Chapter or by other rule of law.

In other words, courts should keep their eyes on the expectancy, as I explain in Chapter 16. Furthermore, because the goal of expectation damages is to put the non-breaching party "in as good a position," as she would've been in had the parties performed, courts must be careful not to overcompensate or undercompensate that party. The warning against "penal damages," for example, tells courts not to award punitive damages, which would overcompensate the non-breaching party.

In applying remedies in an Article 2 transaction, always remember that not all the applicable rules are expressly stated in the Code. Section 1-103(2) states that unless displaced by a particular provision, the general principles of law and equity supplement the Code provisions. Chapter 16 explains a number of these general principles, such as causation, certainty, and mitigation.

Giving the Buyer a Remedy When the Seller Is in Breach

When sellers fail to perform their end of the bargain, buyers are entitled to remedies, which include the following:

- ✔ **Specific performance:** Demanding the promised goods
- ✔ **Cover:** Obtaining the goods from another source
- ✔ **Market:** Not obtaining the goods from another source but calculating damages based on the market price

This section explains these remedies in greater detail. It also explains when to add consequential and incidental damages and what to do when a seller breaches a contract after a buyer accepts goods or services.

Seeking specific performance: Getting the promised goods

With *specific performance,* the court orders the defendant to perform the contract by actually delivering the goods rather than paying money damages for breach. Specific performance is an *equitable remedy* as opposed to a *remedy at law.* Here's what each of these remedies is:

- ✔ **Remedy at law:** Typically money damages

- ✔ **Equitable remedy:** A court-ordered action, such as requiring a party to perform the contract (for more about equitable remedies, see Chapter 18)

If you're seeking an equitable remedy in a court of general jurisdiction, you have to prove that the remedy at law is inadequate. So, with contracts, you have to prove that no matter how much money you get from the defendant, you still won't get the financial equivalent of performance.

For example, outside the UCC are real estate contracts. Courts can enforce land sales by specific performance, because money won't get the buyer the equivalent piece of real estate. Similarly, within the UCC, § 2-716(1) says that "specific performance may be decreed where the goods are unique or in other proper circumstances." So if, for instance, you contract to sell me a particular painting by Picasso, money damages won't get me the equivalent of performance because I can't buy that Picasso painting somewhere else.

The reference in the Code to "other proper circumstances" comes up in long-term contracts for the sale of a commodity. For example, if I contract to sell you 100,000 barrels of Saudi Arabian crude oil and breach, you can probably find the oil elsewhere, even if you have to pay a bit more, because it's fungible. Therefore, you couldn't get specific performance. But if I contract to provide you with 100,000 barrels of Saudi Arabian crude oil each year for the next five years, and then I breach, your expectancy was not just the oil but also a long-term commitment to provide oil. If you're unable to find a seller willing to provide the same long-term contract, specific performance may be appropriate.

Buying substitute goods and calculating cover damages

Most of the time, buyers who don't get the promised goods from the seller *cover* after breach by purchasing the same goods somewhere else and then seeking damages from the initial seller for the difference between what they would've paid under the contract and what they had to pay to cover. The Code contains this formula for calculating damages in § 2-712(2):

Cover price

−Contract price

+Incidental and consequential damages

−Expenses saved by breach

Damages

Here are the main parts of the equation:

- ✔ **Cover price:** The *cover price* is what the buyer had to pay another supplier to buy the same goods elsewhere.

- ✔ **Contract price:** The *contract price* is the price named in the contract.

- ✔ **Incidental and consequential damages:** *Incidental damages* are expenses related to the actual damages, such as storage and shipping costs to return defective goods. *Consequential damages* are losses that result from not receiving what was promised, such as lost sales because a party failed to deliver supplies needed in the manufacturing process. (For information about incidental and consequential damages, see "Adding consequential damages for losses caused by the breach" and "Including incidental damages and subtracting savings," later in this chapter.)

- ✔ **Expenses saved by the breach:** *Expenses saved by breach* are any savings that resulted from the breach; for instance, a lower shipping expense from another supplier.

As with common law, the principle of mitigation requires the buyer to keep the damages as low as reasonably possible (see Chapter 16 for a rundown on the rules of mitigation). So he has to cover in good faith by purchasing within a reasonable time at a reasonable price.

Suppose a buyer in Boston contracted to buy from a seller in Seattle 100,000 bushels of winter wheat at $7.50 per bushel. The buyer agreed to pay the shipping cost of $50,000. The seller later breaches. The buyer finds similar wheat from a seller in Minneapolis for $8.00 per bushel and has to pay shipping costs of $30,000 to get it. Here are the numbers:

Cover price: $800,000

Contract price: $750,000

Incidental and consequential damages: Assume $0 for now

Expenses saved by the breach: $20,000 (because according to the contract, the buyer would have to pay $50,000 in shipping costs but actually paid only $30,000, for a savings of $20,000)

The formula for calculating damages in this case looks like this:

$$
\begin{array}{r}
\$800,000 \\
-\$750,000 \\
+ \qquad \$0 \\
- \ \$20,000 \\
\hline
\$30,000
\end{array}
$$

Even without the formula, you can see that $30,000 is the correct result under the rule of the expectancy (see Chapter 16 for details on the expectancy). Had the seller performed, the buyer would have had the wheat at a cost of $800,000, including the shipping cost. Because of the breach, the buyer has the wheat, but he's out $830,000 instead. To bring the buyer from where he is now (out $830,000) to where he would've been had both parties performed the contract (out $800,000), the seller must give him $30,000.

Making the buyer whole by calculating market damages

Sometimes the buyer doesn't want to cover; that is, she doesn't want to replace the goods she was promised. If the market price of the goods has risen higher than the contract price, which is the usual reason sellers breach, the buyer suffers a loss even if she doesn't cover. Had the seller performed, the buyer would have goods worth more than she paid for them. Contract law allows her to recover that benefit of the bargain. The Code contains this formula for calculating market damages in UCC § 2-713:

$$
\begin{array}{l}
\text{Market price} \\
-\text{Contract price} \\
+\text{Incidental and consequential damages} \\
-\text{Expenses saved by breach} \\
\hline
\text{Damages}
\end{array}
$$

Note: This formula is almost exactly the same as the cover formula in UCC § 2-712 except that it uses "market price" rather than "cover price." When breach occurs at the time of performance, the two formulas produce the same result, because if the buyer had covered, she would've done so at the market price in order to mitigate damages.

Assume you were going to sell me a car that was worth $11,000 for only $10,000. But then you breach. I could cover by purchasing a comparable car, but I elect not to. I'm still damaged, however, because had you sold me the car, my net worth would've increased by $1,000. According to the formula for calculating market damages, I can recover the difference between the market price ($11,000) and the contract price ($10,000), which is $1,000.

Conceivably, I could recover that $1,000 from you and then cover by buying a comparable car. However, doing so would probably make no difference to the outcome. I'd probably still have to pay $11,000 to get the car I wanted at the market price, so I'd end up with no more than my expectancy — an $11,000 car that cost me $10,000. (I would've paid $11,000, minus the $1,000 I received in damages from you.)

Section 2-713 says that the formula uses "the market price when the buyer learned of the breach." This language creates an issue when a seller breaches by *anticipatory repudiation* (breaching before performance is due, as I explain in Chapter 15), because the Code says "learned of the breach" and not "learned of the repudiation." Some courts therefore plug into the formula the market price at the time of performance rather than the market price at the time of the repudiation. The better choice is to use the price at the time of repudiation (or more precisely, a commercially reasonable time after the buyer learned of the repudiation, because the buyer may need some time to shop around for the best price). Why? Because if the buyer starts shopping for cover goods at that time, it reduces the cost of breach, and less money wasted is a good thing.

Suppose a buyer agrees to purchase 100,000 bushels of winter wheat at $7.50 per bushel to be delivered October 1. On August 1, when the market price reaches $7.75 per bushel, the seller clearly and unequivocally informs the buyer that he isn't going to perform. The buyer waits until October 1 when the market price is $8.00 per bushel, and when the seller fails to deliver on that day, the buyer seeks to recover damages. If she plugs into the formula the difference between the market price of $800,000 at the time of performance, October 1, and the contract price of $750,000, then she can claim damages of $50,000.

However, she could've mitigated by buying the goods at the time of the repudiation. Had she done so, the damages would've been the difference between the market price at the time of the repudiation on August 1 ($775,000) and the contract price ($750,000), and she could recover only $25,000. This is the better interpretation of the language because it discourages the buyer from doing nothing at the expense of the seller. Similarly, if a buyer covers but pays more than the market price, her damages are calculated according to the market formula, giving her what she would've had if she had covered in a reasonable manner.

Adding consequential damages for losses caused by the breach

As I explain in the preceding two sections, the formulas for both cover damages and market damages include the buyer's right to recover consequential damages. The UCC incorporates the rule of foreseeability (the Hadley rule) for consequential damages (see Chapter 16). The rule is found in UCC § 2-715(2)(a). As enacted in North Carolina at 25-2-715(2)(a), it provides:

> (2) Consequential damages resulting from the seller's breach include
>
> > (a) any loss resulting from general or particular requirements and needs of which the seller at the time of contracting had reason to know and which could not reasonably be prevented by cover or otherwise;

This section of the Code contains the only express reference to mitigation in Article 2, though you know that the concept should be applied because UCC § 1-102 tells you to supplement the Code with common-law principles.

Suppose the wheat buyer in the example in the preceding section operates a cereal factory and needs the wheat she contracted to buy to make cereal. When she doesn't receive the wheat, she says she can't make the cereal and claims as consequential damages the lost profit from her cereal sales. The seller has two defenses to this claim:

- ✔ **Lack of advance knowledge:** The seller is liable only for consequential damages that, in the words of UCC § 2-715(2)(a), "the seller at the time of contracting had reason to know." Although this seller would probably know that the wheat was used to produce cereal, he wouldn't know that the buyer was running low on inventory and would have to stop production if she didn't get this particular shipment. If the buyer had told the seller at the time they made the contract, "If I don't get that wheat, my assembly line will stop, and I won't be able to make cereal," that discussion would've addressed the foreseeability issue.

- ✔ **Loss prevention:** The seller is liable only for a loss "which could not reasonably be prevented by cover or otherwise." Here, the buyer could've prevented the loss simply by covering — buying the wheat somewhere else. *Remember:* The principle of mitigation doesn't allow a buyer to rack up losses at the seller's expense when she reasonably could prevent them.

Including incidental damages and subtracting savings

Incidental damages is a phrase that's unique to the Code. In the case of a buyer seeking damages, it's defined in UCC § 2-715(1). As enacted in North Carolina at 25-2-715(1), it provides:

> § 25-2-715. Buyer's incidental and consequential damages.
>
> (1) Incidental damages resulting from the seller's breach include expenses reasonably incurred in inspection, receipt, transportation and care and custody of goods rightfully rejected, any commercially reasonable charges, expenses or commissions in connection with effecting cover and any other reasonable expense incident to the delay or other breach.

Incidental damages are really a form of consequential damages, because they're expenses set in motion by a breach. If a buyer doesn't get the correct goods from a seller, he may incur expenses in storing those goods or returning them. If the seller didn't deliver the goods at all, the buyer may incur expenses to find another seller. The main point of this provision is to exempt these expenses from the foreseeability requirement (see Chapter 16 for details). Because these are minor expenses incurred in dealing with the consequence of the breach, contract law can assume that the seller would know that they would result from a breach.

Sometimes a buyer claims that hiring a lawyer to pursue the seller is a reasonable incidental expense or consequential loss, but courts have rejected this argument. Under the American Rule (see Chapter 16), a party isn't entitled to attorney's fees unless they provide for them in the contract or sue under a statute that provides for them, and the UCC doesn't.

The final part of the damages formula, both for cover damages and market damages, is to deduct "expenses saved in consequence of the seller's breach." The principle here is that to the extent the breach saved the buyer some money, the damages should be reduced by that amount. For example, a buyer of winter wheat was going to pay $50,000 in shipping expenses to the seller under the contract. When the seller breached, the buyer covered and paid only $30,000 in shipping expenses to the second seller. The damages the first seller pays should be reduced by the $20,000 that the buyer saved because of the breach.

Keeping the goods and claiming damages

A seller may be in breach even if the buyer accepts the goods from the seller. For instance, perhaps a buyer doesn't discover within a reasonable time after delivery that the goods aren't as promised and he doesn't have the right to revoke acceptance under UCC § 2-608. Or the goods were supplied with a warranty, and a buyer doesn't discover a breach of warranty until later.

When a buyer accepts goods and then finds that the seller is in breach, the remedy is provided in UCC § 2-714(2). As enacted in North Carolina at 25-2-714(2), it provides:

> (2) The measure of damages for breach of warranty is the difference at the time and place of acceptance between the value of the goods accepted and the value they would have had if they had been as warranted, unless special circumstances show proximate damages of a different amount.

The formula under this provision looks like this:

> Value of the goods as promised
>
> –Value of the goods accepted
>
> Damages

Suppose a seller delivers a computer that's warranted to have a 500-gigabyte hard drive. After acceptance, the buyer finds that the hard drive is only 250 gigabytes. The buyer is entitled to the difference in value between what was promised and what was accepted. You could measure this amount in different ways: the difference in the sale price of the computer with the 500-gigabyte hard drive and the same computer with a 250-gigabyte hard drive, or the cost of giving the buyer what it was promised, which is usually the cost of repair.

The seller may claim that its 500-gig computer sells for $1,000, whereas its 250-gig computer sells for $950, making the difference in value $50. But the buyer may claim that to have the 250-gigabyte drive replaced with a 500-gigabyte drive would cost $100, so that repair cost represents the difference in value. This question is a difficult one for a court, but the repair cost appears to be more in line with the principle of the expectancy, because it's the amount needed to put the buyer where he would've been had the seller performed.

The formula for keeping the goods and then claiming damages may not seem fair to the seller in cases where a seller makes rash promises.

Suppose a seller offers $1,000 for a computer that it promises has features only computers that cost $5,000 have. After I buy the $1,000 computer, I discover that it doesn't have all those features — it only has the features of a $2,000 computer. The formula says I have a claim for damages of $3,000 — the difference between the value of what I was promised ($5,000) and what I got ($2,000). The seller may think that's unfair, because I didn't lose any money — in fact, I got a $2,000 computer for $1,000. Furthermore, the seller only got paid $1,000 but has to pay $3,000 in damages. Nevertheless, the rule of the expectancy says that I'm entitled to the benefit of the bargain I made, and had the seller performed, I would've had an increase in my wealth of $4,000. The formula gives me that amount, because I spent $1,000 and got something worth $2,000 plus $3,000 in damages, which leaves me where I would've been: $4,000 ahead.

Providing the Seller a Remedy When the Buyer's in Breach

After you understand the buyer's remedies against the seller (see the earlier section "Giving the Buyer a Remedy When the Seller Is in Breach"), the seller's claims against the buyer are easy, because they're mostly the mirror image of those damages with a few extra wrinkles thrown in. These remedies include the following:

- ✔ **Damages for delivered goods:** Obtaining the contract price
- ✔ **Resale:** Selling the goods to another buyer
- ✔ **Market:** Not reselling the goods but calculating the damages based on the market price

In this section, I explain all three of these remedies as well as what to do when none of them gives a party the benefit of the bargain.

Seeking the contract price as damages

If a seller has delivered goods to a buyer and the buyer breaches the contract, the seller's remedy is simple enough: The seller has performed his part of the contract, so he's entitled to the amount of money that gives him what he would've had: the contract price.

Sometimes this remedy may seem unfair to the seller. Suppose, for example, the seller promises to sell 100,000 bushels of wheat at $7.50 a bushel. The market price of wheat goes up to $8.00 a bushel, but the seller still delivers the goods. The buyer, however, doesn't pay the seller the agreed upon $750,000. Even though the seller has delivered goods worth $800,000, his expectancy was to get $750,000 for them, so that's all he can recover.

You can find this rule in UCC § 2-709(1)(a). As enacted in North Carolina at 25-2-709(1), the rule provides:

§ 25-2-709. Action for the price.

(1) When the buyer fails to pay the price as it becomes due the seller may recover, together with any incidental damages under the next section, the price

(a) of goods accepted or of conforming goods lost or damaged within a commercially reasonable time after risk of their loss has passed to the buyer; and

(b) of goods identified to the contract if the seller is unable after reasonable effort to resell them at a reasonable price or the circumstances reasonably indicate that such effort will be unavailing.

Sometimes the seller can recover the contract price of the goods even if he doesn't deliver them to the buyer. That rule is found in UCC § 2-709(1)(b). This situation usually arises with unusual goods that have no market value.

Suppose a buyer orders a neon sign for $2,000 that says "Eat at Joe's" and refuses to accept delivery when it's finished. The seller has to mitigate by making reasonable efforts to find a buyer for the goods, but finding someone to buy an "Eat at Joe's" neon sign is probably not going to happen. So he can recover the $2,000.

Selling to someone else and calculating resale damages

Most of the time, when a seller finds that a buyer doesn't want the goods he contracted to buy, she sells them to someone else. This resale remedy is similar to the buyer's cover remedy, in which the buyer purchases the goods from someone else and then recovers from the seller who's in breach any additional cost above the contract price (see the earlier section "Buying substitute goods and calculating cover damages" for details).

The resale formula, as found in UCC § 2-706(1) is this:

Contract price

–Resale price

+Incidental damages

–Expenses saved

Damages

One difference between the resale formula and the cover formula in UCC § 2-712 is that the seller's remedies don't include consequential damages, because when the buyer doesn't perform, the seller doesn't get money. To prove that nonpayment by one particular buyer caused a foreseeable loss to the seller would be difficult, so as a matter of policy, don't go there.

Suppose a buyer in Boston contracted to buy from a seller in Seattle 100,000 bushels of winter wheat at $7.50 per bushel. The buyer agreed to pay the shipping cost of $50,000. The buyer breaches. The seller finds a buyer in Minneapolis who will pay $7.00 per bushel, but the seller has to pay shipping costs of $30,000 to get it there. The numbers look like this:

Contract price: $750,000

Resale price: $700,000

Incidental damages: $30,000

Expenses saved by the breach: $0 (The seller saved nothing, because the buyer was going to pay for shipping.)

Plug the numbers into the formula:

$$\begin{array}{r} \$750,000 \\ -\$700,000 \\ +\ \$30,000 \\ -\quad\quad \$0 \\ \hline \$80,000 \end{array}$$

Even without the formula, you can see that $80,000 is the correct result under the rule of the expectancy. If the buyer had performed the contract, the seller would've been out the wheat and would have $750,000. Because of the breach, the seller has only $700,000 for the wheat and is out $30,000 for the shipping. To bring the seller from where he is now (having $670,000) to where he would've been had the contract been performed (having $750,000), the buyer has to give him $80,000.

Deciding whether to complete the manufacture of the goods

The resale remedy assumes that the goods are ready for resale at the time of the breach, but what if they're not? Should the seller continue to manufacture the goods even though doing so may result in the buyer's paying more in damages? The seller has two options:

- ✔ Stop manufacturing the goods.
- ✔ Manufacture the goods and then sell them.

Contract law expects the seller to choose the option that the seller reasonably believes will mitigate her loss to the greatest extent, thus minimizing the buyer's liability.

In the famous common law case of *Rockingham County v. Luten Bridge Co.,* the county ordered a bridge to be built. After construction began, the county breached the contract, saying it didn't want the bridge. The contractor nevertheless finished the job and then sued for the contract price. The court held that the contractor couldn't recover for the completed bridge because of mitigation.

Assume that the contract price was $100,000 and that the contractor was going to spend $90,000 on labor and materials to make a $10,000 profit. As I explain in Chapter 16, at whatever point the county breaches, the contractor recovers enough damages to pay its expenses and end up with a $10,000 profit. So the contractor gets no additional benefit by continuing to work — it always comes out ahead $10,000. But the more work the contractor does, the more money the county loses. To prevent those losses to the county, the contractor must stop work when the county breaches.

However, that common-law rule may not apply to the sale of goods, because the seller can ship the goods elsewhere when they're finished. Assume, for instance, that a buyer contracts with a seller to build a machine for $100,000, and the seller expects to earn a $10,000 profit. After the seller invests $30,000 in the machine, the buyer breaches. To give the seller the expectancy, the buyer would need to pay the seller $40,000 in damages. But if the seller completes the machine and sells it for $80,000, the damages would be only $20,000.

UCC § 2-704(2) allows the seller to complete the manufacture "in the exercise of reasonable commercial judgment." As enacted in North Carolina at § 25-2-704(2), it provides:

> (2) Where the goods are unfinished an aggrieved seller may in the exercise of reasonable commercial judgment for the purposes of avoiding loss and of effective realization either complete the manufacture and wholly identify the goods to the contract or cease manufacture and resell for scrap or salvage value or proceed in any other reasonable manner.

An interesting problem arises if the seller thought it could reduce the damages by completing manufacture, but by the time it finishes, the machine is obsolete and all the seller can get for it is $20,000. The seller would claim a loss of $80,000, but the buyer would claim that the seller could've stopped production and had damages of only $40,000. The outcome of a situation like this probably depends on whether the seller's decision was reasonable at the time it made the decision, not on how it looks in hindsight. Because the policy of mitigation is so important, most courts agree that a party should recover if it took reasonable steps to save the breaching party money — even if those steps backfired.

Making the seller whole by calculating market damages

Just as a buyer can decide not to cover and instead recover the difference between the market price and the contract price, so too can the seller decide not to resell and instead recover the difference between the contract price and the market price. The formula to determine the amount the seller is eligible to recover as market damages, found in UCC § 2-708, is as follows:

Contract price

–Market price

+Incidental damages

<u>–Expenses saved</u>

Damages

The *market price* is the price that the goods can be sold for at the time and place for tender. (*Tender* means offering the performance.) Unless otherwise agreed, when a seller is obligated to send goods to a buyer, UCC § 2-504 says that his obligation isn't to get them to the buyer but to get them to the carrier, such as a delivery service or railroad. In other words, in a shipment contract, the seller tenders the goods when he delivers them to the carrier.

For example, a buyer in Boston contracts to buy from a seller in Seattle 100,000 bushels of winter wheat at $7.50 per bushel. The buyer agrees to pay the shipping cost of $50,000. The wheat is to be shipped from Seattle on October 1, arriving in Boston on October 5. Because this is a shipment contract under which the seller's obligation is to tender the goods to the shipper in Seattle on October 1, the time and place for tender are October 1 in Seattle. So to find the market price, you'd look up the market price in Seattle on that date.

Assume that market price in Seattle was $7.00 per bushel. The numbers look like this:

Contract price: $750,000

Resale price: $700,000

Incidental damages: $0

Expenses saved by the breach: $0 (The seller saved nothing, because the buyer was going to pay for the shipping.)

Plugging the numbers into the formula, you see that the buyer owes the seller $50,000 in market damages:

$$
\begin{array}{rr}
 & \$750,000 \\
- & \$700,000 \\
+ & \$0 \\
- & \$0 \\
\hline
 & \$50,000
\end{array}
$$

Solving the mystery of lost profits

Sometimes remedies formulas don't give a party the benefit of the bargain. In such cases, remember that the overall purpose of the rules is to compensate the injured party for its loss. The Code states in UCC § 1-305 that because compensating the injured party is more important than the literal rules, the Code remedies should be "liberally administered" to fairly compensate the injured party.

A good example of how the Code liberally administers remedies is the *lost profits rule* of UCC § 2-708(2). This rule provides that if the other measures of damage wouldn't give the seller its expectancy, the measure of damages is the profit that the seller would've made. This rule applies only to volume sellers, or those able to sell a number of the goods.

For example, assume that I have a contract to sell you my car for $10,000. You breach, and immediately a third party buys the car for $10,000. Under the seller's resale rule of UCC § 2-706, I received my expectancy. The difference between the contact price and the resale price is $0, so I lost nothing.

The same scenario with a new-car dealer has an entirely different outcome, however. Assume a new-car dealer contracts to sell you a new car for $25,000. You immediately say you don't want it, and a few minutes later, a third party walks into the showroom and buys the car for $25,000. You claim that under UCC § 2-706, the car dealer hasn't suffered any loss because it was able to resell the car. But the dealer may claim that because it can get a supply of cars from the manufacturer, it could've sold cars to both you and the third party, so it's entitled to the profit it lost on your sale. According to the Code, this argument is a good one, but it's not easy to figure out how much that lost profit is — leave that task to the accountants.

In *Neri v. Retail Marine,* Mr. Neri bought a boat from Retail Marine for $12,587. The boat had to be ordered from the manufacturer, but before it arrived, Neri breached and said he didn't want it. The shop spent $674 storing the boat, insuring it, and paying finance charges on it. After four months, Retail Marine sold the boat for $12,587. Retail Marine claimed as damages from Neri the $2,579 profit it would've made, the $674 costs it incurred after the breach, and $1,250 in attorney's fees.

The trial court didn't award any damages to Retail Marine. The appellate court, however, realized that this case was a classic example of when a seller should recover damages even if it resold the goods. The court quoted an authority that stated, "If the dealer has an inexhaustible supply . . . , the resale to replace the breaching buyer costs the dealer a sale because, had the breaching buyer performed, the dealer would have made two sales rather than one. The buyer's breach, in such a case, depletes the dealer's sales to the extent of one, and the measure of damages should be the dealer's profit on the sale." The court awarded the lost profit of $2,579. The court also determined that the $674 was exactly the kind of incidental damages that a seller can recover under UCC § 2-710. However, the court didn't allow the shop to recover attorney's fees, because no provision in the Code provides for them and the contract didn't provide for them, either.

Chapter 18

Checking for Additional Remedies

. . . .

In This Chapter

▶ Knowing when equitable remedies are likely to be granted

▶ Undoing or rewriting the contract

▶ Letting parties specify remedies for breach of contract

▶ Awarding transaction costs in addition to damages

▶ Looking at choice-of-law and choice-of-forum clauses

▶ Resolving disputes through arbitration and mediation

. . . .

Contract law typically provides remedies for breach, but parties have other options as well, including undoing or rewriting the contract, specifying their own remedies in the contract, and resolving disputes outside the courts through arbitration or mediation. (You can read about breach in Chapter 16. Chapter 17 gives you the lowdown on the most common remedies used to address breach of contract.)

This chapter discusses alternative remedies for breach, explores the sorts of transaction costs courts are likely to award in addition to damages, and explains why the courts rarely award attorney's fees or punitive damages in contracts cases.

Deciding Whether Equitable Remedies Should Be Granted

Merry Old England, where most American law came from, had two court systems: courts of law and courts of equity. Each had different authority, which they jealously guarded. As you may imagine, the *courts of law* had authority to grant remedies at law, mainly money damages. The *courts of equity* had authority to grant equitable relief, which mainly means ordering somebody to do or not to do something. If you went to a court of equity, the judge would look down his nose and ask, "Why isn't the court of law good enough for you?" You'd then have to explain why the remedy at law was inadequate.

Suppose back then that your neighbor was building a dam, which, when finished, would cause water to back up and flood your property. You could wait until the property was destroyed and sue him at law for money damages. Or you could explain to the court of equity that a better solution would be to get an injunction to prevent your neighbor from building the dam in the first place.

In most jurisdictions today, the courts of law and equity have been combined into what's known as the *courts of general jurisdiction*. Exceptions exist, notably in Delaware, which still has separate courts of equity. If you see a case on appeal where a chancellor rather than a judge made the decision, you're probably looking at a court of equity case. Also, many courts of limited jurisdiction, such as small claims courts, lack equity powers and can award only money judgments.

Even though the court systems have merged, the rule remains: To get equitable relief, you have to prove that the remedy at law is inadequate. In other words, it's not just about the money.

Courts today award two principal forms of equitable relief:

 ✔ **Specific performance:** Ordering a party to do something — usually what the party promised to do in the contract

 ✔ **Injunction:** Ordering a party *not* to do something

The following subsections describe these forms of equitable relief in detail.

Awarding specific performance . . . or not

Courts typically award specific performance when money damages are insufficient to settle a dispute. The clearest situation in which a court is likely to award specific performance involves real estate contracts. Because every parcel of real property is unique, money can't buy a true substitute, so the court orders specific performance, which the courts can easily enforce — if the seller refuses to convey the property to the buyer, the court can do it for her.

In the rest of the world, specific performance is a common remedy. However, courts in the U.S. are reluctant to award specific performance of a contract for the following two reasons:

✔ **Specific performance could send debtors to prison.** When a court grants a judgment after a trial, such as finding that a defendant breached the contract and the plaintiff is entitled to $10,000 in damages, it doesn't order the defendant to pay the $10,000. If the judge ordered the defendant to pay the money and she doesn't pay up, the defendant would be in contempt of court for violating a court order and could be thrown in jail. This order would amount to imprisoning debtors, and debtors' prison is an institution that was abolished long ago. Instead, the court gives the plaintiff a piece of paper called a *judgment* that says he's entitled to recover $10,000 from the defendant. With a judgment in hand, the plaintiff can use the resources of the state, such as the sheriff, to help collect the money.

✔ **Courts don't want to order specific performance when they would have to supervise the performance.** If a builder doesn't finish a construction project and the court orders her to complete it, the owner would probably return to court whining that the builder wasn't doing a very good job. The court doesn't want to get involved in supervising the dispute. Letting the owner find another builder to finish the job is much easier for the court, so the court awards money damages.

Stopping a party with an injunction

The equitable remedy of an *injunction* is nearly the opposite of specific performance. Instead of ordering a person to do something, an injunction orders her not to do something. As a practical matter, an injunction often induces the parties to work out their dispute.

Suppose New York City's Metropolitan Opera (the Met) hires a star to sing on a particular night. The star gets a better offer from La Scala in Milan, Italy, and says, "Ha-ha! I'm going to sing at La Scala, instead." To get the remedy at law, the Met would need to hire a different singer and claim as damages the difference between what it was going to pay the original singer and what it had to pay the substitute. But the Met claims that this remedy is inadequate because the singer is unique. This argument is probably a good one. After all, fewer people may be interested in seeing the other singer.

The court doesn't want to order the singer to perform because of problems with supervision (imagine the Met complaining to the judge, "She's not singing well enough. Order her to sing better!") and because doing so may amount to involuntary servitude. Instead, the court issues an injunction ordering the singer not to sing on that night for anyone else. This injunction may be enough to convince the singer to resolve her differences with the Met.

KEY CASE

Philadelphia Ball Club v. Lajoie

At the turn of the 20th century, the U.S. had only one predominant professional baseball league, the National League. In 1901, some entrepreneurs formed a rival league called the American League. As often happens in professional sports today, you can imagine that the new league tried to recruit a lot of its players from the existing league. The only problem was that those players had contracts with the National League teams, and the teams didn't want to let the players go.

One such player was Nap Lajoie, a second baseman with the Philadelphia Phillies. He was lured to break his contract and sign with the Philadelphia Athletics of the American League. The Phillies sued for equitable relief, and the court had to resolve the difficult question of whether Lajoie was a unique player. If he was just a run-of-the-mill player, the court reasoned that the remedy at law was adequate — the Phillies could just sign another second baseman and collect the money damages. But if he was unique, equitable relief was appropriate. After examining his statistics, the court concluded that "He may not be the sun in the baseball firmament, but he is certainly a bright particular star." This conclusion was later proved prophetic when Lajoie was inducted into the Hall of Fame.

The court didn't grant an order of specific performance, which would order Lajoie to play for the Phillies. It granted an injunction instead, ordering him not to play baseball for any other team. The action was brought in state court, however, so the injunction was valid only in Pennsylvania, meaning Lajoie wouldn't be able to play any home games for his new team, the Athletics. Rather than play him only on the road (outside the court's jurisdiction), the Athletics traded him to Cleveland. He avoided setting foot in Pennsylvania until the dispute was resolved when the two leagues worked out an agreement in 1903.

Today, the issue of whether a baseball player is unique isn't subject to serious dispute. Most people agree that athletes and star entertainers are unique for the purpose of granting equitable relief when they breach their contracts.

Undoing or Revising the Contract

Courts may employ the remedy of *rescission* to undo a contract or *reformation* to revise the contract. This section explains these two options in detail.

Unwinding the contract through rescission

One alternative contract remedy is to tear up the contract and pretend it never happened. Contract law refers to this remedy as *rescission*. I like to think of it as unwinding the contract, because when the contract is rescinded, the parties are supposed to be returned to their pre-contract positions. Rescission can come about in a number of ways:

✔ **Agreement of the parties:** The parties are free to mutually agree to terminate their contract, as I explain in Chapter 12. The parties can then decide whether to allocate payments. Even if they opt for no allocation of payment, consideration for the agreement to rescind still exists, because each party has gotten something: a release from their contractual obligations.

✔ **A successful defense to contract formation:** After forming a contract, one of the parties may successfully claim a defense to contract formation that *vitiates,* or undermines, the contract (see Chapters 6 and 7). These defenses include illegality, lack of consideration, lack of capacity, fraud, mistake, and the like. When the contract is avoided because of a defense after one party already conferred a disproportionate benefit on the other party, the courts can ensure a fair outcome by using the principles of restitution to compensate the party who conferred the disproportionate benefit.

If I sell my house to you and you prove that we entered into the transaction because of a mutual mistake, contract law rescinds the contract and discharges our duties. You return title of the house to me, and I return the payments you made. However, because you got the benefit of living in the house, the court may require you to make restitution to me for your use of the house before the rescission.

✔ **A material breach:** If we have a contract and you commit a material breach, I have the option of declaring that my performance under the contract is discharged (check out Chapter 14). In addition, I can recover damages for the breach. Whether you can recover restitution for any performance you rendered prior to the breach was at one time hotly debated. Now the position of the Restatement, as found in § 374, is that the breaching party is entitled to restitution.

In the 1834 case of *Britton v. Turner,* Turner employed Britton to work for one year for $120. Britton breached the contract after nine and a half months. Because this was material breach of an entire contract, Turner was entitled to consider the contract at an end and claim damages.

The issue was whether Britton had a claim for the work he had done prior to the breach. The court must have concluded that he couldn't claim damages for breach of contract because he didn't substantially perform. His claim was in restitution for the value of the benefit he had conferred on Turner. Still, at that time, he was mostly out of luck because he didn't have clean hands in the matter — he was the party at fault, and the rule at the time was that the dirty contract-breaker wasn't entitled to restitution.

But the court changed the rule. It reasoned that if a person in Britton's situation didn't recover anything, he had no incentive to continue performing. After all, the more he puts in before breach, the more he'd lose. Furthermore, an employer may have an incentive to make things difficult for an employee and get him to quit before he finishes performing. So the court decided that even a dirty contract-breaker should get restitution.

Calculating the amount of the restitution is a difficult question. Clearly Turner's expectancy has to come first (see Chapter 16 for details on the expectancy). If Turner had to pay someone $30 to finish the job, Britton should get no more than $90, because Turner's expectancy was to get the job done for $120. But if Turner got the contract completed for $20, Britton should get no more than the pro-rata portion of the contract he performed. That is, if the entire job was worth $120 and he completed 9.5/12 of it, he should get no more than $(9.5 \div 12) \times \$120 = \$95$.

Today this problem doesn't come up in employment contracts, because wage and hour laws protect employees by requiring that employers pay them for work done. However, it can still arise in other transactions, such as construction contracts. Most courts follow the rule of this case and grant restitution to the contract-breaker.

Rewriting the contract through reformation

Courts primarily use *reformation* (rewriting the contract) for correcting *scrivener's errors,* or mistakes made as an agreement is being written down. Courts rarely use reformation as a remedy, and when they do, it's usually to conform the written contract to the parties' understanding when they made a mistake in transcribing it. If the parties agreed to certain terms and the person who wrote up the agreement accidentally omitted a term, the writing is reformed to reflect the agreement that the parties made.

A controversial use of reformation arises when an unanticipated price increase of an *input* (something required to produce what's being sold) burdens the seller of the product or service, who then claims he is excused from performing the contract. (See Chapter 13 for more on excuse because of unanticipated events.) A few courts have taken it upon themselves to rewrite the contract in those instances to make it fairer, but most courts say that contracts are for the parties to make, not for the judges to make for them.

Letting the Parties Determine the Remedies for Breach

Contract law supplies rules (referred to as *default rules*), but the parties often have the freedom to contract around those rules. (See Chapter 10 for more about default rules. Chapters 16 and 17 cover the default rules that apply to damages.) Parties often attempt to contract around the rules by doing the following:

✓ Providing for *liquidated damages,* or damages determined in advance of breach

✓ Providing for limitations on the remedies that would otherwise be available

I discuss both of these ways of contracting around the default rules in this section.

Calculating liquidated damages

To avoid the complexity of calculating damages later, parties sometimes agree in advance to *liquidated damages* — what the damages will be in the case of breach. In fact, most economists favor the parties' right to determine damages in advance. However, the courts have a strong policy against *punitive damages* (money awarded to punish the offender rather than to compensate the innocent party) for breach of contract, so most courts allow a liquidated damages provision only if the situation passes the first two or all three of the following tests:

✓ **Damages must be difficult to foresee and calculate.** If a contract is for the sale of goods, calculating actual damages is fairly easy, as I explain in Chapter 17. In a construction contract, however, foreseeable losses, such as those resulting from delay, may be difficult to determine. Subcontractors may not be available at the altered times. And tenants may not be able to move in on time and may have claims against the owner. And the owner may need additional financing to weather the period before rents come in. In such a situation, liquidated damages would be appropriate.

✓ **The parties must make reasonable efforts to calculate the actual damages.** Given the first test, this calculation may seem impossible, but the goal is to have damages that aren't punitive. Come up with a number that's not arbitrary.

To prevent damages from appearing to be punitive, consider calculating them on a per diem basis rather than just ballparking a huge lump sum. For example, on a large construction project, liquidated damages measured on a daily basis (say, $25,000 per day) would probably be more reasonable than a lump sum, such as $500,000, because damages for 1-day's delay can't reasonably be the same as damages for a 20-day delay.

✔ **In some jurisdictions, liquidated damages can't exceed the actual damages that occurred after the breach.** This rule is known as the *hindsight rule,* because it disallows liquidated damages based on what happened after the breach even if the first two rules were followed at the time the parties agreed to the contract. Liquidated damages in excess of actual damages appear to be punitive, especially where the actual damages are minimal, so a court may disallow liquidated damages and award actual damages instead.

The courts closely scrutinize liquidated-damages provisions, especially if the provision appears to penalize the breaching party rather than compensate the non-breaching party.

For example, say you hire me as an employee for a year for $100,000. Our contract says that I owe you $50,000 as liquidated damages if I breach. The problem is that because you could probably hire a substitute employee for less than $150,000 if I breach, the provision appears to be in the contract to prevent me from breaching rather than to compensate you for my breach. The courts also scrutinize such provisions when a party has little or no bargaining power (as in the case of consumers) and the liquidated damages seem unreasonable.

Down payments or deposits that a buyer makes in advance of a purchase are generally not considered liquidated damages because the parties didn't necessarily agree that the down payment was a reasonable amount for the seller to retain in the event of the buyer's breach. The parties are free to contract around this rule by expressly agreeing that the down payment is forfeited as liquidated damages. For example, when a buyer agrees to purchase real estate, the agreement usually requires that the buyer pay a certain amount as a down payment, sometimes called an *escrow deposit.* If the buyer goes through with the purchase, this amount is credited to the sale price, but if the buyer breaches, the agreement provides that the seller may retain this amount as liquidated damages.

An interesting problem arises when parties include a liquidated-damages provision in their contract but a breach results in no actual damages. The question that arises is whether a party is eligible to recover the liquidated damages even though it suffered no loss.

For example, suppose a builder is ten days late and the owner demands the $25,000 per day in liquidated damages they agreed to in their contract, even though the owner admits that he suffered no actual damages. Contract law has at least three different thoughts on how to resolve the issue:

✔ **The economist's view:** Each party took a risk that the actual damages may be more or less than the actual damages. For instance, if the owner had actually been damaged in the amount of $500,000, he would still get only $250,000. Therefore, the liquidated damages should be recovered even in the absence of actual damages.

✔ **The hindsight rule:** Many courts apply the hindsight rule — now that they know from hindsight the actual damages, they refuse to enforce a liquidated damages clause if the actual damages turn out to be nonexistent or minimal.

✔ **The middle road:** Some courts take a middle road, allowing the liquidated damages unless the difference between the liquidated damages and the actual damages is so great as to be unconscionable.

As you can see from this discussion, contract law leaves a lot of room to challenge a liquidated damages clause. The fact that a device designed to prevent litigation may actually end up causing a lot of litigation is unfortunate.

California and Hawaiian Sugar Co. v. Sun Ship, Inc.

California and Hawaiian Sugar Co., or C&H Sugar, grew its sugar cane in Hawaii and processed it in California. In 1979, C&H Sugar decided it would save a lot of money if, instead of paying a number of carriers to transport its sugar, it built a giant ship just for this purpose.

So in the fall of 1979, C&H Sugar contracted with Sun Ship to build the sugar ship for about $25 million, with a delivery date of June 30, 1981. The parties realized that if the ship wasn't delivered on time, C&H Sugar would be in a pickle, because it would then have to find alternate shipping and may have to pay premium prices to get it at the last minute. Because the damages would be difficult to estimate, this situation warranted a liquidated damages provision, thus satisfying the first test for enforcement of liquidated damages. The parties agreed to liquidated damages of $17,000 for every day

delivery was late. Because these were sophisticated parties who were trying to work out a reasonable formula for liquidated damages, they passed the second test.

Sun Ship experienced many problems building the ship and delivered it on March 16, 1982, almost nine months late. C&H Sugar demanded $4.4 million in liquidated damages. Fortunately for C&H Sugar, many ships were available at the time, so it suffered only $368,000 in losses because of the breach. Sun Ship tried to invoke the hindsight rule, claiming that it shouldn't have to pay liquidated damages that were so far out of proportion to the actual damages. But the Ninth Circuit Court of Appeals, applying Pennsylvania law, refused to apply the hindsight rule, determining that because the parties had determined the computation of the damages, the court wasn't going to interfere.

Providing for limited remedies

Parties often add a provision to their contract to limit the remedies for breach. As I explain in Chapter 10, merchant sellers often limit the remedies for breach by disclaiming the implied warranty of merchantability and adding a limited express warranty of their own, which usually specifies available remedies and the amount of consequential damages. Alternatively, they may give the implied warranty of merchantability but limit the remedies available for its breach. This section discusses how to limit available remedies and consequential damages.

Limiting available remedies

Manufacturers often limit the remedy for breach of warranty to "repair and replace." For example, instead of giving you money damages for breach of warranty, an automobile manufacturer promises to repair or replace defective parts for a certain period of time. This remedy leads to an interesting situation when the repair doesn't take and the buyer has to keep bringing the goods back for repair after repair.

The Code has a solution to this problem in UCC § 2-719(2). As enacted in North Carolina at 25-2-719(2), it provides:

> (2) Where circumstances cause an exclusive or limited remedy to fail of its essential purpose, remedy may be had as provided in this act.

Most courts find that the remedy "fails of its essential purpose" when the buyer doesn't get what she reasonably expected — goods that work properly. In the event that a buyer doesn't get what she expected, a common remedy is *revocation of acceptance* under UCC § 2-608, which allows the buyer to return the goods and get her money back. Many states have supplemented this rule with a *lemon law* that permits the buyer of a car under warranty to return the car if it's not fixed after a certain number of attempts at repair or a certain number of days in the shop.

Limiting consequential damages

The default rule is that a buyer can recover as consequential damages the losses set in motion by a breach (see Chapters 16 and 17 for details). Sellers are particularly concerned about the amount of these damages, which can easily exceed the cost of their product, so they often limit the damages in the contract.

The rule for the sale of goods is in UCC § 2-719(3). As enacted in North Carolina at 25-2-719(3), it provides the following:

(3) Consequential damages may be limited or excluded unless the limitation or exclusion is unconscionable. Limitation of consequential damages for injury to the person in the case of consumer goods is prima facie unconscionable but limitation of damages where the loss is commercial is not.

As you can see from the Code, parties have freedom of contract to limit consequential damages, but the seller in a consumer goods transaction can't limit liability for personal injury.

Suppose a company buys accounting software for $499. After it's installed, the system crashes due to a bug in the software. The company spends thousands of dollars to reboot its system and work around the system while it's down. When the company makes its claim against the software vendor, the vendor offers to give it $499, pointing out that the contract says, "Damages for breach, including consequential damages, are limited to the amount of the purchase price of the product." These limitations are generally enforceable. Note that this example involves software, which is probably not a "good" under Article 2, which defines goods as things that are movable. Nevertheless, the warranty provisions of most software contracts are structured like those in contracts for the sale of goods, and courts frequently apply the same rules. Because the rule wasn't written for this transaction, judges say it's applied *by analogy*.

In a typical warranty provision, the seller limits the remedy for breach and excludes consequential damages. An interesting question arises in such a case when the court finds that the limited remedy fails of its essential purpose and the court therefore strikes it from the contract. Does the court strike the consequential damages exclusion as well? Jurisdictions take three different approaches to this problem:

✔ They strike both provisions.

✔ They strike only the limited remedy, not the consequential damages exclusion.

✔ They strike both provisions if included in the same paragraph but only the limited remedy if the provisions appear in separate paragraphs. (I call this the *arbitrary approach*.)

Awarding Transaction Costs on Top of Damages

The plaintiff in a contracts case has a tough time coming out ahead or breaking even. In theory, the injured party gets what he would've had if both parties had performed. However, to recover those damages, he incurs *transaction costs,* including attorney's fees and the cost of litigation. This section explores whether a plaintiff can obtain money from the defendant to pay for some of these transaction costs. I also include a subsection on the rare instances when courts award punitive damages to help plaintiffs recover their costs.

Getting attorney's fees

The general rule in U.S. law is that each side pays its own attorney's fees, win or lose. This rule, which is called the *American Rule,* differs from the *English Rule,* which requires the loser to pay the winner's attorney's fees.

Consider the American Rule when planning whether to bring a contract claim. Because contract damages are fairly predictable, you can tell your client how much she's likely to recover and the likely cost to get that recovery. Your client can then make a business decision as to whether pursuing the claim is worth it.

The American Rule is a default rule, so parties can contract around it. In fact, sometimes these provisions are one-sided. A bank, for example, may put in the contract that the bank gets attorney's fees from the customer but not vice versa. Most jurisdictions consider these one-sided provisions unfair, and by either statute or case law they require that the provisions be read as reciprocal.

Some statutes provide for attorney's fees, so a plaintiff may want to bring a claim under such a statute instead of or in addition to making a claim under the common law or the UCC. For example, most consumer protection statutes provide for attorney's fees on the theory that by bringing such a claim, the attorney is serving the public good. Read the statute carefully, however, because some statutes provide that only the plaintiff can recover fees, whereas others provide that either party can recover fees.

Recovering transaction costs

You often see at the end of a case that one party is allowed to recover its costs. Unfortunately, the party isn't allowed to recover all the expenses he incurred in bringing the suit. Civil procedure statutes strictly enumerate which costs a party may recover, and typically they allow the recovery of only limited expenses, such as filing fees and the cost of depositions. They don't include the main cost, which is usually attorney's fees.

Punitive damages? Fuhgeddaboudit!

Punitive damages are rarely awarded in contracts cases, because such damages would discourage breach. You may think it strange not to discourage breach, but breach can be "efficient." Economists say that goods and services should be free to flow to where they can be most efficiently used, not necessarily to where they've been allocated by contract. For example, a person shouldn't be discouraged from taking a better job out of fear of having to pay damages in excess of the employer's actual loss. The employee who leaves her employer in the lurch may commit a moral wrong, but contract law is concerned only with the legal wrong — and that wrong can be righted with compensation.

One of the few times courts may award punitive damages is in bad-faith insurance claims. If the insured person makes a valid claim but the insurance company refuses to pay in bad faith (with no good reason) and compels the insured to sue in order to recover, the court may grant punitive damages to discourage this behavior from the insurance company. Some courts have said that punitive damages may be available when the parties have a "special relationship," but the only relationship that's been found to clearly fit this category is between insurance company and insured. In addition, some consumer-protection statutes provide for punitive damages in order to discourage a business from engaging in unfair or deceptive acts or practices.

Of course, if you can make a claim for a *tort* (a wrongful act that results in injury) that's independent of the contract, you can bring a tort claim and possibly receive punitive damages. Malpractice claims are a good example. If you have a contract with a professional, such as a lawyer or a doctor, she probably breaches the contract when she doesn't perform in a reasonable manner. You could bring the claim for breach of contract, but bringing the claim in tort may have its advantages, including the chance to recover for pain and suffering and to possibly receive punitive damages.

Finding the Law that Governs the Contract

Through freedom of contract (see Chapter 10), parties may choose which set of rules govern the contract and where the trial is to take place in the event of breach. How these two issues play out follows the usual pattern: The default rules are in place, but the parties are free (with certain exceptions, of course) to contract around those rules.

When disputes arise over which set of rules govern the contract or the location of the forum for dispute, contract law offers some guidance, as I explain next.

Selecting the governing law through a choice-of-law clause

The phrase *choice of law* means choosing the law that governs any possible contract disputes. A body of law called *conflict of laws* governs the choice-of-law rules. Unfortunately, these rules aren't very tidy when it comes to choosing the law that governs a contract dispute, and different jurisdictions have different rules. These rules can be divided into two categories, the old rule and the modern rule, as I explain in this section.

Examining the old rule

Under the *old rule,* the law that applies is the law of the place where the last act occurred that resulted in contract formation. This act is usually the acceptance. If one party signs the contract in Ohio and the other signs in Indiana, the second signature is the acceptance (the contract is formed at that point), so Indiana law governs. Drafters may manipulate this rule. For example, the business in Ohio may add to the contract language stating, "No contract is formed unless approved by our home office in Omaha, Nebraska." In that case, the contract is formed in Nebraska, so Nebraska law governs.

This rule isn't very helpful in cases where the issue is whether a contract *was* formed. In the famous case of *Leonard v. Pepsico,* for example, Pepsi claimed that no contract was formed. The judge wasn't sure which law to apply but said it didn't really matter because the case concerned fundamental principles of contract law that are pretty much the same everywhere.

Studying the modern rule

Under the *modern rule,* the law that applies is the law of the jurisdiction that has the most significant contacts with the transaction. So if a builder in Montana agrees to build a home for a Washington resident in Idaho, and the contract is signed in California, Idaho law would probably govern. Although four states have contacts with the transaction, the most significant contacts are with Idaho, where the real property is located and the performance will take place. In a contract for the sale of goods, the place where the goods are delivered is generally the most significant contact.

Parties are generally free to use their freedom of contract to choose the law that will govern their agreement as long as the contract has some reasonable connection with that jurisdiction. If, for example, parties in Montana were to enter into a songwriting agreement, they could probably provide that California law governs the contract. Even though the contract doesn't have any direct connection with that jurisdiction, providing for California law to govern is reasonable because California has a significant body of law related to entertainment contracts, and Montana doesn't.

The parties can't choose the law of a jurisdiction that offends the policy of the law of the jurisdiction whose law would've applied if the parties hadn't chosen the law. In other words, parties can't expect a jurisdiction to apply laws that offend it. But a court can manipulate the rule in order to apply its own law to the case.

In a famous case involving the arbitration clause in a contract for a Subway sandwich shop franchise in Montana, the contract provided for Connecticut law, which is where Subway has its headquarters. This connection was strong enough to permit the parties to choose Connecticut law, but the Montana court objected to Connecticut's policy of giving favorable treatment to arbitration clauses and refused to apply that law. Having thrown out the choice-of-law clause, it then applied the law of the jurisdiction that had the most significant contacts with the transaction — Montana!

If a court is asked to apply law other than the *law of the forum* (the jurisdiction where the court is sitting), the lawyers must supply information about the law in that other jurisdiction to the court to aid its decision making. So if the rules of civil procedure lead you to litigate your case in Montana but you've agreed to apply California law, you have to educate the court on the relevant California law. This situation happens frequently in federal courts that often handle cases based on diversity of citizenship. Federal contract law doesn't exist, so the federal court must determine which state's law applies to the transaction.

Selecting the place of trial through a choice-of-forum clause

Whereas a choice-of-law clause gets you the law you desire, a *choice-of-forum* clause allows you to require that a suit be brought in a particular court. A party may add such a provision to a contract because a particular forum is convenient and perhaps provides a home-field advantage.

The U.S. Supreme Court doesn't hear many contracts cases (see why in Chapter 1), but it does have jurisdiction over disputes that arise under *admiralty law* (law on the high seas). One such case involved a choice-of-forum clause. In *Carnival Cruise Lines v. Shute,* Mrs. Shute was injured when she fell on a Carnival ship at sea. The Shutes sued Carnival in Washington state, where the couple lived. But Carnival claimed they had to bring suit in Florida, where Carnival is headquartered, because the contract contained a choice-of-forum clause. The Shutes claimed the clause was unconscionable, because it was buried in the fine print of the contract and would cause inconvenience and financial hardship. The court nevertheless upheld the clause, explaining that even though the agreement was a *contract of adhesion* (one party drafts it for the other party to sign without negotiation), the clause was fair and the Shutes had reason to know of it.

A case decided by the Supreme Court in admiralty has mandatory authority only in admiralty-law cases. State courts, or federal courts using state contract law in diversity cases, are free to ignore the holding of admiralty-law cases like the *Shute* case when deciding contracts cases. Nevertheless, such cases have persuasive authority.

Resolving a Dispute through Alternative Dispute Resolution

Although the default rule says that cases are heard in the court system, parties are free to contractually opt out of the court system and agree on an *alternative dispute resolution* (ADR) approach instead. They can bind themselves in their contract to ADR, or they can agree to ADR after the dispute arises. The two most common ADR methods are arbitration and mediation, which I describe in this section.

Litigation is an all-or-nothing proposition, and many parties agree to a settlement along the way. The court system often has procedures that encourage settlement. Many court systems have procedural rules that require mediation at some point, and frequently they offer an arbitration alternative. For example, if you go to small-claims court, the judge may give you the alternative of having the case heard by a volunteer arbitrator rather than the judge. In fact, those TV show "judges" you see are really arbitrators who are resolving disputes that the parties have agreed to have heard by the arbitrator.

Resolving disputes through arbitration

The most common method of ADR is *arbitration,* in which the parties refer the case to a presumably impartial third party who acts like a judge and decides the case. Arbitration is binding (most common) or nonbinding. With *binding arbitration,* the parties agree upfront that the arbitrator's decision can be entered and enforced just like a judgment in court. With nonbinding arbitration, a party can opt out after the arbitrator presents her decision. In automobile warranty disputes under the Magnuson-Moss Warranty Act, for example, the arbitrator's decision is binding on the automobile manufacturer but not on the consumer.

If you're negotiating a contract that has an arbitration clause, consider choosing an arbitrator who brings particular expertise to the case. For example, if the dispute is about a construction contract, you may want to choose someone who's knowledgeable in construction matters.

Although arbitration has some drawbacks, it offers the following benefits over litigation:

- **Less expensive:** You have to pay the arbitrator, which costs more than the "free" judge, but you usually spend less on attorney's fees and pre-trial procedures.

- **Faster:** Arbitrators can limit or expedite the *discovery* (pretrial procedures that enable a party to obtain information from the other party) that bogs down so many court cases.

- **More flexible:** Arbitrators aren't bound by the rules of law, so they can be more flexible in developing solutions to resolve the parties' dispute. Nor do arbitrators have to follow the rules of evidence, so the parties have little to appeal from in an arbitrator's decision — an error of law is generally not appealable.

- **Less formal:** Arbitration proceedings are usually less formal than trials, often leading to a less adversarial and more collaborative atmosphere.

- **Less controversial:** Most arbitrator decisions simply say, "I find for A in the amount of $X," which gives the parties little to quarrel over.

- **Private:** Arbitration is private, resulting in no public record of the proceedings.

In the old days, courts were concerned that arbitrators were taking business from the courts, but now the diversion of cases from an overburdened court system is generally welcomed. No one objects to instances where the parties agree to take their dispute to arbitration after the dispute arises (as opposed to when they bind themselves ahead of time by contract).

So what's not to like in arbitration? Sellers in consumer transactions often include an arbitration clause in a contract of adhesion to restrict the consumer's options and avoid litigation. To protect a party that lacks bargaining power, a court may declare a term unconscionable (as I explain in Chapter 6), and some courts have used this power to strike down arbitration clauses.

The U.S. Supreme Court, however, has issued a string of opinions strongly supporting arbitration by applying the Federal Arbitration Act (FAA) to arbitration cases in state courts. The FAA provides that a court may not invalidate an arbitration clause "save upon such grounds as exist at law or in equity for the revocation of any contract." In other words, a court can't say that the clause is unconscionable just because it's an arbitration clause. Although this battle is likely to continue, courts are finding their hands tied in resisting arbitration clauses unless the arbitration clause itself is so one-sided as to be unconscionable.

Trying mediation

Mediation differs from arbitration in that the third party who was asked to mediate a dispute doesn't have the power to make a decision that's binding on the parties. Instead, the mediator tries to get the parties to reach a settlement of their dispute that satisfies both parties' interests. Sometimes a contract provision requires the parties to mediate, but this provision only requires them to make a good-faith effort to resolve their dispute. If they're unable to reach an agreement, they're free to walk away.

Mediators cite several benefits of mediation over litigation:

- **Personal empowerment:** Parties have more control over the dispute resolution process. They don't simply hand the dispute over to lawyers to resolve.

- **More conducive to peacemaking:** Mediation is less adversarial and more collaborative. The focus isn't on winning but on finding a solution that's mutually satisfactory.

- **More-durable solutions:** The parties take ownership of the dispute and the resolution of it, so they tend to buy into the solution. As a result, the parties are more likely to comply with and less likely to appeal the decision.

- **Fewer unresolved issues:** Often disputes are about more than money damages. Mediation enables the parties to address personal losses and emotional issues that fall outside the law. Parties are able to mend their relationship or part on more amicable terms.

Part VI
Bringing Third Parties into the Picture

"...and, as the men's union representative, I'd like to go over a few things in the contract they're not very merry about."

In this part . . .

Most of contract law concerns only the relationship between the parties to the contract, and normally only two parties are involved. *Third parties* are people or groups who aren't parties to the original contract but have an interest in it. The most significant third parties arise in transactions that involve third-party beneficiaries, tortious interference, assignment of rights, and delegation of duties — all of which are addressed in this part.

Chapter 19

Deciding Whether a Third Party Can Enforce or Interfere with a Contract

In This Chapter

▶ Understanding how third parties may get involved

▶ Recognizing and establishing third-party beneficiaries

▶ Checking whether a party qualifies as a third-party beneficiary

▶ Steering clear of tortious interference with contract

*T*hird parties often get involved in contracts and contract disputes. For example, third parties may have an interest in enforcing a warranty (see Chapter 18 for details). If I give you food at my house and the food makes you sick, you may want to bring a claim against the seller who sold me the food, even though you're not a party to the contract between me and the seller, making you a third party. Provisions in the UCC resolve whether you can bring such a claim.

Third parties may also get involved in other ways — by becoming third-party beneficiaries, by interfering in the performance of a contract between two other parties, or by having the rights or duties of the contract assigned or delegated to them. This chapter focuses on third-party beneficiaries and people who interfere in another parties' contract by inducing one of them to breach. Here, you find out how to determine whether someone is a third-party beneficiary. You also see the potential consequences a third party may suffer as a result of interfering in a contract between other parties. (For more about assignment and delegation, see Chapter 20.)

Determining Whether a Party Is a Third-Party Beneficiary

In a *third-party beneficiary* transaction, a party who's not a party to the contract sues to enforce a promise that one of the parties made. Contract law had trouble finding a theoretical justification to allow this but ultimately allows it as part of the role of contract law to carry out the parties' intent.

Everyone agrees that whether a party is a third-party beneficiary hinges on whether the parties intended that party to be a third-party beneficiary of the promise. The challenge is to find that intent. The Second Restatement of Contracts (which has been around since 1981 and has become so familiar that I simply call it the *Restatement*) takes a somewhat circular approach to this problem. In § 302, the Restatement creates two categories of beneficiaries: intended and incidental. It goes on to say that a beneficiary of a promise is an intended beneficiary if the parties so intend and one of the following applies:

> (a) the performance of the promise will satisfy an obligation of the promisee to pay money to the beneficiary; or

> (b) the circumstances indicate that the promisee intends to give the beneficiary the benefit of the promised performance.

The First Restatement of Contracts, which came out in the 1920s, is somewhat more helpful because it provides names for these two categories of third-party beneficiaries:

- ✓ **Creditor beneficiary (a):** One to whom one of the parties to the contract owed money that he arranged to pay

- ✓ **Donor beneficiary (b):** One to whom the parties to the contract intended to make a gift

This section explores these two categories in turn, describes a third category for parties who have only an incidental interest in the contract, and introduces three key questions you can ask to determine whether a third party is likely to qualify as a third-party beneficiary. It also discusses the rights of third-party beneficiaries and whether the parties to the contract can change those rights.

Creating a creditor beneficiary by telling someone to pay your debt

The parties intend to create a creditor beneficiary when performance of the promise will satisfy the promisee's obligation to pay money to the beneficiary.

In other words, A and B make a contract in which B promises A that he'll do something for C. They intend to make C a creditor beneficiary if B's performance will satisfy an obligation of A to pay money to C.

For example, John owes Terry $100. John sells a widget to Peter for $100 and as part of the contract, John tells Peter to pay the $100 to Terry rather than to John. Peter doesn't pay. Terry asks whether she can sue Peter for the $100. Terry is obviously a third party, but contract law must determine whether she qualifies as a third-party beneficiary, which she must be in order to have the right to sue.

Here's how to determine whether the parties to a contract intended to create a creditor beneficiary:

1. **Identify the promise that the third party is seeking to enforce.**

   In this example, Terry is seeking to enforce Peter's promise to John.

2. **Ask whether the performance of the promise will satisfy an obligation of the promisee to pay money to the beneficiary.**

   Yes, the performance will satisfy John's obligation to pay Terry. Therefore, Terry is a creditor beneficiary and, as a third-party beneficiary, can sue Peter to enforce the promise.

Securing the rights of third-party beneficiaries

For a long time, American contract law had a hard time recognizing the rights of third-party beneficiaries simply because it couldn't see how a person who wasn't a party to the contract could sue to enforce the contract. The principal case that changed the rule in the U.S. was the 1859 New York case of *Lawrence v. Fox*. Holly owed Lawrence $300. Holly loaned Fox $300, and in return, Fox promised to pay the $300 to Lawrence to satisfy Holly's debt to Lawrence. When Fox didn't pay him, Lawrence sued Fox.

The court had trouble finding consideration from Lawrence that would allow him to enforce Fox's promise to someone else. But it claimed it found a principle in the law of trusts that in the case of "a promise made to one for the benefit of another, he for whose benefit it is made may bring an action for its breach." This sounds like a conclusion rather than a justification, but the long and short of it is that the promise became enforceable.

Curiously, two years later an English court decided on similar facts that the beneficiary couldn't recover. Third-party beneficiaries in England finally got the right to enforce the promises through legislation rather than through court decisions.

This situation arises in many real-world transactions, such as real estate contracts. Suppose I buy a house from you, and in the process, I take out a $100,000 mortgage from the bank. I then sell the house to Terry, and she assumes the mortgage; that is, she promises me that she'll pay the bank. However, she doesn't pay the bank. The bank can still come after me (if you don't understand why, see Chapter 20), but the bank wants to know whether it can go after Terry. Here's how to decide whether the bank is a third-party beneficiary:

1. Identify the promise that the bank is seeking to enforce: Terry's promise to pay the bank.

2. Ask whether the performance of the promise will satisfy an obligation of the promisee (me) to pay money to the beneficiary (the bank). Yes, that's why I got Terry to make the promise to me. Therefore, the bank is a third-party beneficiary and can sue Terry to enforce the promise. (By the way, most mortgages today have a provision expressly saying that the mortgage isn't assumable and that the balance is due on sale of the property.)

Creating a donor beneficiary by making a gift

According to the Restatement, a third party is a third-party beneficiary if "the promisee intends to give the beneficiary the benefit of the promised performance." This third party is referred to as a *donor beneficiary* (*donor* meaning the giver of a gift). In other words, A and B make a contract in which A gets B to promise to give something to C.

For example, John sells a widget to Peter for $100. As part of the contract, John tells Peter to pay that $100 to John's favorite charity. Peter doesn't pay. The charity asks whether it can sue Peter for the $100.

To determine whether the parties to a contract intended to create a donor beneficiary, here's what you do:

1. **Identify the promise that the third party is seeking to enforce.**

   The charity wants to enforce Peter's promise to pay the charity $100.

2. **Ask whether the promisee intends to give the beneficiary the benefit of the promised performance.**

   Yes, John (the promisee) said he intends to give the charity (the beneficiary) the benefit of the $100. Therefore, the charity is a donor beneficiary and, as a third-party beneficiary, can sue Peter to enforce the promise.

The most common example of a donor beneficiary is the beneficiary in a life insurance policy. I agree to pay the insurance company a premium in return for its promise to pay my beneficiary upon my death. The third party is clearly an intended beneficiary and can sue to enforce the insurance company's promise. Notice that the beneficiary gave no consideration in return for being named as a beneficiary. As I explain in Chapter 3, this is a gift promise and is not binding. Therefore, I can generally revoke (take back) this promise to make someone my beneficiary, such as by designating a new beneficiary. However, my promise may be enforceable on a theory of reliance (see Chapter 4 for details on reliance).

Creating an incidental beneficiary: Another name for loser

After defining what qualifies someone as a third-party beneficiary, the Restatement says that if you're not a third-party beneficiary, you're an *incidental beneficiary,* which really means you're a loser — you have no right to enforce the contract. To determine whether someone's an incidental beneficiary, look for a third party who benefits from the contract and then ask whether the reason the parties entered into the contract was to benefit that third party. If the answer is no, then the third party is an incidental beneficiary.

For example, suppose I hire you to do some research for me for the summer. I promise that in payment, I'll buy you a new Mercedes from Midtown Motors. Needless to say, you accept my offer. You do a fantastic job on the research, and I say, "Let's go down and pick out that Mercedes." You say, "Professor Burnham, I didn't do it for the Mercedes. I did it for the love of contract law. That's good enough for me, and you don't have to get me the Mercedes." You're happy, I'm happy, but unfortunately the third party to our contract, Midtown Motors, is unhappy. They sue to enforce the contract, claiming to be a third-party beneficiary. Would they have benefitted from performance of the contract? Yes, indeed. Did we enter the contract with the intention of benefitting them? Nope. That makes Midtown Motors an incidental beneficiary — they lose.

Asking three key questions to identify third-party beneficiaries

As a quick check to determine the likelihood that a third party qualifies as a third-party beneficiary, ask the three questions I present in this section. The answers to these questions won't give you a definitive determination, but they can be helpful in making the determination.

Is the third party named in the contract?

A third-party beneficiary is usually named in the contract. This alone isn't enough to make someone a third-party beneficiary, however. When you name the beneficiary of an insurance policy, you most certainly intend that party to be a third-party beneficiary. But if I name Midtown Motors as the place I'll purchase a car to pay you for your research work, I probably didn't intend Midtown Motors to be a third-party beneficiary. The intent all depends on the context in which that party is named.

When writing a contract that names a beneficiary, consider adding that the parties expressly do or do not intend the party to be a third-party beneficiary.

Does performance run to that third party?

Another test is whether performance of the contract runs to that third party. If so, an intent to benefit that party is more likely. In a life insurance contract, the insurer will perform directly to that third party (the beneficiary) by paying that person the money. In our research contract, in which I promise to buy you a car in payment for your work, my performance runs to you, not to Midtown Motors. (We could say it runs *through* them but not *to* them.)

In a case where an insurance company promised the buyer of an automobile that it would provide liability insurance, a person injured by the buyer sued the insurance company. Obviously, the injured person was not specifically named in the contract, but the purpose of the contract was to compensate those who were injured by the buyer, so that was close enough to name the injured person as a third-party beneficiary.

This issue of who performance runs to sometimes comes up with government contracts that intend to serve a public interest. Did the government intend to benefit those directly affected by the contract or to benefit the general welfare? Courts have generally determined that such a contract wasn't intended to benefit any particular person unless the terms of the contract provided for that.

For example, suppose the government contracts with a business to retrain unemployed workers in a particular city, and the business doesn't do it. Do the unemployed workers have a claim against the business? Probably not. The government's intent in contracting with the business was to serve the general good by reducing unemployment, not to benefit any particular unemployed worker.

Did the promisee intend to benefit the third party?

Questions about third-party beneficiaries all come back to intent. One way to focus on that intent is to think of the promise from the point of view of the promisee — the one to whom the promise was made. If someone is a third-party beneficiary, then the scope of the promisor's obligation has been expanded from the promisee to the third party as well.

After that's been established, ask whether the promisee bargained for that expanded obligation. In the case of the auto insurance policy, that answer is easy, because the promisee sought the promise of the insurance company to benefit the injured party in case of an accident. But if you agreed to be my research assistant in return for a Mercedes, did you intend for me to promise to benefit Midtown Motors? Probably not. You were most likely looking after yourself.

Changing a third-party beneficiary's rights

The parties to a contract are generally free to modify their contract, changing their duties to each other, as I explain in Chapter 12. Similarly, the parties are generally free to change the beneficiary of a contract. However, exceptions arise when the rights of the beneficiary are said to have *vested,* meaning they can't be changed without her consent.

The rights of a beneficiary usually vest in the following situations:

- **Express agreement:** A term in the contract provides that the beneficiary can't be changed.
- **Reliance:** The beneficiary changes her position in reliance on the promise.

Changing a named beneficiary can be an issue with life insurance policies. If the beneficiary of a life insurance contract has relied on the promise, the insured may not be able to change the duty to the beneficiary — for example, by changing the person named as beneficiary. In many jurisdictions, courts found that the insured was unable to change the beneficiary unless he or she reserved that power in the policy. Most policies now provide that the insured party has the power to change the beneficiary.

Interfering with Someone Else's Contract: A Big No-No

Tortious interference arises when a third party induces one of the parties to the contract to breach the contract. This gives the injured party a couple of options: She can sue the party to the contract for breach of contract, and she can sue the third party for tortious interference with contract.

Tortious interference is a tort claim, not a contract claim. Some describe it as a "business tort," and maybe because tortious interference is less common than other torts, it's often not studied in Contracts or Torts classes. But it's important because a person may not be aware that he's setting himself up for a tort claim when he induces a party to breach a contract. Of course, the tort is committed only when the interference is "improper," and the problem that usually arises is in trying to determine whether the person's interference was improper or justified.

This section explains how to recognize tortious interference with a contract and how the courts determine whether such interference is improper.

Finding the tort of tortious interference with contract

A party can't get punitive damages for a breach of contract claim. However, a party may be able to get punitive damages for proving an intentional *tort* (wrongful act resulting in injury), such as tortious interference with contract.

In fact, one of the biggest judgments in U.S. legal history came when Pennzoil sued Texaco for tortious interference with its contract to buy Getty Oil. The jury found Texaco liable for tortious interference and assessed damages of more than $10.5 billion (reduced to a mere $8.5 billion on appeal), forcing Texaco into bankruptcy.

Restatement of Torts § 766 describes *tortious interference:*

> One who intentionally and improperly interferes with the performance of a contract (except a contract to marry) between another and a third person by inducing or otherwise causing the third person not to perform the contract, is subject to liability to the other for the pecuniary loss resulting to the other from the failure of the third person to perform the contract.

Why is the contract to marry exempt?

Marriage is at root a contract. Think of grounds for annulment as circumstances that avoid the contract, and think of grounds for divorce as material breach of the contract. No-fault divorce is mutual rescission.

In the old days, a person who had a romantic relationship with one of the parties was liable for tortious interference with the marriage contract. The tort was called *alienation of affections* or *criminal conversation,* suggesting that it could be a crime as well. Nowadays, although we don't condone this behavior, most jurisdictions have statutes that bar civil or criminal liability for it.

Engagement to marry is also a contract. But if one party breaks off the engagement, the other party usually can't sue for damages for breach of contract. The so-called *heartbalm statutes* in most jurisdictions have eliminated that claim, with the exception of recovering out-of-pocket expenses incurred in preparing for the wedding.

Tortious interference can apply to interference with the formation of a contract, just as it can apply to the contract itself. In the movies, the hero is always sweeping in at the last moment to snatch the bride away from Mr. Wrong. This sounds like tortious interference, but the Restatement specifically provides that this behavior carries no tort liability.

The most difficult of these elements to prove is that the interference was improper, because the party who interfered usually claims that its interference was justified. The next section tackles that issue.

Considering claims that the interference is improper

The defendant in a tortious interference claim usually defends by saying that if it did interfere, its interference was not improper but justified. For example, not long ago, every night people across America got annoying phone calls at dinnertime with offers from long-distance services. Everyone already had a long-distance service, so if you accepted one of these offers, you had to break your existing contract with another service. Although the calls may look like tortious interference, they were probably not heavy-handed enough to qualify as improper. The company offering the service could claim that its action was justified by free enterprise, with competing parties free to offer their wares to customers, who could then decide whether they wanted to get out of their existing contracts in order to accept.

A more heavy-handed example was dramatized in the movie *The Insider.* Jeffrey Wigand was a scientist employed by Brown & Williamson Tobacco Company. In his contract, he promised not to divulge corporate secrets to anyone. Nevertheless, he made some disclosures to the CBS team that produces *60 Minutes.* Brown & Williamson could've sued Wigand for breach of contract, but they went after the deeper pocket: They threatened to sue CBS for tortious interference. CBS's defense would've been that they're in the news business and the public had a right to know this information. Nevertheless, the threat worked, and *60 Minutes* didn't air the episode.

The case of *Phillips v. Montana Educational Association* (MEA) is not an important one, but it nicely illustrates the analysis of a claim for tortious interference with contract. Phillips was an employee of the MEA who was fired. Instead of suing his employer for breach of contract, he sued the Board of Directors of the Association for tortious interference with contract. Clearly he and the Association had a contract, and the directors had caused it to be terminated. The only issue was whether their action was improper.

The court found that the duty of the board of directors of a corporation is to act in the best interests of that corporation. It may be in the best interests of the corporation to breach a contract the corporation has with some other party. As long as they were acting in good faith, then the board of directors was justified in inducing the corporation to breach the contract with Phillips.

Chapter 20

Acknowledging the Rights and Duties of Third Parties

. . . .

In This Chapter

▶ Getting to know each party's rights and duties

▶ Recognizing when a party can or can't assign rights to a third party

▶ Knowing when a party can or can't delegate duties to a third party

▶ Novation: Rewriting a contract to remove a party

. . . .

The parties to a contract may assign their rights or delegate their duties to a third party. For example, if Acorn Industries buys out Hickory, Inc., then Acorn buys Hickory's contract rights and obligations. If prior to the buyout, Hickory had contracted with Filberts to purchase 3,000 rubber duckies for $1,250, then Hickory assigns to third-party Acorn its right to purchase those rubber duckies, and it delegates to Acorn its duty to pay the $1,250 to Filberts. Likewise, Hickory assigns its right to the services of its employees to Acorn, and it delegates its duty to pay those employees to Acorn.

This chapter describes what constitutes each party's rights and duties under their contract and explains how to determine when a party to the contract is allowed to assign her rights or delegate her duties or is prohibited from doing so. You also find out how to write language into a contract that prohibits assignment or delegation or both, and you see how to remove a party from a contract so the person no longer has the duty to perform under it.

Breaking Down a Contract into Rights and Duties

Before trying to figure out whether a party to a contract is allowed to assign his rights or delegate his duties to a third party, you need to be able to recognize each party's rights and duties as specified in the contract:

✔ **Right:** As a promisee in a contract, a party has the *right* to the promisor's performance.

✔ **Duty:** As a promisor, a party has the *duty* to perform.

After you've identified what constitutes the rights and duties of each party, you can develop a better understanding of how the parties may be able to transfer those rights and duties to a third party.

The following examples examine rights and duties in three different types of contracts: the sale of goods, construction, and services.

In a contract in which a seller agrees to sell a buyer all the widgets it requires for $100 each, the buyer's and seller's rights and duties look like this:

	Right	*Duty*
Buyer	Receive the widgets	Pay for widgets
Seller	Receive the payment	Tender the widgets

In a contract in which a builder agrees to build a house for an owner for $300,000, the builder's and owner's rights and duties look like this:

	Right	*Duty*
Builder	Receive $300,000	Build the house
Homeowner	Get the house	Pay $300,000

In a contract in which a famous artist agrees to paint the president's portrait for $50,000, the president's and painter's rights and duties look like this:

	Right	*Duty*
President	Have his portrait painted	Pay $50,000
Painter	Receive $50,000	Paint the portrait

Determining Whether Rights May Be Assigned

A contract right is a piece of property that can be bought and sold. The party to the contract that assigns the right is the *assignor,* and the third party who receives the right is the *assignee.*

If you took out a student loan from Bank A, for example, you might receive a letter from the bank telling you that from now on, you should send your payment to Bank B rather than Bank A. What happened behind the scenes is that

Bank A had a contract with you and assigned the right to receive your payments under that contract to Bank B. After you get an effective notice of the assignment, you should perform for the assignee, Bank B, which now has the right to your performance. Transfers of the right to receive money constitute a substantial part of the world economy.

This section explains how contract law applies the general rule and examines exceptions to that rule.

Applying the general rule: Freely assigning rights

The general rule is that parties may freely assign contract rights. The assignee "stands in the shoes of the assignor," who essentially drops out of the picture. This rule is pretty much the same in the common law and in the Code. You can find it in the UCC in § 2-210(2). As enacted in North Carolina at 25-2-210(2), it provides in part:

> (2) Unless otherwise agreed all rights of either seller or buyer can be assigned except where the assignment would materially change the duty of the other party, or increase materially the burden or risk imposed on him by his contract, or impair materially his chance of obtaining return performance.

The right to receive money is an example of a freely assignable right. Applying the general rule, you can see that assigning this right doesn't materially change the duty of the *obligor* (the party who promised to perform), because it's just as easy for the obligor to pay the assignee as to pay the assignor. All three hypothetical contracts in the earlier section "Breaking Down a Contract into Rights and Duties" contain a right to receive money.

When the right involves something other than receiving money, assignment can be more problematic, as I explain next.

Spotting exceptions to the assignment of rights

As the UCC states, the rule of free assignment of rights has a number of exceptions. One is the usual exception to default rules: The parties can agree to some other arrangement in their contract (see "Prohibiting Assignment and Delegation," later in this chapter, for details). The other exceptions occur when the assignment would do one of the following:

- ✔ "Materially change the duty of the other party"

- ✔ "Increase materially the burden or risk imposed on him by his contract, or impair materially his chance of obtaining return performance"

Here's how these exceptions might play out in the three examples I introduce earlier in the section "Breaking Down a Contract into Rights and Duties":

- ✔ **Potential changes in quantity — a material change in duty:** In a normal situation for the sale of goods, the buyer can often assign its right to receive the goods, as long as delivery to the assignee isn't any more difficult for the seller as a result. But consider an example in which the seller is obligated to tender all the widgets the buyer requires. In this requirements contract, the quantity to be supplied depends on the buyer's needs (see Chapter 2 for details on requirements contracts).

  Assume that a giant corporation buys out the business that originally contracted to buy the widgets. The original buyer assigns the rights under its contracts to the business that takes it over. The new company would then tell the seller under the widgets contract that the right to all the widgets the business requires have now been assigned to it. This could disrupt the seller's expectations, because it probably entered the contract based on the size of the original buyer's business. It could object to the assignment on the grounds that the assignment materially changed its duty.

- ✔ **Reducing the assignor's motivation to pay — impaired chances of return performance:** In the construction example, a builder agrees to build a house for an owner for $300,000. Suppose the owner tells the contractor that he has assigned the right to have the house built to his neighbor, who owns a nearby lot. Even though building the house for the neighbor is no more difficult for the contractor, the original owner now has no incentive to pay for the house, because this was an assignment of the right to get the house, not a delegation of the duty to pay. So the contractor may claim that the assignment has impaired his chance of getting the return performance of payment.

- ✔ **Choice of person — a material change in duty:** In the artist example, an artist is to paint the president's portrait. This is a personal services contract. If the president decides he doesn't have time to get his portrait painted, he might tell the painter, "I've assigned my right to Professor Burnham. Paint his portrait instead." Although painting my portrait would be no more difficult for the painter, he can object to the assignment on the grounds that the contract involved a *choice of person* — it mattered to him who he was going to paint.

Determining Whether Duties May Be Delegated

The general rule in contract law is that parties may freely delegate their duties under the contract. The party doing the delegating is the *delegating party* or *delegator,* and the one to whom the duty is delegated is the *delegate* or *delegatee.*

The big difference between assigning rights and delegating duties is that the assignee takes the place of the assignor, whereas the delegatee doesn't take the place of the delegator; hence, the delegating party remains liable for performance and breach. In other words, an obligor can't get out of his contractual duties by delegating them.

This section examines how contract law applies the general rule and looks at exceptions to that rule when parties delegate their duties.

Applying the general rule: Freely delegating duties

The rule allowing parties to freely delegate their duties under the contract is essentially the same in the common law and the Code. You can find it in the UCC in § 2-210(1). As enacted in North Carolina at 25-2-210(1), it provides:

> (1) A party may perform his duty through a delegate unless otherwise agreed or unless the other party has a substantial interest in having his original promisor perform or control the acts required by the contract. No delegation of performance relieves the party delegating of any duty to perform or any liability for breach.

You may be surprised that duties can be so easily delegated, but when you think about it, this happens all the time. For example, you're working for Homebrew Software. On Friday, you get notice that Megasoft has taken over the company, and starting Monday, you'll be working for them. What's happened is that Homebrew assigned its right to your services and delegated the duty to pay you to Megasoft. You may despise Megasoft, but that doesn't matter. As long as your duties are unchanged, contract law says that the party you perform for makes no difference. And as long as you're paid, who's paying you doesn't matter.

Construction contracts commonly employ delegation. An owner probably hires a particular contractor, such as ABC Construction, because she heard that they're very reliable and do excellent work. Imagine her surprise when XYZ Construction shows up to do some of the work. But the delegation of performance of parts of a construction contract is very common. That's what *subcontracting* is all about: The prime contractor has delegated some of its duties to the subcontractor.

One of the reasons subcontracting is widely permitted is that the original party remains liable for performance and breach, even after the delegation. Because ABC Construction promised the owner they would do the job, delegating their duties to XYZ Construction doesn't relieve ABC of that obligation, and they can be sued for XYZ's breach.

Back to the source: Spotting exceptions to the delegation of duties

The exception to free delegation arises when the "other party has a substantial interest in having his original promisor perform or control the acts required by the contract." With the sale of goods, a seller is generally free to delegate his duty to tender the goods, because if the goods are *fungible* (the same regardless of the source), who provides them makes little difference. On the other hand, if the source of the goods or services makes a substantial difference in performance, then the party can't delegate the duty.

For example, suppose the famous artist tells the president, "I've delegated my duty to paint your portrait to someone else." Even if that person was a reputable artist, the president would likely object, claiming he had a substantial interest in having his original promisor perform because of that person's particular abilities as an artist.

In *Macke Co. v. Pizza of Gaithersburg, Inc.,* a company called Virginia had a contract to install and service vending machines at Pizza's pizza shops. Macke then purchased Virginia's assets, which included an assignment of Virginia's rights, including the right to receive money from Pizza, and a delegation of Virginia's duties, including the obligation to install and service Pizza's vending machines. Pizza refused to accept performance from Macke, claiming that the delegation was not effective, and Macke sued for breach.

The trial court found that because Pizza had picked Virginia on account of its skill, judgment, and reputation, the contract involved a choice of person, so the duties couldn't be delegated. But the appellate court explained that even though services were involved, this was the kind of service that any company in that line of business could perform. The court cited language from a California case that held that duties under a contract to grade a street could be delegated:

> All painters do not paint portraits like Sir Joshua Reynolds, nor landscapes like Claude Lorraine, nor do all writers write dramas like Shakespeare or fiction like Dickens. Rare genius and extraordinary skill are not transferable, and contracts for their employment are therefore personal, and cannot be assigned. But rare genius and extraordinary skill are not indispensable to the workmanlike digging down of a sand hill or the filling up of a depression to a given level, or the construction of brick sewers with manholes and covers, and contracts for such work are not personal, and may be assigned.

Using UCC § 2-609 to get assurances

If the contract doesn't involve fungible goods, a buyer may be concerned about whether the delegate is going to do the job. Sure, the buyer can always sue the delegating party in the event of breach, but she doesn't want a lawsuit; she wants performance. A party who's concerned that the other party may not perform can demand assurances, as I explain in Chapter 15.

The Code provides for a party in this situation to similarly demand assurances from the delegate. UCC § 2-210(6), as enacted in North Carolina at 25-2-210(1), provides:

> (6) The other party may treat any assignment which delegates performance as creating reasonable grounds for insecurity and may without prejudice to his rights against the assignor demand assurances from the assignee (Section 2-609).

For example, if I ordered food from a certain caterer and the caterer later tells me that another caterer will be providing the food, I may be concerned because I was relying on the reputation of the original caterer. I could demand assurances from the new caterer, and if I didn't get reasonable assurances, then I could regard the delegation as ineffective.

Prohibiting Assignment and Delegation

As with most default rules, the rules on assignment and delegation are generally subject to the agreement of the parties. The parties may put language in the contract to prohibit assignment and delegation. This section explains how to draft language to prohibit assignment and delegation and describes the limitations that pertain to such prohibitions.

Drafting an effective prohibition

When drafting a prohibition, use specific language to clearly express what the parties intend to prohibit: assignment of rights, delegation of duties, or both. If you want to prohibit both assignment and delegation, for example, spell it out by saying, "Rights under this contract may not be assigned, and duties under this contract may not be delegated."

Don't draft something vague like "This contract may not be assigned." Contracts are not assigned; rights are. Did the drafter mean to prohibit the assignment of rights, the delegation of duties, or both? This problem arises so often that the UCC has a rule that addresses it. UCC § 2-210(4), as enacted in North Carolina at 25-2-210(4), provides:

> (4) Unless the circumstances indicate the contrary a prohibition of assignment of "the contract" is to be construed as barring only the delegation to the assignee of the assignor's performance.

Under this rule, if you prohibit "assignment of the contract," the result is that you've prohibited only the delegation of duties and not the assignment of rights. Although this result may seem surprising, it makes sense in light of the rules of interpretation I explain in Chapter 11. The goal of interpretation is to carry out the intent of the parties. Parties are generally more concerned about delegation than assignment, so they probably intended only to prohibit delegation. Furthermore, because the general policy is to permit assignment and delegation, this interpretation supports that policy by giving the language a narrow reading.

Recognizing key limitations on prohibition

Because contract law strongly supports assignment and delegation, parties may encounter limitations on their ability to prohibit assignment and delegation. The two key limitations are these:

- ✔ Limitations on prohibiting the assignment of the right to receive money
- ✔ Limitations on the remedy, even if a prohibition is effective

This section explains these limitations in detail.

Restricting the assignment of the right to receive money

The right to receive money for goods sold or services rendered on credit is called an *account*. Businesses commonly sell their accounts or use their accounts as collateral to secure a loan — a practice known as *accounts receivable financing*, which is an important part of commerce.

A gym, for example, having gotten you to sign a contract for a year's membership at $100 per month, has an account — the right to receive $1,200 from you over the next 12 months. It can convert that contract to cash now by selling the contract rights at a discounted (reduced) rate (say, $1,000) or by borrowing money and using the account as collateral. The buyer or lender, as an assignee, can then go after you if you don't pay.

To prevent restrictions on accounts receivable financing, Article 9 of the UCC provides that prohibitions on assignment aren't effective with respect to contracts used in financing. For example, if a contract for the sale of goods contains a provision that states, "Rights under this agreement may not be assigned," then the buyer would be prohibited from assigning its right to receive the goods. However, the seller still would be able to assign its right to receive the money in order to get financing, because that prohibition on assignment isn't enforceable.

Figuring the consequences of breach of a prohibition

Not all courts agree on the effect of the breach of a clause that prohibits assignment and delegation. The majority rule is that the assignment or delegation is still effective, but the other party can recover damages. The minority rule is that the assignment or delegation is not effective.

For example, you contract to have work done by ABC Construction, and you don't want them to subcontract the work. You put in the contract, "Duties under this contract may not be delegated." You then see that XYZ Construction is doing the work. Under the majority rule, the delegation is effective and you're entitled to any damages. This rule makes little sense to me, because you're entitled to damages anyway if XYZ doesn't perform properly, so the prohibition doesn't get you anything. Under the minority rule, the delegation is not effective and you can refuse to accept performance by XYZ.

If you're in a jurisdiction where the only consequence is damages, you can put language in the contract to provide for the consequences you intend. You can say something like, "Duties under this contract may not be delegated, and any attempted delegation is ineffective."

If the other party breaches the contract by delegating their duty when the contact says they can't delegate, that's probably not enough to allow the non-breaching party to terminate the contract. You can terminate a contract only if the other party commits a material breach, and breaching the clause prohibiting delegation is probably not material. However, you're free to draft an express condition to that effect (see Chapter 14 for details). You can say something like, "Duties under this contract may not be delegated. If duties are delegated, then the other party does not have to accept performance from the delegate and can terminate the contract."

Substitutions: Making a New Contract through Novation

People sometimes forget the rule that delegation doesn't relieve a party of their obligations, which may lead to unfortunate consequences. The solution to this problem is to enter into a *novation* — a new contract under which the original party is discharged and another party is substituted.

For example, a husband and wife jointly take out a car loan and agree to repay the loan to the bank. Then the couple decides to separate. In their separation agreement (the contract that provides the terms for their separation), they state that the husband will own this car and will make the payments to the bank. Later, the husband doesn't pay the bank, and the bank comes after the wife. The wife explains that the husband is now responsible for those payments. But what really happened is that the husband and wife delegated to the husband the duty to make the payments. The delegation doesn't relieve the delegating party, who remains liable for performance and breach. The wife has to pay. Here, instead of delegating the duty to the husband, the couple should've asked the bank to agree to a novation — a new contract in which the bank would discharge the husband and wife from the original contract and enter into a new contract with the husband.

Part VII
The Part of Tens

The 5th Wave   By Rich Tennant

THE JUSTICES RULE ON PAPER vs SCISSORS vs STONE

In this part . . .

This part is comprised of two chapters. The first one explains how to solve contract law problems, whether you're encountering them on an exam, interviewing a client, or analyzing a contract. This chapter provides ten essential questions you need to ask in your contract analysis — a checklist of sorts that you can use to be sure you haven't overlooked a key issue.

The second chapter introduces you to ten A-listers in the history of contract law. It explains why each individual is important, describes the person's philosophy of contract law, and highlights the significant contribution he made to the evolution of contract law.

Chapter 21

Ten Questions to Ask When Analyzing a Contracts Problem

In This Chapter

▶ Taking the IRAC approach to resolving contract issues

▶ Asking questions about contract formation, enforceability, and defenses

▶ Posing questions about where to find and how to interpret contract terms

▶ Asking about breach, remedies for breach, and third-party rights and duties

*L*aw school exams and the essay portion of the bar exam present you with facts to analyze. The key word here is *analyze*. Your assessors don't want to hear you advocate a position, and they aren't very interested in your conclusion. They're interested in your *analysis* — your ability, given certain facts, to reason from issues to possible outcomes.

When answering an exam question or fielding such a question from a client, start with the facts and then engage in the following thought process, which law school instructors refer to as IRAC (Issue, Rule, Analysis, Conclusion):

1. **Issue: Identify the issue.**

   To identify an issue, ask lots of questions about the legal consequences of the facts that you're given. When you see the issue, asking the right question should lead you to the applicable legal rule.

2. **Rule: State the appropriate rule to resolve this issue.**

   The rule may be a black-letter rule, a principle, or a case or series of cases relevant to the issue.

3. **Analysis (or Application): Perform your analysis.**

   The outcome of a legal case is a function of both facts and rules. Your analysis of the problem demonstrates how well you've mastered the interplay of facts and rules in a given situation to predict what the outcome is likely to be. In the process, you may identify additional sub-issues and have to loop back to the *I* in IRAC.

4. **Conclusion: State the tentative solution to (the predicted outcome of) the legal problem raised in the issue.**

   Don't worry about having a firm conclusion. Raising questions is more important than answering them.

IRAC in action

Here's a sample question. It's probably too simple to be representative of law school exams, which often have fact patterns that raise multiple issues. However, this example gives you a general idea of how to answer a question by using the IRAC approach:

Question: John Brown orally agrees to buy Mary Smith's house for $300,000. Mary then goes to see her lawyer, but he is not in the office, so she leaves a note on his desk that says, "Just agreed to sell my house for $300,000 to John Brown. Please draw up papers. [signed] Mary Smith." The next day, someone else offers Mary $325,000 for the house. She asks you whether her agreement to sell the house to John Brown is binding. Is it?

1. **Identify the issue.**

   The key fact here is that the agreement was oral. So you form the issue around the legal significance of that fact: Is Mary's agreement to sell the house to John enforceable even though it's oral?

2. **State the rule required to resolve the issue.**

   Agreements to convey real estate are within the statute of frauds and are not enforceable unless evidenced by a writing.

3. **Perform your analysis.**

   Apply the rule to the facts: This is an agreement to convey real estate, so it's within the statute of frauds. It's not enforceable unless evidenced by a writing, which raises a sub-issue: Is there a writing that evidences this contract? The rule is that the writing must identify the subject matter of the contract, show that a contract was made between the parties, contain the essential terms of the transaction, and be signed by the party against whom enforcement is sought.

   The writing Mary left on the lawyer's desk evidences the agreement. It indicates that the agreement is between John and Mary and that it is for the sale of Mary's house, and the writing states the sales price. These terms are probably sufficient, because other terms could be supplied by custom and usage and the default rules. Mary, who is the person against whom John would be enforcing the agreement, signed the writing. It would not bind John if he were the person who refused to perform the contract.

4. **Compose your conclusion.**

   Therefore, it appears that the agreement is binding on Mary because even though it's oral and therefore within the statute of frauds, there's a writing signed by Mary that contains the essential terms of the agreement.

Use the ten questions in this chapter as a checklist to ensure that you've identified all the issues surrounding a given legal problem. This checklist is like a condensed outline, so you have to flesh it out with answers to follow-up questions. For example, stating "Is a contract formed?" is too broad of a question to state as an issue on an exam. You need to narrow it down by asking which facts suggest that a contract may not have been formed and think through subtopics of contract formation.

The questions and explanations for each question in this chapter can help you flesh out the broad questions raised by the issues and tip you off to facts that often signal a particular issue. Memorize these ten questions!

Law school exams and the essay portion of the bar exam serve as realistic training, because you can expect to have similar experiences with clients. When a client comes to see you, relates some facts (or at least their version of the facts, as you will sometimes discover to your sorrow), and asks what the likely outcome will be, you don't give an answer. You look very thoughtful and say, "It depends." What the outcome primarily depends on is the answers to the issues that arise. Those issues are the questions about the legal significance of the facts that you need to ask in order to solve your client's problem (or the problem on the exam).

Was a Contract Formed?

The first question to ask is "Was a contract formed?" Formation issues often ask whether the offer, acceptance, and consideration necessary for a contract are present. If the facts are "A and B agreed that B would buy a widget from A for $400," then don't bother looking for formation issues.

But if the facts don't say that an agreement was made, look for facts that make you wonder whether someone presented an offer, whether someone accepted, and whether consideration was present. For example, suppose the facts are "A wrote to B that for the next ten days, he would sell his widget for $400. On the ninth day he said he changed his mind, and on the tenth day B accepted." Now you have an issue: Was A's offer still open when B accepted it?

Like the answers on Jeopardy, your issues should always be in the form of a question. Don't start by answering, "A's offer was not open when B accepted it," and then explain why. That's not raising an issue — that's defending a conclusion. If your analysis is wrong (for example, maybe A was a merchant making a firm offer under UCC § 2-205), you won't get much credit. But if you raised the right issue and then went off the track in your analysis, you'll still get some credit.

Is a Promise Enforceable without a Contract?

If your analysis leads you to conclude that the parties don't have a contract, don't stop there. Contract law is more generally about the enforcement of obligations. Look for whether the transaction includes a promise and, if it does, whether the promise is enforceable without a contract. A promise may be enforceable without a contract if the doctrine of reliance or restitution comes into play (see Chapter 8 for details):

- ✔ **Reliance:** Look for reliance on a promise, and if you find it, analyze it under Restatement § 90. Remember that the remedy in reliance may be limited to the extent of the reliance. If I promise you $1,000 and you reasonably rely on the promise by spending $700, you'll probably recover only $700. (If you spend $1,200, this raises the issue of whether spending $1,200 in reliance on a promise of $1,000 is reasonable.)

- ✔ **Restitution:** If the parties have no contract but one party has conferred a benefit on another party, ask whether the principle of restitution compels that party to give up the benefit. Sometimes an obligation to pay for a benefit is a contract "implied in law," which really means restitution. The remedy in restitution is generally the value of the benefit conferred, which can be difficult to measure.

Does a Party Have a Defense to the Contract That Was Formed?

Even if the parties formed a contract through offer and acceptance, one of the parties may be able to raise some affirmative defense that voids or avoids the contract. If the defense *voids* the contract, the parties didn't form a contract, but if the defense *avoids* the contract, then presumably the parties had a contract initially. The affirmative defenses include illegality, unconscionability, capacity, fraud, duress, undue influence, and mistake. (See Part II of this book for details on contract defenses.)

Don't make up facts to raise issues that can lead to a contract defense. For example, if the facts are "A and B entered into a contract," don't raise an issue like "What if A was mentally incapacitated?" when no facts suggest it. On the other hand, if the facts say, "A and B, *who was 17 years old,* entered into a contract," raise an issue about the legal significance of that fact: "Is the contract voidable because B was a minor?"

Be on the lookout for contracts within the statute of frauds, because that raises the issue of whether the contract has to be evidenced by a writing. A tipoff is a fact like "A called B *on the telephone* and ordered a widget for $600." When you see the words "on the telephone," a light should go on, and you should raise the issue of whether this contract is enforceable if it's oral.

If a defense is successful, then the court usually tries to put the parties back where they were before the agreement was made, which may require using principles of reliance and restitution. For example, if you see that a real estate contract is not enforceable because it's oral, look for a fact that says one party made a down payment to the other. The issue is then whether that party can get the down payment back through restitution.

Where Do You Find the Terms of the Contract?

Often after the parties reduce their agreement to a signed writing, one party claims that the agreement includes another term that they discussed during negotiations. This issue invokes the parol evidence rule, as I explain in Chapter 9.

The fact that parties had a side understanding before they signed an agreement can tip you off to a parol evidence rule issue. Look for facts like "*Just before they signed their agreement,* A said to B, 'Will you agree to tear down that icehouse?' and B responded, 'I will.' They then signed the agreement."

There's a difference between the parties' agreement — what they in fact agreed to — and their contract — the sum of their legal obligations. One big difference is that parties can't possibly include language that addresses every aspect of the transaction or everything that might happen in the future.

Make sure you know which terms a court will supply under the gap-fillers or default rules. For example, if the facts say that "A agreed to sell a widget to B," then you must raise issues such as whether the fact that the parties didn't agree on a price is fatal to the contract and, if not, what the rule is for price in the absence of an agreement. A court will also read in the parties' course of performance, course of dealing, and applicable trade usage. In a sale of goods transaction, it will read in the implied warranties. And in all transactions, it will read in the obligation of good faith and fair dealing. See Chapter 10 for more about finding contract terms that aren't written down.

If you don't know a rule, ask what's reasonable — you won't be far off.

Do the Parties' Interpretations of the Contract's Language Differ?

After you find the terms of the contract, a dispute may arise as to the meaning of the words the parties used, which raises an issue of interpretation. In such a situation, the court will determine whether the language is ambiguous. One of the issues is which *extrinsic* evidence (evidence outside the contract) the court will admit to resolve this question. The court will also use some rules of interpretation for guidance, so know those rules, which I explain in Chapter 11. If the court concludes that each party had its own meaning for an essential term and those meanings are equally reasonable, then the issue is whether the court will have to throw up its hands and say there is no contract because of a misunderstanding.

Is a Party in Breach?

Breach means not doing what you promised to do. Often issues arise because a party didn't perform and then claims it's not in breach because its performance was discharged. Discharge may arise by modification or by accord and satisfaction, as I explain in Chapter 12.

To spot a modification issue, look for facts that show the parties changed their initial agreement *after* it was formed. For example, the facts say, "On June 1, A agreed to sell a widget to B for $400. On June 2, B asked if A would reduce the price to $350, and A agreed." Because the second agreement took place after the initial agreement was made, the issue is whether the modification is enforceable. If they instead agreed to another term *before* they signed the agreement, it is likely to be a parol evidence rule issue. Look to see whether the agreement has a NOM (no oral modification) clause. If so, and the parties made an oral modification, raise an issue as to the enforceability of the modification under the *waiver* doctrine.

The claim of discharge may arise because of impracticability or frustration, as I explain in Chapter 13.

To find impracticability and frustration issues, look for an event *after* the contract was formed that did one of the following:

- ✔ Made performance impossible or very difficult for a seller
- ✔ Took the value out of the performance for a buyer

If you see a fact like "Farmer A agreed to sell his crops to B. Just before the harvest, a plague of locusts wiped out the crop," the issue is probably whether A's nonperformance is excused by the occurrence of the event. If the parties had a belief that was not in accord with the facts *before* they entered the contract, it's a mistake issue instead.

Did a Condition Have to Occur Before a Performance Was Due?

The Restatement defines a *condition* as an event that is not certain to occur but that must occur before performance is due (see Chapter 14). This description helps you see the issue when the facts show that a party claims that it's not in breach because its performance was conditional.

Look for some event that had to occur before performance was due. For example, if A and B agreed that A would buy B's house if A could get a mortgage, then when A refuses to buy the house, you need to raise the issue of whether A's performance was excused because the event of getting a mortgage had not occurred.

In addition to conditions that the parties expressly state, watch out for *implied conditions* (conditions supplied by the court), including the other party's performance in an exchange. If A promised to build a house for B for $300,000 and B refuses to pay, ask whether A has brought about the event that had to occur before B had to pay: building the house. B may claim that A didn't do everything he promised, which may raise an issue of substantial performance — contract law will cut some slack and say that if the breach by one party is only immaterial, then the other party still has to perform. Look for facts that raise an issue of substantial performance, like "A finished building a house for B except that A used Cohoes pipe for the plumbing, although the specifications required Reading pipe."

Don't forget that a party's "substantial performance" doesn't necessarily excuse their breach. The other party still has to perform but may deduct damages. For example, suppose a builder completes a house that he promised to build for $300,000; however, he used Cohoes pipe rather than the Reading pipe he promised, and the owner refuses to pay. First ask whether the builder substantially performed. If the answer is yes, then you can say that the condition occurred that had to occur before the owner had to perform by paying for the house. But because the builder is in breach, the owner may deduct damages for the breach (wrong kind of pipe) from the payment.

Did a Breach Occur Before Performance Was Due?

Breach prior to the time of performance is called *anticipatory repudiation.* Whether a breach occurs at the time for performance or in advance of that time often doesn't matter. Problems arise, however, when one party treats a breach as material breach by anticipatory repudiation, thus discharging their obligations under the contract, and the other party claims it didn't breach. (For more about anticipatory repudiation, see Chapter 15.)

To find an anticipatory repudiation, look for waffling words in the facts, such as "A and B agreed that A would sell B his entire potato crop on August 1. On July 1, the market price was going up, and A said to B, *'I'm not sure you are going to get my potatoes.'*" The issues here are whether what A said constitutes an anticipatory repudiation and what B can do to be sure.

What Are the Remedies for Breach?

If the parties have a contract and a party breaches, then you may need to look for issues involving the remedies. The general remedy is money damages, measured by the *expectancy* — the amount of money required to put the non-breaching party where he would've been had the contract been performed (see Chapter 16). In computing the expectancy, you may have to deal with the issues of foreseeability, certainty, and mitigation:

- ✔ **Foreseeability:** Look for facts that indicate damages that don't involve the direct loss of the subject matter of the contract but that were triggered by the breach. For example, if the facts say, "When A didn't get the grain on time, *he was unable to make any money from his bread factory,*" then you have an issue of whether that type of loss, called *consequential damages,* is recoverable.

- ✔ **Certainty:** When the issue is certainty, the facts raise questions about whether the party can compute her loss to a reasonable certainty. For example, if the facts say, "When A didn't publish the book, *the author lost royalties.*" That's undoubtedly true, but the issue is whether the royalties can be calculated to a reasonable certainty.

- ✔ **Mitigation:** With mitigation, the issue is whether the non-breaching party is making efforts to reduce the losses. For example, if the owner of the bread factory claims that she couldn't make bread because the grain was delivered late, ask what efforts she made to get the grain from another seller.

The issue of whether *specific performance* (a court ordering a party to perform instead of paying money damages) is appropriate may be raised if the facts suggest that the subject matter of the contract is unique. Look also at whether the parties agreed to the amount of damages in a *liquidated damages clause,* and if they did, raise the issue of whether that clause is enforceable.

Look at your old friends reliance and restitution as remedies that the non-breaching party can claim, particularly if measuring the expectancy is difficult. Look for losses they've suffered that they might not get back any other way. For example, an actress agrees to appear in a Broadway musical and then breaches before rehearsals begin. The producer is entitled to the money he would've made had the show opened on Broadway. This amount is impossible to determine to a reasonable certainty, so he may recover in reliance the out-of-pocket expenses he incurred prior to the breach.

Finally, an issue as to whether the breaching party may be able to claim restitution might be present, particularly if the breaching party can't recover on the contract because she didn't substantially perform. For example, if a contractor promised to build a house with Reading pipe and built it with Cohoes pipe, your analysis may lead you to the conclusion that the contractor did not substantially perform. Therefore, under the contract, the owner's duty to pay for the house is discharged, excusing him from paying the builder. You now have another issue: Can the builder recover in restitution for the part of the house that she completed?

How Does the Contract Affect Third Parties?

If the facts show that the contract involves a *third party* (one who's not a party to the contract), then an issue may involve that party. Here are some issues relating to third parties:

- **Enforcing promises:** If the third party is trying to enforce a promise made under the contract, then the issue is likely whether that party is a third-party beneficiary (see Chapter 19).

- **Warranty claims:** The party may also be a third-party beneficiary if it's making a warranty claim under the UCC when that party isn't a party to the contract. For example, if the facts say, "A borrowed B's Powerco electric drill that B bought at Megamart. The drill fell apart, injuring A," then an issue exists as to whether A can make a warranty claim against Powerco or Megamart.

- ✓ **Tortious interference:** If the third party induces the breach, the issue is likely to be whether one of the parties to the contract has a claim against the third party for tortious interference with contract.

If contract rights are assigned or duties are delegated, then issues may arise as to whether the assignment or delegation is permissible under the default rules or under any language in the particular contract. If it's not permissible, an additional issue may arise as to the remedy. (For more about the assignment of rights and delegation of duties, see Chapter 20.)

Chapter 22

Ten Notable People (And Philosophies) in Contract Law

In This Chapter

▶ Identifying some of the key names in contract law

▶ Picking up on the philosophical theories behind contract law

▶ Obtaining suggestions for further reading

Contract law isn't just a bunch of rules handed down and enforced by some centralized rule-making authority. It has evolved over several centuries and is a community project. This chapter shines the spotlight on several key figures, past and present, and their contributions to contract law. In describing these authorities, I reference some of the legal theories associated with them, including formalism, legal realism, relational contract theory, and law and economics. If you're interested in further exploring these theories of contract law, I recommend Robert Hillman's *The Richness of Contract Law* and Peter Linzer's *A Contracts Anthology*.

Lord Mansfield

William Murray, the Earl of Mansfield (1705–1793), was the Chief Justice of the King's Bench of England during the late 18th century. He's credited with modernizing English commercial law at a time of rapid industrialization. Mansfield revived a centuries-old tradition of having juries of merchants decide commercial cases not on the basis of some abstract law imposed from on high but on the basis of what was customary practice. This tradition continues in the Uniform Commercial Code (UCC), where an important source of the parties' agreement is usage of trade and where standards are frequently found in what is "commercially reasonable."

Christopher Columbus Langdell

Christopher Columbus Langdell (1826–1906) was a Contracts professor and dean of Harvard Law School. Langdell is credited with replacing lectures with the case method of instruction, so you can thank him for the fact that it's hard (and rewarding!) to figure out contract law by reading cases (and I can thank him for the fact that the case method probably drove you to buy *Contract Law For Dummies*). Curiously, although his method is still in use today, the reason for it has completely changed. In an age of science, Langdell thought that the cases were scientific data from which the principles of contract law could be extracted through dissection. Today, contract law uses the case method to compare and contrast decisions made in different fact situations in order to appreciate the complexity of a rule in action.

Samuel Williston

Samuel Williston (1861–1963) was a professor of contract law at Harvard and the principal Reporter for the First Restatement of Contracts (1932). Williston's monumental treatise on contract law, first published in 1920, is considered the first work that established Contracts as a field of its own. Williston was a bit rigid, exemplifying a school known as *legal formalism,* which relies heavily on logic and form rather than on context and substance. Formalists tend to see law as a closed system, separated from social policy, and are reluctant to explore what the law should be as opposed to what it says. Williston's treatise is being revised and updated by other scholars, so if you check out *Williston on Contracts,* use the 4th Edition if you want to get the modern take on the subject and the older editions if you want to get a flavor of Williston.

Arthur Corbin

Arthur Corbin (1874–1967) was a professor of contract law at Yale Law School whose monumental treatise on contract law was first published in 1950. Corbin had a greater capacity than Williston for recognizing that one rule could not fit all situations, and the two scholars often clashed philosophically. You frequently see their opposing views being voiced in the cases.

Corbin was more of a legal realist, interested in context such as the agreement the actual parties made, whereas Williston, as a formalist, often looked at the contract more bloodlessly, as if abstract objective parties made it. Corbin's treatise was subtitled *A Treatise on the Working Rules of Contract Law,* with the word *working* indicating that the rules are not immutable. If there was no good reason for a rule, he thought it should be replaced. Other authors are revising Corbin's treatise in a Revised Edition. If you want to get some flavor of his thinking and winning writing style, pick up the original edition, especially Volume 1.

Benjamin N. Cardozo

Benjamin N. Cardozo (1870–1938) worked his way up through the New York state court system, being appointed to the Court of Appeals (the highest court in the state) in 1914. His decisions in the area of contract law are remarkable for their elegance of expression and insight into doctrine. In decisions such as *Wood v. Lucy, Lady Duff-Gordon* (1917) and *Jacob & Youngs v. Kent* (1921), he dragged contract law kicking and screaming into the 20th century by recognizing the significance of context over formal logic.

At the end of his career, Cardozo took the seat of another great thinker on contracts, Oliver Wendell Holmes, on the United States Supreme Court, serving from 1932 until his death.

Karl N. Llewellyn

Karl Llewellyn (1893–1962), a law professor at Columbia University and the University of Chicago, was the principal author of the UCC. Llewellyn is associated with the movement known as *legal realism,* which saw law not as a discrete study but as one of many social sciences, including psychology, sociology, and anthropology, that can be used to solve human problems. His study of the Northern Cheyenne tribe, *The Cheyenne Way* (1941), is said to have influenced his drafting of the UCC, which frequently relies on cultural norms and shared values. Law students are sometimes forced to read his introduction to law, *The Bramble Bush* (1930), which has some sound ideas that, like much of his work, is obscured by an inelegant writing style.

E. Allan Farnsworth

Allan Farnsworth (1928–2005) was a professor of law at Columbia University and the principal Reporter for the Second Restatement of Contracts (1981), taking over that position on the death of Robert Braucher, another great Contracts scholar. Although Farnsworth was not an innovator, he had an enormous talent for synthesis and clear expression. His treatise, *Farnsworth on Contracts,* now carried on by Larry Garvin, is the most comprehensive and readable single-volume work on contract law. When you want to know more about the topics that I cover in *Contract Law For Dummies,* I recommend that you check out Farnsworth.

Ian Macneil

Ian Macneil (1929–2010), who served as a professor of contract law at Cornell, the University of Virginia, and Northwestern, is closely associated with the concept of *relational contract*. This view finds shortcomings in looking at a particular contract in isolation as a transaction between two autonomous parties, as a legal formalist might look at it. Instead, relational theory looks at the contract in the context of a web of exchange relationships. Macneil's book, *The New Social Contract* (1980), explains this theory.

Richard Posner

Richard Posner (1939–), a law professor at the University of Chicago who was appointed to serve as a judge on the 7th Circuit United States Court of Appeals, is a leading exponent of the Law and Economics movement and a very prolific writer on legal subjects. His book *Economic Analysis of Law* introduces the reader to economic principles and then shows how to use them to solve problems in all areas of law, not just Contracts. He and the "Chicago school of economics" have many disciples today, making it a major force in the field of law. His well-crafted opinions often provide great insight into how economic principles can solve problems in contract law.

Stewart Macaulay

Stewart Macaulay (1931–), a professor at the University of Wisconsin School of Law, wrote a groundbreaking article called "Non-Contractual Relations in Business: A Preliminary Study" (1963), which showed that in practice, businesspeople often follow their own norms based on what makes sense to them rather than what contract law or their contract says.

Macaulay's writing is full of insights into the way things really work. Law professor Grant Gilmore, in a very provocative and readable book, *The Death of Contract* (so titled because he thought reliance theory was going to overtake contract law), called Macaulay "The Lord High Executioner of the Contract is Dead Movement."

Appendix

Glossary

acceptance: An offeree's giving what the offeror requested in order to form a contract, such as a promise to do something or actually doing it.

accord and satisfaction: An *accord* is an agreement to discharge a debt by the payment of less than the amount owed. *Satisfaction* is performance of that accord.

agreement: The bargain of the parties in fact, whether or not it is legally enforceable.

anticipatory repudiation: A party's breach of contract by express or implied refusal to fully perform before the contract's performance is due.

assignment: The transfer of a contract right from the person who has that right under the contract (the *assignor*) to a third party (the *assignee*).

avoid: To declare that a presumptively valid agreement isn't enforceable because of the existence of a defense to its formation. See also *voidable contract.*

breach: A party's unexcused nonperformance of what that party promised in the contract.

condition: An event that must occur before some contract performance is due.

consideration: Whatever each party brings to the table in a bargained-for exchange; one of the necessary elements of a contract.

contract: A legally enforceable promise or exchange of promises.

contract defense: A challenge to a contract's formation or enforceability.

course of dealing: An understanding between the parties to a contract that has been established by their previous transactions. Refer to UCC § 1-303.

course of performance: An understanding between the parties to a contract that has been established by repeated occasions for performance under that contract. Refer to UCC § 1-303.

default rule: The rule of law that applies in the absence of the parties' agreement.

expectancy: The measure of damages that puts the non-breaching party where it would've been if the contract had been fully performed.

extrinsic evidence: Evidence not included in the written contract; also called *parol evidence.*

force majeure: A clause in a contract that enumerates events that excuse a party's nonperformance if the event makes the party's performance impracticable (very difficult or impossible).

frustration of purpose: The occurrence of an unforeseen event that removes the value of performance for one of the parties to such an extent that the party's performance is excused.

gap filler: A term that contract law reads into the contract when the parties didn't include it at the time of contract formation.

gift promise: A promise that's made without requesting anything in exchange.

good faith: An immutable rule in all contracts (whether stated or not) that requires the parties to act honestly and reasonably.

implied terms: Terms supplied by the court based on the assumption that the parties would have agreed to such terms had they thought of it.

impracticability: The occurrence of an unforeseen event that makes performance very difficult or impossible, thereby excusing a party's nonperformance.

knockout rule: A method of dealing with conflicting terms in the forms that the parties exchange; the court discards both terms and reads in a default rule from the Code or common law.

mailbox rule: The rule that acceptance of an offer is effective on dispatch; that is, when it leaves the offeree's hands, not when it's received by the offeror.

merger (integration) clause: Language in a contract stating that the written contract is the final and complete expression of the terms of the agreement. The purpose of the merger clause is to bar the admission of parol evidence to supplement or contradict the written agreement. See also *parol evidence.*

mistake: A contract defense claiming that the contract can be avoided because one or both parties entered into the agreement based on a belief that was not in accord with the facts.

misunderstanding: A problem of interpretation that makes the agreement void because each party ascribes a different meaning to an essential term and each meaning is reasonable.

mitigate: To lessen the damage that results from breach. The "duty to mitigate" means that the non-breaching party can't recover for losses it could've prevented.

option: A type of contract in which an offeror agrees to keep the offer open in exchange for a consideration from the offeree.

parol evidence: Evidence not included in the written contract; also called *extrinsic evidence.*

parol evidence rule: According to the rule, after the parties have reduced their agreement to a writing that they intend to contain the final and complete statement of their agreement, extrinsic evidence is not admissible to supplement or contradict the writing.

performance: The execution of what the parties promised in their contract.

pre-existing duty rule: According to the rule, consideration is absent if a party merely promises to do what it's already bound to do.

promise: A commitment to do or not to do something.

promissory estoppel: A party's reasonable reliance on the other party's promise that prevents the promisor from denying that the promise is enforceable merely because consideration is absent. Refer to Restatement § 90.

reliance: See *promissory estoppel.*

reliance damages: Out-of-pocket expenses incurred because of reliance.

rescission: The process by which the parties mutually tear up their contract or by which a court unwinds a contract that it has avoided.

Restatement: Short for *The Second Restatement of Contracts* — a compilation of the rules of contract law based on past judicial decisions.

restitution: A claim requiring a party who has received a benefit that was not a gift and was not forced on the party to return the value of the benefit received.

satisfaction: See *accord and satisfaction.*

statute of frauds: The collective name for statutes that require certain types of transactions to be evidenced by a writing signed by the party against whom enforcement is sought. For example, all real estate contracts are within the statute of frauds.

unconscionability: The doctrine that a court may use to strike down a contract or a contract term that shocks the conscience of the court. Refer to UCC § 2-302.

Uniform Commercial Code (UCC): A body of laws enacted by each state that governs commercial transactions in the United States. Article 2 of the UCC governs the sale of goods.

unliquidated debt: An obligation that has not been fixed in amount by either the parties or a court.

usage of trade: A practice or method of dealing that is so commonly found in a particular business or industry that it's assumed to be part of a contract between parties in that trade. Refer to UCC § 1-303.

void contract: An agreement that can never be enforced because it was never properly formed.

voidable contract: An agreement with obligations that may be escaped by a party due to some defense to formation. See also *avoid.*

waiver: The voluntary surrender of a legal right.

Index

• E •

• F •

• S •

Apple & Macs

iPad For Dummies
978-0-470-58027-1

iPhone For Dummies,
4th Edition
978-0-470-87870-5

MacBook For Dummies, 3rd
Edition
978-0-470-76918-8

Mac OS X Snow Leopard For
Dummies
978-0-470-43543-4

Business

Bookkeeping For Dummies
978-0-7645-9848-7

Job Interviews
For Dummies,
3rd Edition
978-0-470-17748-8

Resumes For Dummies,
5th Edition
978-0-470-08037-5

Starting an
Online Business
For Dummies,
6th Edition
978-0-470-60210-2

Stock Investing
For Dummies,
3rd Edition
978-0-470-40114-9

Successful
Time Management
For Dummies
978-0-470-29034-7

Computer Hardware

BlackBerry
For Dummies,
4th Edition
978-0-470-60700-8

Computers For Seniors
For Dummies,
2nd Edition
978-0-470-53483-0

PCs For Dummies,
Windows
7 Edition
978-0-470-46542-4

Laptops For Dummies,
4th Edition
978-0-470-57829-2

Cooking & Entertaining

Cooking Basics
For Dummies,
3rd Edition
978-0-7645-7206-7

Wine For Dummies,
4th Edition
978-0-470-04579-4

Diet & Nutrition

Dieting For Dummies,
2nd Edition
978-0-7645-4149-0

Nutrition For Dummies,
4th Edition
978-0-471-79868-2

Weight Training
For Dummies,
3rd Edition
978-0-471-76845-6

Digital Photography

Digital SLR Cameras &
Photography For Dummies,
3rd Edition
978-0-470-46606-3

Photoshop Elements 8
For Dummies
978-0-470-52967-6

Gardening

Gardening Basics
For Dummies
978-0-470-03749-2

Organic Gardening
For Dummies,
2nd Edition
978-0-470-43067-5

Green/Sustainable

Raising Chickens
For Dummies
978-0-470-46544-8

Green Cleaning
For Dummies
978-0-470-39106-8

Health

Diabetes For Dummies,
3rd Edition
978-0-470-27086-8

Food Allergies
For Dummies
978-0-470-09584-3

Living Gluten-Free
For Dummies,
2nd Edition
978-0-470-58589-4

Hobbies/General

Chess For Dummies,
2nd Edition
978-0-7645-8404-6

Drawing
Cartoons & Comics
For Dummies
978-0-470-42683-8

Knitting For Dummies,
2nd Edition
978-0-470-28747-7

Organizing
For Dummies
978-0-7645-5300-4

Su Doku For Dummies
978-0-470-01892-7

Home Improvement

Home Maintenance
For Dummies,
2nd Edition
978-0-470-43063-7

Home Theater
For Dummies,
3rd Edition
978-0-470-41189-6

Living the
Country Lifestyle
All-in-One
For Dummies
978-0-470-43061-3

Solar Power Your Home
For Dummies,
2nd Edition
978-0-470-59678-4

Available wherever books are sold. For more information or to order direct: U.S. customers visit www.dummies.com or call 1-877-762-2974.
U.K. customers visit www.wileyeurope.com or call (0) 1243 843291. Canadian customers visit www.wiley.ca or call 1-800-567-4797.

Internet

Blogging For Dummies,
3rd Edition
978-0-470-61996-4

eBay For Dummies,
6th Edition
978-0-470-49741-8

Facebook For Dummies,
3rd Edition
978-0-470-87804-0

Web Marketing
For Dummies,
2nd Edition
978-0-470-37181-7

WordPress
For Dummies,
3rd Edition
978-0-470-59274-8

Language & Foreign Language

French For Dummies
978-0-7645-5193-2

Italian Phrases
For Dummies
978-0-7645-7203-6

Spanish For Dummies,
2nd Edition
978-0-470-87855-2

Spanish
For Dummies,
Audio Set
978-0-470-09585-0

Math & Science

Algebra I
For Dummies,
2nd Edition
978-0-470-55964-2

Biology For Dummies,
2nd Edition
978-0-470-59875-7

Calculus For Dummies
978-0-7645-2498-1

Chemistry For Dummies
978-0-7645-5430-8

Microsoft Office

Excel 2010 For Dummies
978-0-470-48953-6

Office 2010 All-in-One
For Dummies
978-0-470-49748-7

Office 2010 For Dummies,
Book + DVD Bundle
978-0-470-62698-6

Word 2010 For Dummies
978-0-470-48772-3

Music

Guitar For Dummies,
2nd Edition
978-0-7645-9904-0

iPod & iTunes For
Dummies, 8th Edition
978-0-470-87871-2

Piano Exercises
For Dummies
978-0-470-38765-8

Parenting & Education

Parenting For Dummies,
2nd Edition
978-0-7645-5418-6

Type 1 Diabetes
For Dummies
978-0-470-17811-9

Pets

Cats For Dummies,
2nd Edition
978-0-7645-5275-5

Dog Training For Dummies,
3rd Edition
978-0-470-60029-0

Puppies For Dummies,
2nd Edition
978-0-470-03717-1

Religion & Inspiration

The Bible For Dummies
978-0-7645-5296-0

Catholicism For Dummies
978-0-7645-5391-2

Women in the Bible
For Dummies
978-0-7645-8475-6

Self-Help & Relationship

Anger Management
For Dummies
978-0-470-03715-7

Overcoming Anxiety
For Dummies,
2nd Edition
978-0-470-57441-6

Sports

Baseball
For Dummies,
3rd Edition
978-0-7645-7537-2

Basketball
For Dummies,
2nd Edition
978-0-7645-5248-9

Golf For Dummies,
3rd Edition
978-0-471-76871-5

Web Development

Web Design
All-in-One
For Dummies
978-0-470-41796-6

Web Sites
Do-It-Yourself
For Dummies,
2nd Edition
978-0-470-56520-9

Windows 7

Windows 7
For Dummies
978-0-470-49743-2

Windows 7
For Dummies,
Book + DVD Bundle
978-0-470-52398-8

Windows 7 All-in-One
For Dummies
978-0-470-48763-1

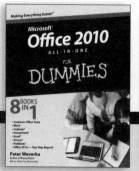

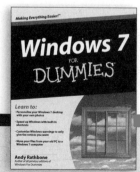